"This is a seminal book in every sense of that word… Seminal in that by addressing the implications of Emergence and Emergence Christianity for the religious formation of children and youth, it addresses one of (and arguably *the*) central questions facing 21st-century Christianity in the West. Seminal in that for the first time it brings together in one place the insights, wisdom, and practical suggestions of our most experienced and inspired leaders and thinkers in the field. Seminal in that, with vigor and candor and the unbeatable virtues of fine writing and good editing, it describes for us an entirely accessible landscape of hope and holy purpose. In sum, this is a seminal book."

Phyllis Tickle, author of *The Great Emergence* and *Emergence Christianity*

"The future of our faith traditions has everything to do with the formation of our youth, and the vitality and well-being of our young people is deeply connected to the ways they learn their faith. I am often concerned that religion is presented in ways that strike youth as uninspired and irrelevant, 'as an old man saying no' as the saying goes. But not in this book. *Faith Forward* is full of light and warmth. It is a treasure for coming generations, and the present one as well."

Eboo Patel, Founder and President, Interfaith Youth Core, and author of
Acts of Faith and *Sacred Ground*

"This book is a treasure trove of wisdom from leaders who share the best of what they have to offer in the quest to nurture faith and spirituality among the young. Dave Csinos and Melvin Bray invite us to a banquet of good words and good work. Here we can spend time in the company of authors, activists, and ministers who inspire and challenge us to imagine how we might share our faith with young people *and* how we might open ourselves to being changed by the faith that animates the lives of the young."

Parker J. Palmer, author of *Healing the Heart of Democracy*, *The Courage to Teach*, and *Let Your Life Speak*

"Thinking about, writing about, and trying to ~~...~~ hese days, especially in the dysfunctional city c ~~...~~ uncommon it really is. And it surprises people tc ~~...~~ e say and do *inside* our households, with the p ~~...~~ more for the common good than all we can acc ~~...~~ how we raise our children. So this book has the ~~...~~ rity and I hope many people read it."

Jim Wallis, President, Sojourners, and author of
God's Politics and *On God's Side*

"All the world religions are finding it very hard to pass on their faith to the next generation in a mature way. How do you make faith something real, personal, and loving, while still honest, intelligent, and inclusive? It takes real pastoral and practical genius to do this – and here it is!"

Fr. Richard Rohr, O.F.M., Center for Action and Contemplation, Albuquerque, New Mexico

"Those of us who care deeply about the future of our children (who are, of course, *all* children) will find this collection to be a great gift and a magnificent challenge, pressing us to recognize our crucial roles in nurturing our younger companions on the way of life. *Faith Forward* calls us to see the need for rethinking, renewing, and revisiting the stories of faith that originally nurtured many of us in order to help such stories become more fully available to our children as they set out on their own contemporary journeys of hope and great possibilities. Such rediscovering of faith is certainly a challenge well worth wrestling with – for our children, for our faith communities, for our nations, and for ourselves."

Vincent G. Harding, Co-founder and Chairperson, Veterans of Hope, and Professor Emeritus of Religion and Social Transformation, Iliff School of Theology

"Why do we try to give children a version of Christianity that hasn't worked for so many adults? *Faith Forward* challenges us to rethink how we offer the gospel to children and youth without the baggage our generation has added to it."

Mary Hawes, National Children's Advisor, Church of England

"Dave Csinos and Melvin Bray have compiled an invaluable book for anyone seriously interested in doing effective ministry with children and youth in the 21st century. *Faith Forward* will help pastors and youth ministers in their efforts to minister the Gospel of Jesus Christ in culturally competent ways that speak to youth from all across the spectrum of humanity. I highly recommend it not only to pastors, youth ministers, seminary professors and seminarians, but also to parents who are trying to understand the cultures that shape our young people."

Jeremiah A. Wright, Jr., Pastor Emeritus, Trinity United Church of Christ, Chicago, Illinois

"This is an extremely stimulating, mind-stretching collection of presentations that articulate the emerging contours of Christianity the authors believe are needed for new times. Beyond broad strokes, the authors provide concrete ideas with respect to how these core emphases can be part of good ministries to children and youth. As such, this is an invaluable resource for Christian leaders who – like the hockey superstar – are skating not to where the puck is, but to where it is going to be."

Reginald W. Bibby, Board of Governors Research Chair, Department of Sociology, University of Lethbridge

"It is so important, and yet so hard, to fuse ideas with action, action with reflection. David Csinos and Melvin Bray have picked up this challenge in *Faith Forward* and wonderfully pushed us in this direction. Each chapter provides rich thoughts that draw the reader deep into thinking about her own ministry, seeing the connections between church and ministry, theology and life, youth ministry and children's ministry. This is a book that will challenge you and draw you into the fusion of new thoughts and actions."

Andrew Root, author of *The Relational Pastor, The Theological Turn in Youth Ministry*, and the Theological Journey Through Youth Ministry series

"Read this book with a pencil nearby. Read this book if you want to draw outside the lines of ministry with children and youth. Taste from the potluck of stories, ideas, and challenges from a remarkable group of women and men who care about how faith is nurtured and lived with all of God's children."

Elizabeth F. Caldwell, Harold Blake Walker Professor of Pastoral Theology, McCormick Theological Seminary

"When David Csinos, Melvin Bray, and others assembled 450 youth ministry and children's ministry leaders for the CYNKC conference in Washington, D.C., something truly extraordinary happened. They curated an ingenious environment in which prophetic imagination erupted, birthing innovative ways of thinking and dreaming about a new Christian renaissance of spiritual formation and living for children and youth in the world through the church of Jesus Christ. This book gives you a glimpse into some of the ideas that fueled this generative dialogue and will invite you to join the dialogue as God's Spirit woos us into God's good future."

Mike King, President of Youthfront, Executive Editor of *Immerse Journal*, author of *Presence-Centered Youth Ministry*

"The old institutions of Western Christianity have passed away. In *Faith Forward* you have the opportunity to listen to the pioneers of the coming era. Listen and be inspired by the creative, enlivening, and compassionate forms of community that emerge from those called to cultivate the freedom of Jesus among our children and youth."

Mark Yaconelli, author of *Contemplative Youth Ministry*

"*Faith Forward* makes important contributions to the discussion of how young people will participate in emerging church communities. The book offers a wide array of considerations and practices that should or could be brought into new contexts, including some gems on including children often marginalized and a new look at the idea of mission in today's diverse world. With 21 widely varied chapters to choose from, it's a book that can be enjoyed as the topics call to you."

Catherine Maresca, Director of the Center for Children and Theology,
Washington, D.C.

"Don't be fooled, this book is not just for those involved in children's and youth ministry! It's for all adults willing to wrestle with their own faith development. Before inspiring your next Sunday school plan, I hope this book challenges you to examine your own assumptions about what it means to be Christian today."

Joanna Shenk, editor of *Widening the Circle: Experiments in Christian Discipleship* and co-producer of the *Iconocast* podcast

"If you are looking to be engaged by some innovative and forward-thinking ideas about 21st-century children's and youth ministry, *Faith Forward* is a stimulating read. Moving us beyond the status quo, each chapter gives us a new lens for practicing a new evangelization."

Frank Mercadante, founder and Executive Director, Cultivation Ministries

What I love about *Faith Forward* is the breadth of the conversation and richness of the stories of its contributors. The narratives in these chapters are adventurous, inspiring, provocative, courageous, and full of practical wisdom. They invite us not simply to do things differently *to* young people, but to seek to become with them the kind of church that God is (re)shaping.

Craig Mitchell, Director of Christian Education and Discipleship, Adelaide College of Divinity and Flinders University, South Australia.

Faith Forward

Faith
Forward

A Dialogue on Children, Youth,
and a New Kind of Christianity

Edited by
David M. Csinos and Melvin Bray
Foreword by Shane Claiborne

CopperHouse

Editor: Ellen Turnbull
Cover design: Cyrus Gandevia
Interior and pre-press production: Cyrus Gandevia
Cover image: © Chris Schmidt/iStockphoto
Proofreader: Dianne Greenslade

CopperHouse is an imprint of Wood Lake Publishing, Inc. Wood Lake Publishing acknowledges the financial support of the Government of Canada, through the Canada Book Fund for its publishing activities. Wood Lake Publishing also acknowledges the financial support of the Province of British Columbia through the Book Publishing Tax Credit.

At Wood Lake Publishing, we practise what we publish, being guided by a concern for fairness, justice, and equal opportunity in all of our relationships with employees and customers. Wood Lake Publishing is committed to caring for the environment and all creation. Wood Lake Publishing recycles, reuses, and encourages readers to do the same. Resources are printed on 100% post-consumer recycled paper and more environmentally friendly groundwood papers (newsprint), whenever possible. A percentage of all profit is donated to charitable organizations.

Library and Archives Canada Cataloguing in Publication

Faith forward : a dialogue on Children, Youth, and a New Kind of
Christianity / edited by David M. Csinos and Melvin Bray ; foreword by
Shane Claiborne.

Includes bibliographical references.
ISBN 978-1-77064-574-5 (pbk.)

1. Church work with children–Congresses. 2. Church work with youth–Congresses. 3. Children–Religious life–Congresses. 4. Youth–Religious life–Congresses. I. Csinos, David M., 1984-, editor of compilation II. Bray, Melvin, editor of compilation III. Children, Youth, and a New Kind of Christianity Conference (2012 : Seattle, Wash.)

BV4447.F35 2013   259'.2   C2013-903171-5

Published by CopperHouse
An imprint of Wood Lake Publishing Inc.
9590 Jim Bailey Road, Kelowna, BC, Canada, V4V 1R2
www.woodlakebooks.com
250.766.2778

Printing 10 9 8 7 6 5 4 3 2 1
Printed in Canada by Marquis

To those who nurtured our faith

Patricia and Michael Csinos
and
Lorine Draughon and Melvin Bray, Jr.

and to those we hope to nurture

Jaya, Kari, and Melvin IV.

Acknowledgements

Pulling together this book has only been possible because of the contributions, assistance, and support of many individuals and organizations.

It all started with a conference, so it seems only fitting to begin by acknowledging our gratitude to the friends who tirelessly worked toward making a dream come alive. The planning team of the 2012 Children, Youth, and a New Kind of Christianity conference came together as an ad hoc community with a shared vision of making a historical impact the future of children's and youth ministry. Our thanks go out to our fellow planning team members: Danielle Shroyer, Michael Novelli, Amy Dolan, Amy Butler, and Ivy Beckwith. Although not an official member of the planning team, Brian McLaren has been an invaluable mentor and a true champion of our cause, and Jenny Csinos put in countless hours behind the scenes ensuring that everything from name tags to recordings ran smoothly.

Calvary Baptist Church showed the true spirit of hospitality as they welcomed 450 people for those four inspiring days in May 2012. From the time the conference was only a seed of an idea, the leadership of this congregation nurtured it through their encouragement, collaboration, and desire to be part of the journey at every step. In addition to Amy Butler, Senior Pastor at this church, our thanks extends to Paul Rosstead, Jason Smith, Leah Grundset Davis, Edgar Palacios, and the team of staff and volunteers at Calvary who caught the vision and took it to new heights.

From the moment he first heard about the conference and our desire to capture the event in the pages of a book, Mike Schwartzentruber had a feeling that we were onto something. He and the rest of the team at Wood Lake Books – particularly Ellen Turnbull, who worked with us throughout to give shape to this project – rallied around our efforts to produce this volume and offered helpful feedback throughout the process. Their genuine humility and faithful passion show us the very best of a new kind of Christianity.

The extraordinary group of authors and speakers whose words enliven these pages have been insightful partners on this journey. As they poured out their hearts, minds, and souls, they wove inspiring visions and offered prophetic challenges that add up to make this book what it is.

Our families have walked with us on every step of this pilgrimage and words fall short of conveying our appreciation to them. In particular, our wives, Jenny and Leslie, have graciously given us the gifts of space and time needed to undertake this project. They have showered us with support, offered copious amounts of patience, and – perhaps most importantly – pulled us away from this project when we needed to be pulled away.

Contents

FOREWORD

I think one of the most important things that the church can talk about today is spiritual formation, or what it means to grow up young Christians. But as I look at the church, it seems to me that we've got a problem on our hands.

There's a great book that Dave Kinnaman and Gabe Lyons wrote called *unChristian*. They travelled around the United States asking young non-Christians to describe their perceptions of Christians. Some of the top answers were that Christians are anti-gay, judgmental, and hypocritical – and the list doesn't get much better from there.

Clearly, we've got an image crisis on our hands. And if we're honest with ourselves, much of it is well-deserved. These perceptions are what people have seen and tasted and heard from Christianity.

The deep irony is that these aren't the perceptions that people walked away with when they met Jesus. They didn't meet Jesus and go away thinking, "Man, that brother doesn't like gay people." They walked away fascinated by his love.

We've tried all kinds of things in the church to help young people encounter Jesus. I grew up in the Bible belt where we played youth group games like chubby bunny. But youth group games don't really offer young people a chance to know Jesus and be one of his disciples. They may entertain young people, but they don't offer them a chance to become fascinated by Jesus' love.

We've also tried fear tactics. In one of the churches I attended, I remember watching a youth group skit about several teens riding in a car that hits a bus. Demons come out from stage left and drag all the kids who didn't know Jesus to hell. The dude who was playing the devil was

 **Shane Claiborne** unveils the tragic messes we've made of our world and the tangible hope that another world is possible. His ministry experience varies from working alongside Mother Teresa in Calcutta to serving a wealthy mega-congregation near Chicago. Shane is a founding partner of The Simple Way and author of several books, including *The Irresistible Revolution*.

so good at evoking fear that when the leaders gave an altar call even the associate pastor came forward.

We've even tried picketing. One of my friends recently told me about a music festival that he went to with his kids. As they walked up to the gates, they saw a group of Christians outside holding signs saying "Bob Marley is in hell" and "Janis Joplin is in hell." My friend looked at his kids and asked them what they thought about this situation. His son replied, "I didn't know they had such good music in hell."

Christians have tried youth group games, fear tactics, judgmental picket signs, and all sorts of other strategies for getting and raising new Christians. But I think that these sorts of things lead young people away from Christianity rather than towards it. They deform Jesus' message instead of forming people who love and live by that message.

We've got to recapture what it means to do formation and to grow up young people into the way of Jesus. Rather than just entertaining, or just preaching the bad news, we need to share the good news. That's what led me down the path of discipleship. Despite game after game of chubby bunny, and scare-you-straight youth group skits, in the end I didn't choose Jesus because I was scared to death of going to hell or because I loved games. I chose Jesus because he's good, and he's beautiful, and I fell in love.

I am convinced that the gospel, the good news, spreads best not through force but through fascination. It's not just something that is taught; it's something that's caught as we see folks who love in ways that we want to love, and act in ways that we want to act. This idea of formation is at the very heart of what it means to be Christian.

This is one of the reasons I love what happened at the 2012 Children, Youth, and a New Kind of Christianity conference, and why I have so much respect for Dave and Melvin and all the other folks who organized and attended this event. I think it demonstrates a maturing of conversations about what it means to be Christian in our world today. That event and this book remind us that we need to recapture what it means to disciple and be discipled. As Bonnie Raitt said, "Let's give them something to talk about." (Although I think she was talking about something else...)

Those of us who were part of this conference (and countless others like us) want a Christianity that we can touch and see and feel. We want a Christianity that fascinates the world by the way that we love. We want a Christianity that gives young people something to talk about.

Speaking of fascination, one of the cool things that I like about living in Pennsylvania is that we've got the Amish. I love the Amish. I was blown away by how the Amish responded after a terrible school shooting. In 2006, a man walked into an Amish school, shot ten little girls – five of whom died – and then shot himself. The Amish community responded by going to the shooter's family and asking them if there was anything they could do to help them in their time of grief. People from all over started pouring out money to the Amish and the community took this money and created scholarships for the children of the shooter. And they not only went to the funerals of their own children who died that day; they went together to the funeral of the shooter.

I was in Australia when this incident happened. Australia is very post-Christian and there aren't a lot of "good news stories" about Christians in the headlines in this country. Yet what made headline news when this horrific incident occurred was an article titled "Amazing Grace." The article asked why this Amish community would do what they did amidst this terrible tragedy. It told the story of not just the horror, but of the response and the love and grace of the Amish, love and grace which don't just happen, but which come with discipline and community cultivation. This community caught the whole world's attention with its love. It gave the world something to talk about.

What if the rest of Christianity had that imagination?

The word discipleship shares the same root as discipline. We need to remember this. We need to cultivate holy habits in children and youth, the disciplines of love and grace. We need to talk with young people about what it looks like to live as God's holy counterculture in the world. We need to talk about what it means not to conform to the patterns of this world, but to imagine new ways to live.

But we need to do more than just talk. We need to live in ways that make this counterculture come alive. We need to embody our new imaginings.

This is what saints do. People admire saints because saints hear the beat of a different drum. We know they live in ways that don't compute with the world around them. One of my favourite saints is St. Juniper, who followed St. Francis in the 13th century. He was notorious for giving away his clothes to the poor to the point that he sometimes went naked. And when the authorities told him never to give his clothes away again, he encouraged a beggar to steal them from him.

Imagine raising up a generation that has such imagination and boldness. Imagine raising up a generation that thinks to love their neighbours as themselves. Imagine raising up a generation that fascinates people with love.

Jacques Ellul was right when he said, "Christians were never meant to be normal. We've always been holy troublemakers, we've always been creators of uncertainty, agents of dimension that's incompatible with the status quo; we do not accept the world as it is, but we insist on the world becoming the way that God wants it to be. And the Kingdom of God is different from the patterns of this world."

Faith Forward talks about what it means to raise up young disciples. It suggests that spiritual formation involves a kind of faithfulness that's formed in community. It advocates new patterns for our communities too, through which children and youth become fascinated with the beauty of Jesus. That's right on the money. But as we strive to fascinate young people with the Jesus way, we're going to mess up along the way. So we have to continue to be honest about our contradictions and our hypocrisies. I don't think young people are looking for a church that's perfect. They're looking for a church that's honest. And I think that the problem is that we haven't been honest. We've pointed fingers at other people and yet we haven't been honest about ourselves and our own struggles. There's nothing fascinating about that. Young people need churches that can admit to the struggles and places we fall short, even as we strive to live in the way of Jesus.

So I'm excited and inspired by this book. I'm excited that Dave and Melvin brought together this eclectic group of voices that offer new hope and vision for the church and its young people. It leaves me hopeful that a generation of children's and youth ministers are asking how they can form young disciples who live in Jesus' way of love. And it gives me something to talk about.

Shane Claiborne

Introduction

Many Paths, One Journey

Both of us have always been people who play with our faith, in all the best senses of the phrase. Inspired by curiosity and imagination, we've experimented and tinkered with faith in all sorts of ways throughout our lives. And while the quests and paths on this journey are many, they are brought together through two common passions: a passion for faith formation with children and youth, and a passion for faithfully following Jesus.

Over the past decade or so, our own journeys led us to explore "new kinds of Christianity," those missional, emerging, forward-thinking expressions of following in the way of Jesus that continue to interrogate what it means to be disciples of Christ in our present age. Although our paths did not cross until a few years ago, by the time we connected with each other through a mutual friend we had both been swimming in this sea of fresh expressions for some time. And although we both felt at home in this water, we agreed that something seemed to be missing.

In different ways, we were both disconcerted by the lack of serious consideration about how to help youth and children swim in these waters with us. While there were a few resources bobbing around that addressed this topic, it seemed to us that conversations about young people within new kinds of Christianity remained marginal.

In 2009, Dave decided that enough was enough: it was time to bring the topic of faith formation with children and youth to the forefront of contemporary expressions of Christian faith and discipleship. He decided to hold a conference about this very topic and began contacting friends and colleagues, feeling out who would be interested in collaborating in such an event. And when Melvin heard about this guy who wanted to organize a conference, he got so excited that he moved to rally sponsorship even before he knew who this guy was. Later, he got in touch with Dave and offered to help in any way possible.

Children, Youth, and a New Kind of Christianity (CYNKC), as the conference was called, was born out of a desire to help practitioners, parents, pastors, professors, and all sorts of other folks spend time together in conversation and contemplation about nurturing faith in young people; faith that is generous, innovative, contextual, and even controversial. The conference was a conversation shared among many kinds of people: mainline and evangelical, Catholic and Protestant, believer and skeptic, young and old, novice and expert. All in all, about 450 people, from seven different countries and dozens of denominational inflections, gathered at Calvary Baptist Church in Washington D.C., for this event.

From the beginning, CYNKC was meant to be a place of dialogue, a coming together across lines of difference in order to explore common questions and share uncommon experiences. Grassroots, ecumenical, forward-thinking, innovative, collaborative – these values were at the heart of the conference. Many of the contributors to this event (and subsequently this book) did not live at the intersection of new kinds of Christianity and children's and youth ministry; many pitched their tent in either one camp or the other. But united by a desire to help young people on their journeys of faith, people from dissimilar ministry contexts and different areas of expertise and interest came together to step outside of their respective comfort zones and engage in mutually respectful conversation, exploration, and learning.

From May 7 to 10, 2012 the Spirit stirred as this eclectic rabble of disciples and allies joined forces at that church on the corner of 8th and H Streets. It was a sacred time for us, the fulfillment of a dream and the beginning of what would become an ongoing quest, one that led to the founding of Faith Forward, an organization dedicated to seeking ideas and practices for sharing new kinds of Christian faith with children and youth. And it seems only natural that we would continue the journey together by co-editing a book based on ideas shared at the conference. So we have done just that. Our hope is that the calls to action found herein will dare and delight readers in deeply meaningful ways, no matter one's ideological disposition.

Potlucks and Travel Journals

It's difficult to organize and pare down a collection of conference presentations into a book with some cohesion. The myriad of traditions, perspectives, and ideas at CYNKC collided to create something that was beautiful but also fleeting. In the process of developing this book, we've often asked ourselves and one another how we might coherently organize the diverse collection of authors and topics joined together in these pages.

Drawing imagery from the culinary world, books are often like meals with many courses. Each course brings something new to the table: mouth-watering hors d'oeuvres, savoury soup, fresh salad, succulent meat, and sweet dessert. Chefs carefully select ingredients and form flavour combinations for each course in ways that allow the meal to build on itself throughout the dining experience.

But as we collected pieces of this book, it didn't seem like we were preparing a multi-course dinner. Chapters came in all sorts of shapes and in all kinds of flavours. Some pieces seemed to be missing while other pieces seemed similar-yet-distinct from one another. Some chapters expressed deep theological and pedagogical theories, while others were based on years of experience in ministry with youth and children. This was no multi-course meal. It was a *potluck!*

While multi-course meals are neat and organized, potlucks are messy – even chaotic. Sometimes no one brings any dessert and other times everyone brings their favourite dessert. Sometimes there are no two dishes alike and at other times multiple people bring variations on a similar dish. Foods mix together as guests take spoonfuls from one another's offerings. Each plate ends up being a unique creation.

What potlucks lack in refinement they make up for in good-heartedness and passion for good food. At potlucks, people bring the best food they have to offer, whether it's a simple dish of rice and beans or a seven-layer carrot cake. At potlucks, no master chef is required. All are welcome to share what they like.

At our potluck, we have sought to give authors freedom to bring their best dishes to the table, spiced with their unique blends of traditions, beliefs, and ways of seeing the world. True, some of us who dine at this table may prefer different flavour profiles. But rather than seasoning one another's food so that it fits with our preferred tastes, our hope is to provide all with some comfort food, and stretch all by offering flavours that may be new for them.

While the image of a potluck offers one way of seeing this book, there's another metaphor that guided our task of collecting and editing this book. This metaphor also offers a way of reading it. This book chronicles a sojourn of our time together at CYNKC that was part of an ongoing journey that welcomes new pilgrims and offers guidance with each new step. In a sense, then, this book is a *travel journal*, a record of thoughts, ideas, practices, and moments shared on our common quest to ask new questions (and ask not-so-new questions again and in new ways) about nurturing young disciples. Each chapter is a field excursion on this journey, offering particular views and perspectives for reflection.

During your journey through this book you'll come across four signposts, each of which comes before a chapter that marks what appears to be a significant crossroad along the way of faith formation. You'll see each signpost coming into view in the chapters that precede it. And as you proceed from it, the themes and ideas spotlighted in the signpost continue to resonate throughout the chapters that follow. Like signposts on a trail, these signpost chapters not only recommend a course to follow, they also provide a reference point from which one can chart investigative excursions off the beaten path.

The quest begins with Brian McLaren's chapter. Although this marks the beginning of our common journey through this book, it is offered as a signpost rather than a starting point, for we all began our pilgrimages before opening this book. But our journeys merge at this first signpost. Brian calls us to disarm ourselves of weapons and relieve ourselves of baggage that we carry with us on this journey, weapons and baggage that we may not even know we are carrying. We should reflect upon this so that we don't unwittingly pass them on to younger generations.

As this first signpost fades behind us, a new one becomes visible on the horizon. At our second marker, Ivy Beckwith makes a passionate call for rediscovering imagination in our ministry with children and youth. She reminds us that imagination is at the heart of Christianity and it is through imaginative eyes that we can catch glimpses of God's reign, glimpses we can share with young people.

After moving through some chapters that carry on this call for imagination, the scenery begins to change and our eyes start to focus on the third signpost. As we reach Almeda Wright's chapter, the book shifts toward discussions surrounding how formational work with young people can lead them (and us) to infiltrate the world with God's love. Almeda invites us to cultivate young people who go public with their faith, who are active catalysts for positive change in the world. She calls us to nurture this spirit of public theology, reminding us of the prophetic nature of discipleship with young people.

And as we move on from this signpost, we are nearing the end of our common journey. But not before one final marker. We pause again as John Westerhoff, III reminds us that we are a pilgrim people, a Body of Christ always on the move. Young and old, we undertake our faith journeys in community, and it is through this community that the pilgrimage becomes sacred. It is in walking together that our lives are filled with faith.

And after this final signpost, the journey continues beyond the pages of this particular travel journal. We continue to question, seek, and forge new practices for nurturing – and being nurtured by – our young travel companions.

So let us walk together as a pilgrim people, doing so at our own pace and stopping to reflect as necessary. At times the road will be challenging and at times we may want to turn back. But fear not: we will find nourishment, rest, and encouragement for the journey. We can press onward in the hope proclaimed together at each corporate session of our time at CYNKC, led in song by our resident chorister, Bryan Moyer Suderman:

There's a new world coming, it's already here
There's a new world on its way.

There's a new world coming, it's already here
Let's begin to live that way.[1]

Unloading Our Ideological Guns

> I can hear your message
>
> I can listen to you
>
> I can pay attention 'cause
>
> I know your words are true
>
> I can let them change me
>
> What I say and what I do
>
> I can hear your message
>
> And I can be your messenger too.

-Bryan Moyer Suderman[1]

Bryan Moyer Suderman has a gift for writing songs that celebrate what God is doing in the world and invite everyone to join in. Bryan's "songs of faith for small and tall" have become favourites of families and congregations and have been published in many resources. He is a member of Community Mennonite Church in Stouffville, Ontario, where he lives with his wife and son.

Chapter 1

After the Maps Change:

Children, Youth, and a Church Yet to Be

Brian D. McLaren

In 1991, maps of Europe were divided by a line called the Iron Curtain. To the east of the line were the former Soviet Union and its allies, dominated by Communism. To the west was "the free world," dominated by capitalism. But the Berlin Wall fell in 1989 and the former Soviet Union collapsed in 1991. The Iron Curtain disappeared as a result.

In 1996, I travelled in Eastern Europe, visiting missionaries who had poured into lands that had formerly been under Soviet rule. In one city, my travelling companion and I arrived at a large house that was being used for youth ministry. Shortly after we arrived, young people started streaming in. I had never seen so many piercings, tattoos, metal studs in clothing, wild hairstyles, and garish goth clothing crammed together in one place.

Then the singing began. And prayer. And discussion around an open Bible. I couldn't understand a single word of the local language, but I could feel the sincerity, the faith, the love, the joy of these young people. It was clear that in the aftermath of a repressive regime there was a growing spiritual hunger.

After the last young person left, I asked the couple who led this

Brian D. McLaren is an author, speaker, activist, and former pastor. Brian's groundbreaking books include *A New Kind of Christian*, *A Generous Orthodoxy*, *A New Kind of Christianity*, and *Why Did Jesus, Moses, the Buddha, and Mohammed Cross the Road?* Brian and his wife, Grace, live in Florida and have four adult children and four grandchildren.

BRIAN D. MCLAREN

ministry a question that had been burning in my mind all evening: "The churches in this country have a reputation for being very conservative – legalistic, even. How are these young people being accepted in the churches?"

The wife and husband exchanged a quick glance.

"Should we tell him?" the wife asked.

"Go ahead," the husband answered.

She said to me, "The church that survived Communism needs to be celebrated for the courage and endurance of its members. But the changes that have come so quickly since 1991 are paralyzing for many, if not most, church leaders. We came here to do youth ministry to support the existing church, but now we realize we are training the next generation of church leaders. So this looks like a youth ministry, but we now see it as a seminary for the Eastern European church of tomorrow – the postmodern, post-industrial, post-colonial, post-Communist church that does not exist – yet."

At that time, I was in the early stages of my own paradigm shift. I was realizing that in the United States, my home, a similar chasm existed between younger and older generations. Modern, industrial, colonial, capitalist/Communist-era Christianity had effectively (and in many cases, tragically) adapted to its context. But now a new generation of young adults was spiritually hungry. They were seeking, asking questions, looking for meaning and hope and values. But was the only option open to them a modern, industrial, colonial, Cold War version of the faith?

If not, who would go through the challenging task of disentangling the Christian gospel from its accepted and normative cultural forms so that its treasures could be shared with a new generation?

A few years later, I wrote a book called *The Church on the Other Side*. The "other side" referred to the emerging culture beyond modernity, the world after the maps changed, the world taking shape within a new paradigm. Shortly after that, I wrote *A New Kind of Christian*, and some years later, *A New Kind of Christianity*. In each book, I grappled with the same issue I saw so clearly that night in Eastern Europe: the church that heroically survived the challenges of modernity was in a defensive posture. Asking the church to quickly change its posture so as to welcome in this new generation of spiritual seekers was asking too much.

Some of us needed to do the hard work of theological reformulation, liturgical renewal, missional retooling, and so on, whether or not our work would be accepted or even understood by the existing church. We needed to invest in the church of tomorrow, with or without the support of the church of today.

Predictably, young adult ministers and church planters were attracted to this challenge. A wide range of fresh expressions began springing up – mostly aimed at young adults outside the paradigms of modern, colonial, industrial, capitalist Christianity. These fresh expressions of Christian faith didn't fit into the old dichotomies of Protestant/Catholic or liberal/conservative or charismatic/non-charismatic. Rather, they responded to a whole new set of issues, problems, and questions that Protestants, Catholics, liberals, conservatives, charismatics, and non-charismatics were all oblivious to.

And although there is still so much more work to be done, we have made some small advances over the last decade or so.

But again and again over this last decade, many of us said, "While we're innovating for young adults, we're still teaching our children and youth with the same old off-the-shelf curricula that are based on the same old assumptions as before." True, many of those off-the-shelf curricula have gotten flashier and more hi-tech. And true, there are growing numbers of curriculum designers and religious educators who are far ahead of the curve. But there was still a huge vacuum in a well-thought-out approach to the spiritual formation of children and youth that would prepare them for Christian faith, life, and mission in the new emerging world.

As David Kinnaman had made clear in *You Lost Me*, "The church is not adequately preparing the next generation to follow Christ faithfully in a rapidly changing culture."[1] Instead, the church is too often seen as overprotective, shallow, anti-science, repressive, exclusive, and doubtless.[2]

As a result, the church is facing a largely unacknowledged retention crisis. We're raising kids who will drop out in large numbers (probably around 80%) when they come of age. We're catechizing young people into failing forms of Evangelicalism and Pentecostalism, failing forms of institutional or mainline Protestantism, and failing forms of Roman Catholicism and Eastern Orthodoxy. We try harder and spend more, but retention rates only get worse. We hope the young people will come back when they're older, but when they don't, we feel guilty and depressed.

Sooner or later, of course, we'll realize that harder work, more spending, and ever-increasing guilt and depression are not great ways forward. And that's when we'll start to envision, talk about, and experiment with a new kind of whole-life spiritual formation intended to form disciples who practise a new kind of Christian faith.

Now, when I say "new kind," I realize that Christian faith has always been evolving and emerging, even though many of its loudest proponents seem to deny that fact. So in that light, the new kind of Christianity I'm advocating is actually the old kind, the kind that has always been; the evolving, learning, growing kind. To continue evolving and emerging is actually to be faithful to our living, growing, organic tradition. The kinds of faithful evolution and change that Christians have traditionally practised have been both conservative and progressive – careful to retain what must be retained and eager to embrace what should be embraced. And that conservative/progressive balance has always been notoriously hard to maintain, with the real danger that the faith can go off the road into one of the ditches on either side by refusing the right innovations or embracing the wrong changes.

Many of us are in greater danger of the former, but we're more afraid of the latter, and we are "policed" by those who share the latter fear. That fear must be faced and overcome so that we can engage in the challenge wisely articulated in words attributed to organizational theorist Otto Scharmer:

> What's missing today is a high-quality discourse on rethinking the design and evolution of the entire system from scratch.

> The quality of results produced by any system depends on the quality of awareness from which the people in the system operate.

Our challenge, if Scharmer is right, is two-fold. First, we need to rethink our entire system, and do so from an extraordinary quality of awareness. That quality of awareness, I believe, requires us to join together two things that we so often put asunder. Firstly, we need a profoundly receptive spiritual consciousness, open to guidance from the living God, that intentionally seeks wisdom from beyond ourselves, including an openness to divine wisdom coming from unexpected sources. Secondly, we need a radically engaged thought process. In other words, we don't need human rationality alone, nor do we need a mystical mindset alone. But rather we need a mind-heart attitude that goes to the limits of our own understanding and welcomes resources that come from beyond those limits.

Such an attitude brings us to our second challenge. We need to "let go" of long-held assumptions, many of which we are hardly aware of. We then need to "let be," to not rush or push, but maintain a posture of receptivity. In that posture of heart, we can "let come" and see what new possibilities emerge.

Of course, this process is already ongoing, and those of us who have been deeply engaged in the letting go, letting be, and letting come process can report that at least seven areas are full of rethinking at this moment.

1. Theological Detoxification

There is a profound theological detoxification going on in which we face the ways that our resources – the Bible, theology, liturgy, mission – have been used for violence and harm. A tragic episode from my home state of Florida can serve as an analogy. A five-year-old child brought a loaded gun to school. After it fell out of his pocket, authorities scrambled to figure out how on earth this child got access to a loaded gun in the first place. It turns out the weapon was in his stepfather's truck and the boy found it in the glove box on the way to school. Fortunately, no one was injured, but the incident highlighted how easily tragedies can occur.

Similarly, there are Bible verses lying around our churches and homes that are like loaded guns. We've got loaded weapons in our nightstands in the Gideon Bible – words that have been used to harm Jews, Aboriginal peoples, women, LGBTQ people, Muslims, and others. Of course, similar statements can be made about the sacred texts of other faiths, but we need to deal with the logs in our own eyes. If we're going to be responsible ministers to children and youth, and if our next two millennia are to be less violent than our first two, we need to find and unload the weapons that are lying around our ecclesial households, and we must remove toxic, hostile elements from our theological identities for our own spiritual health, and of course for the well-being of "the other" as well.

2. Identity Formation

This theological detoxification leads to a radical re-exploration of Christian identity formation. How do we form (and reform) Christian character that is distinguished not by strength and hostility to the other on the one hand, or by weakness and tolerance of the other on the other hand, but by strength and benevolence to the other?[3] How can we develop in young generations of disciples a strong sense of us-ness that welcomes otherness – cultural, political, economic, sexual, spiritual, and religious – and leads to one-another-ness?

We know how to have strong Christian identities that are hostile to other faiths, and we know how to have weak Christian identities that are tolerant toward other faiths. But we haven't figured out how to have a strong Christian identity that is benevolent to people of other faiths, so that the stronger our Christian commitment is, the more benevolent it will be.

Christian identity is largely formed by the kinds of people who would take the time to read this book, people who care about children and youth enough to make concerted efforts to learn how to minister with them in better ways. How do we turn otherness into one-another-ness in which each identity is respected and intact? This is a huge challenge for us as we move forward together.

3. Integral Mission

Fresh thinking and practice in the first two areas lead to new approaches to integral mission, where we face brokenness and sin on many levels – personal, institutional, social, economic, ecological, spiritual – and we seek to heal that brokenness with the *shalom* of God.

For the sake of our young people and that new kind of Christianity that's in the process of being born, we've got to embed in children and youth a sense of integral mission, mission that helps them come to a vital spiritual life by integrating the personal with the institutional.

Institutions are important. Anything that lasts more than a generation involves an institution. So contrary to the opinions of some, institutional survival is not negative in and of itself. But we need to ask questions about the nature and purposes of an institution, about whether or not it is doing a good job fulfilling these purposes, and about whether or not it deserves to survive.

But institutional mission is not nearly enough. We need to help children and youth form a wide sense of mission that makes room for social mission, economic mission, and ecological mission, to name a few. This idea hits home for me when I consider that many of the young children in our churches and families will likely be alive at the beginning of the 22nd century. But I wonder what the sea level will be then? How many nuclear wars will be fought between now and then? How will the culture wars in society have evolved? These sorts of questions remind me how important it is to help young people have a sense of mission in the world in order for them to thoughtfully and courageously address the big issues of our time and of times to come.

4. Lifelong Spiritual Formation
Fresh thinking and practice in the first three areas lead us to grapple with questions of lifelong spiritual formation. How can we lead people into lifelong growth that is developmentally sensitive, that employs needed rites of passage, that makes appropriate calls to commitment, that never implies "you've arrived – there's nothing more for you to learn," that avoids dead ends and false promises, that draws from wise educational theory, and that employs appropriate technology?

For many years, it was commonly held that children and youth grow, and adults just stay the same. But we now know better. The truth is that adults are dynamic, and grow as much as anyone else. So we need to think about the spiritual life in a holistic sense. This opens up many doors to exciting possibilities for new practices of faith, including rites of passages and spiritual exercises.

My sister-in-law is a math educator. She has a Ph.D. not in math, but in *math education*. Speaking with her about her work over the years, I have come to realize that we know a lot about how to teach people counting, then adding and subtracting, then multiplying and dividing, then geometry and fractions, then algebra and trigonometry, and so on. We have a well-developed sense of scope and sequence, and we know a lot about how kids learn math. But the sad truth is that we don't know much about how to teach children to love their enemies. We don't know much about how to teach teens to walk the extra mile. And we don't know much about how to teach kids how to love God with the whole self. We tell them they ought to, but we don't tend to give them the tools they need for loving God. We don't have curricula for these sorts of topics that are vital to the Christian life of faith.

But before we move onto the *how* questions, we need to wrestle with the questions of *who* and *what*. Who is it that we are teaching? Who are we who are doing the teaching? What are we called to pass on to younger generations?

5. Healing Doctrine

Surely this theological fomentation will not leave our doctrinal formulations untouched. How can we rediscover the root meaning of doctrine as healing teaching rather than destructive dogma? How can we write creeds and confessions that address the questions and challenges of our day with no less faithfulness and courage than our ancestors brought to their creeds and confessions?

This need became clear to me when I was in South Africa a few years ago and learned about the Belhar Confession. Alan Boesak and others in the Dutch Reformed church realized that after 2,000 years of Christian history we had lots of creeds that grappled with all kinds of dogmatic issues protecting the church from heresy, but we had nothing – absolutely nothing – in our essential doctrinal documents dealing with injustice. We were well protected from Arianism, but not well protected from apartheid. The same could be said about anti-Semitism, Islamophobia, consumerism, and environmental irresponsibility.

So these South African leaders decided it was about time that someone did something to address this gap. They wrote a confession that acknowledges God as just and identifies racism as sin. Their bold action raises the question of us today: what is it time for us to say? What needs to be acknowledged centre stage in our theological teaching?

6. Branding and Rebranding

On a more practical level, all of this reformulation presents what marketing specialists would call branding problems. How can we communicate both fidelity to our past and faithful breaks with this past?

Although there are limitations and problems with using business-related terms, I think that speaking of this issue as one of branding and rebranding helps to clarify the serious problems and struggles we face. As the research of David Kinnaman demonstrates, we Christians have done all sorts of things to damage our brand.

When we think about branding, we might think about the difference between Coca-Cola and Pepsi. From what I hear, most people prefer Pepsi in blind taste-tests. But when they are told that the cup on the right contains Coke and the the one on the left is filled with Pepsi (regardless of what is actually in the cups), people tend to prefer Coke. The actual taste of the product is less significant than what the brain associates with a brand. And Coca-Cola knows this and has expertly branded itself.

Another big player in the world of branding is Disney. Disney pours time and talent into thinking about how to win four-year-olds to their brand and how to prepare them to be 14-year-olds and 24-year-olds who continue to remain faithful to their brand. I wouldn't be surprised if Disney starts opening up senior citizen communities, because they'll have studied these people from birth to old age, and they'll have learned how to keep them loyal to their brand for life!

We've got a lot to learn about branding and rebranding. We've got a lot to think about as we seek to pass on a Christian faith that people can fall in love with and remain faithful to for life.

7. Regenerative Christian Practice

How can we grapple with the challenges outlined above without exhausting ourselves, creating havoc in our communities and institutions, and destroying the very community that we love and seek to serve? How can we sustain our own morale – and income – in draining, uncertain, and turbulent times?

More and more, issues of sustainability are arising in all sorts of fields (such as economics, environmental practice, and business, to name a few). We in the church need to think about sustainable Christian practice. But we can't stop there. We need to go one step further and think about what my friend Pamela Wilhelms calls *regenerative* Christian practice.

Although I've recently met all sorts of people who excel at and are enlivened by their vocations as youth and children's ministry workers, I speak mostly to senior pastors and denominational officials – and I don't run into too many who are feeling great about their calling and their work. I'm finding that many of these leaders are less healthy than they were six months ago; and already at that time they were less healthy than they were a year before that. They're losing momentum little by little and just hanging on because they operate in systems that aren't sustainable, let alone regenerative. Their own life energy is being drained to keep the system operating.

It can get somewhat depressing to think about all the work that is before us if we're going to make our discipling of children and youth sustainable or, better yet, regenerative. But from another perspective, it is exciting to think that we are in on the ground floor of something very important. If we pay proper attention to self-care and self-renewal, if we wisely keep things in perspective, 20 or 30 years from now we could leave a much more robust legacy for the next generation of children and youth workers than the one we have inherited. That's one of the reasons we need each other in professional friendships, associations, networks, and movements; we can help one another stay renewed and refreshed for the long run, so that together we have maximum impact.

The Most Important Work

These are, no doubt, among the deepest possible questions that can be asked. They're on a very different level from "How can we get more butts in seats?" or "Who is our target audience?" or "What is our budget shortfall this year and how can it be reduced?" or "Which curriculum will we buy for VBS this summer?" The deep questions acknowledge that we are in the midst of a profound shift, a shift that requires us to rethink everything.

If the falling of the Berlin Wall in 1989 signalled the beginning of the end of the Communist bloc, perhaps we are now witnessing the crumbling of a capitalist bloc, a colonialist bloc, and the passing of an era of Western hegemony for which Christendom served as a kind of chaplaincy. Perhaps this Christendom should and must pass away. But from its tomb, something beautiful is arising: a new kind of Christianity. It has been gestating for a long, long time. In fact, its genes have been present since the beginning, and conditions today are calling for it to evolve, to emerge, to be born.

This emergence explains why we can no longer afford to think creatively about adults and young adults while leaving children and youth in their classrooms with the same old curricula based on the same old educational assumptions, rooted in unquestioned theological dogma. We need leaders – thousands of them, our very best and most talented leaders – to devote their whole lives to this work. What we create may, on the surface, still look like ministry for children and youth as we know it now. But at a deeper level, we must – like my friends in Eastern Europe back in the 1990s – see it as a seminary for the church that is yet to be, the postmodern, post-industrial, post-colonial, post-Communist, post-capitalist, post-Christendom church that does not exist – yet.

This may be the most important work of all. After all, Jesus said, "Of such is the kingdom of heaven."

Chapter 2

Confessions of a
Sunday School Superstar

Janell Anema

If there was a hall of fame for Bible-thumping, my portrait would surely hang upon those sacred walls. My stories of Sunday school superstardom are tall tales of epic proportions. I have years of material, enough to keep my Millennial peers laughing (and some days crying) for hours.

I grew up in church. Stories from my childhood watch like one of those drug education commercials from the early 1990s, but instead of featuring the hard-lit egg frying on a stove, the story would be blanketed in Presbyterian stained glass light and animated across felt boards. "This is Janell's brain. This is Janell's brain on Christianity!"

I came to faith at a young age because, truth be told, I fell quickly for the man with the lamb – the captivating Christ. You know the one, with the long locks and the deep blue eyes. I was head over heels for dreamy Jesus.

In the midst of what must have been the party for my fifth birthday, I quietly slipped past the amateur distractions of cake and presents into my darkened bedroom, to kneel down in front of my bed. Assuming the position of a Precious Moments figurine, hands clasped at heart's centre, I invited that blue-eyed dreamboat to take up residence inside my heart. My parents had told me that Jesus was the greatest gift of all, and

Janell Anema has been a waitress, professor, church secretary, and avid vacationer who recently relocated to Philadelphia, Pennsylvania. She hopes to continually integrate her passions for travel, the Lord, people, and the church as she seeks to love God and love people in communities around the world.

seeing how it was my birthday, I was going to put that gift on lockdown. It seemed only fitting.

I became a Christian that September afternoon, and then again a few months later at a Christmas Eve service. Over the next decade, in variations on the themes of the four spiritual laws, I invited Sweet Blue Eyes into my heart anytime I heard the "Sinner's Prayer." But I often found myself wondering if I had accidentally cancelled out my salvation. Can two prayers negate a conversion? Does the second, fourth, or 128th prayer cancel the first, third, or 127th? Am I on odds or evens? At best, it was recommitment; at worst it was obsessive-compulsive. Yea, though I walk through the valley of the shadow of over-analysis…

My faith as a child and adolescent was all-consuming – and this all-consuming fire of a faith wasn't just about conversion; it was also about fashion. I certainly looked the part of a Sunday school superstar. Every Wednesday night I buttoned up a maroon polyester vest accessorized with three plastic crowns, each about the size of a silver dollar; crowns with holes so small one might not notice them, were it not for the jewels. The crowns were studded with small-yet-oh-so-sparkly sapphires, rubies, and emeralds earned by doing chores around the house, memorizing scripture verses, and participating in the Bible Olympics. No need to cast blame and judgment toward my parents. My mom was creative, sure, but this system of jewel distribution was not her idea. This was the doing of our local Sunday school. My relationship with God became limited to my ability to perform and gather treasures that were redeemable in heaven. I could collect blue ribbons and tiny jewels and my faith was substantiated and quantified. And I loved it! I loved being good at religion.

Graduating from jewels as I entered junior high youth group, I began collecting whatever sort of religious currency the church was passing out like Monopoly money. I took a ride on the reading railroad, travelling through Kings, Chronicles, and Corinthians. Twice. My mom would often take my brothers and me to drop off Thanksgiving baskets to kids whose parents were in jail. Bail money is hard to come by when there's no such thing as a Free Parking. I avoided landing on Marvin Gardens of Gethsemane, but worked to build a hotel on Saint James Place and consecrate it to the lord of prosperity. Another Easter. Another Advent. Pass Go. Collect $200. Tithe $20. And round the board I went.

Ever the overachiever, I was at church Tuesdays, Wednesdays, Fridays, and twice on Sundays. I was baptized at 14, not as a symbol of my discipleship, but to ensure my eligibility to cast a vote at budget meetings as a full member of the congregation. I worked tirelessly to become an informed voter, taking notes during Sunday night business meetings as earnestly as I took sermon notes on Sunday mornings. Colour-coded, doodled memory verses and Lottie Moon offering estimations filled my journals.

I was being informed yes, but I was also being trained and equipped. During "Big C" church I often found myself battling in prayer for the pastor: "Lord, prohibit the enemy from distracting us with coughing and cellphone rings. Surely you will silence the mouths of crying babies seeking to detract from what the pastor has to say!" Never had I felt like such an integral part of the Lord's army.

I loved the militarism of my faith. It was rigid and ritualistic. And I was always on the winning team. Our youth group summer games of capture the flag easily informed my growing understanding of missions, my birthright as an American Christian, and my responsibilities as such.

I'm sure we've all heard these kinds of stories before from people of my generation. With a dash of wit and a pinch of cynicism, from conferences to camp reunions, I have swapped stories with fellow Sunday school superstars (we're everywhere!); we who revelled in our religiosity, we who celebrated our cultural Christianity – American Christianity, our mother tongue.

But what happens when we grow up?

Heading off to a state university and then choosing to study abroad, I left my Christian subculture and then the continent. I moved to Switzerland for a semester and in ironic providence the only bag that was lost en route contained my electronic converters, my belts, and my Bible. I would be alone in "post-Christendom" Europe without those things that were supposed to gird me – to protect me – from strange currents and strange customs.

On yet another September afternoon, in a conference room in Geneva, I listened to the communications director from Doctors without Borders share about their most recent expedition to West Africa. He told harrowing tales of life in post-conflict Liberia, about the last capital city in the world without municipal power and running water, about a nation where less than 10% of the population had access to health care and upwards of 90% of the women had been victims of gender-based violence.

Questions flooded my mind. Where is Liberia? Why does their flag look so much like ours? What did he just say? They performed surgeries on children who had been wounded in war – not as mere victims, but as soldiers? Did he just say *child* soldiers? How could this be real? How could they skip over the wounds of these wars on global missions Sundays at my church back home? And what kind of God allows this horror and trauma to ravage humanity? I thought Jesus loved the little children, all the children of the world. At least that's what I had been singing.

The world was broken. It was more damaged and disregarded than I knew what to do with. I questioned. I wept. No easy answers came. In those 90 minutes the world unexpectedly became too big and too broken for my one-dimensional Jesus, and my Sunday school religion and I experienced an acute sensation of unravelling. I was in foreign territory and found that I was fluent in a faith that no longer made sense. I suddenly became wildly uncomfortable with the militaristic connotations, nay, *integral components* of my religious vocabulary. I didn't want to be a soldier in the Lord's army anymore. I didn't want to be a soldier at all.

My understanding of God was all too elementary. It now seemed more important to find God living in and among this world and its people than to believe that God lived only in my heart. How could I wait patiently, looking to heaven, when there was a lived hell for so many here and now? The jewels I had collected from childhood and worn proudly were tarnished, representative of little more than my ability to memorize words and phrases. Those words, those scriptures as I knew them, bore no direct correlations to the way I was now encountering the world. I was undone.

I returned to the United States wanting to exchange my outdated religious currency. But my local church was still setting the rate. Sunday services seemed irrelevant to all that I had experienced and learned in my months away. Messages were preached according to the same sort of isolationist Christianity that had precipitated my crisis of faith, this great unravelling.

As it often goes, a loss of innocence can lead to an increase in humanity – and I was desperate to engage this new paradigm, to know more of humanity, to know more of this big, broken, and beautiful world. Not knowing how to engage the deep pain and brokenness of the world in the church, but hungry for answers, I went back to school.

During my first semester at Eastern University in the Campolo College for Graduate Studies I enrolled in a course entitled "Economic Development for Developing Nations." My beloved professor, Dr. John Stapleford (who had the imagination to assign a Bonhoeffer text in an economics course), asked us to write a reflection paper on the interface between economic systems and the kingdom of God. And what did I do?

I Googled "kingdom" + "of" + "God."

I was a Sunday school superstar. I was raised in church. I had been digesting spiritual truths as long as I had been eating solid food. And I was 24 years old when I first learned about the kingdom of God – on the interweb rather than in a pew.

I spent the rest of my semester with Brian McLaren, John Howard Yoder, Stanley Hauerwas, and Lesslie Newbigin – my theological boyfriends (later I drew insight from Lauren Winner, Joan Chittister, Cynthia Bourgeault, and Anne Lamott – my spiritual sisters). Bonhoeffer finally felt like an ally and not an accuser. Slowly, every scripture verse I had hidden in my heart was illuminated and translated in ways that brought me such life. I was child-like in my faith once again, but it felt honest and fresh. It was enlivening. I was being knit back together. So this is what it feels like to be born again...

I was ravenous for this new knowledge – this new kind of Christianity, this new kind of king, and this new kind of kingdom. A kingdom that is now and not yet realized. God's dreams for the world coming true. The mustard seed. The yeast. The pearl. I devoured the texts and relished every word.

In the perfect combination of my naïve persistence and God's infinite kindness, I was given the chance to go to Liberia and work among those very children whose existence had sparked my personal reformation. I couldn't wait to put my love into practice – to have my faith inform my praxis. I was equipped, but this time I had Derek Webb on my iPod and a fresh pair of Toms shoes.

I set out to love the world, one child at a time.

I lived and worked in Monrovia, Liberia's capital city, in the equivalent of Child Protective Services. There was one incredible project our organization was running where young women who had been perpetrators and victims of war were living together. A home functioned as a rehabilitation centre for 25 female former child-soldiers and other vulnerable females and their children (this particular cycle had young women ranging from 12 to 24 years old and ten of them had children, ranging from a few months to five years old). The girls lived at the home for nine months and took accelerated learning programs in the morning and vocational skills training classes in the afternoon, as well as participating in twice-daily devotional times, social skills/health dialogues, and one-on-one counselling opportunities with their social worker. This home was a safe place where the women's physical, emotional, educational, and spiritual needs could be met.

The housemothers and counsellors approached me, hoping I would spend the afternoons doing physical activities with the young women and facilitating some sort of Christian Bible study. Eager to share about God with those girls, those babies with babies, I mapped out a nine-week curriculum on the fruit of the spirit. I stopped at the market to purchase markers and coloured papers. I arts-and-crafted each fruit, each characteristic, carefully and with great attention to detail.

Week one: apples and love. With the "o" in the word "love" I drew a leaf and a stem so when I brought a bag full of apples to share that afternoon, the women might see the connection between the sweet fruit of the spirit and the sweet fruit in their mouths.

Genius, I thought.

I talked about how much God loved them. How he loved them so much that he gave his one and only son. I'm certain that we ended the day with *my* recitation of John 3:16. I'm not sure they even understood my English, but that was not important to me. The speaking of the word would certainly be planting seeds, just like the apple, that would bear fruit in this life and the next.

Week two: bananas and joy. I spoke of the kind of deep joy that we can have even if circumstances are painful. Joy is not happiness, I was sure to remind them, and I may or may not have performed "I've got the joy, joy, joy, joy down in my heart."

It wasn't until week three that I even *noticed* the disconnection between the words that I was reciting and the realities of life for those young women in Liberia. I had brought pineapple because that day we were going to talk about peace, and the platitudes rolled so quickly off my tongue: pineapple and peace. I liked the sound of that! I told the ladies that God gives them peace like rivers in their souls (unlike the rivers in Nimba County that were dyed red with the blood of a nation only a few short years ago). I shared that Jesus is the Prince of Peace (not like Prince Johnson, the warlord who murdered so many Liberians, maybe even some of their own family members). I preached about the peace that passes understanding to children of a nation recovering from 14 years of civil war.

Week four: oranges and self-control. I passed the orange slices along as I asked the young women – girls who had been abused, girls who had been raped, child brides, child soldiers – to brainstorm times when they had seen people exhibit self-control. Our lesson was short that day.

During my final week in Liberia, I gathered the last $83 stashed in my suitcase and used it to purchase gifts for the young women. I racked my brain thinking about the ways that I could most effectively put my money to use. I couldn't pay for all of their school fees, and while Susanna's young child clearly had tuberculosis, how could I neglect the wounds and illnesses of the other young children at his expense? With the pressing needs of child health in front of me, I settled on a gift that moths and rust would not destroy. I purchased 25 hardcover, gold-paged, red-lettered King James Bibles.

I preached at those girls, educating them about kindness and goodness and faithfulness. With each lesson, I found I was not sharing words of love, but telling lifeless stories about a God I didn't understand, and a Christ I didn't know. I didn't know a Christ who was the word, the word made flesh, the word who entered the world and its sciences, its humanity and its suffering, its wars and its wounded.

Paralyzed by the sorrow and brokenness in the world and in the lives of those young women, and in a cheap effort to alleviate my own discomfort, I handed out religious presents instead of offering my presence as a follower in the way of Jesus. I didn't know how to share kingdom theology or how to speak new kinds of Christianity, so I quickly transitioned back into my first language: evangelical fundamentalism in a mission trip dialect. As the weight of the disconnect grew heavier, I rooted myself more firmly in my old-time religion, a version of Christianity that I had spent so much time trying to unlearn.

I had lost the language of the kingdom.

Ralph Waldo Emerson once said that "the world is all gates, all opportunities, strings of tension waiting to be struck."[1] I had set out into the world ready to pass through the gates and take advantage of opportunities before me. But I had not yet developed a theology of tension, the kind of theology that lets us live well as faithful, integrated, connected followers of Jesus. I was a Sunday school superstar, but I didn't know a compassionate Christ who was unimpressed with my crown of jewels, yet ardently, patiently, and passionately in love with his child.

As I think about my life as a Sunday school superstar, I struggle with tenses. It sounds much better to say that I *was* a Sunday school superstar. My faith *was* disconnected. I *was* impotent. I *was* paralyzed.

But I still find it much easier to be good at religion than to press in and ask for revelation. My native tongue is one of platitudes and parables that read much more like Aesop's fables than the living and active word of God. If I'm not careful I *still* live like a Sunday school superstar.

I've exchanged my polyester vest for a social justice sash. Instead of jewels for scripture memory, I now earn merit badges for new, emerging kinds of Christianity. There's the relocate-to-abandoned-places-of-the-empire badge. The fair-trade-shopping badge. The pacifism badge. I'm more green, more locally rooted, more affirming. And I've found that I can also be good at this new kind of Christianity.

But I want more.

So those who have ears let them hear. Let these words fall on soft soil, that we might look at those eager children and active youth in our churches and in our families and be compelled to speak life into them, model an integrated faith for them, and press into the tensions of this world with them, groaning and longing for the kingdom that is not yet and is now coming. Together.

As I've learned to question and be questioned by scripture, I have come to affirm its power. My confessions are not accusations against the Bible, but evidence of my inability to use it as a translator to engage the world. My words are evidence of my incapacity to know the Word as Emmanuel, God with us.

Let me affirm that in the midst of my striving and failing, in the midst of my disconnection, God was (and is) still sovereign. God was still on the move, gathering sons and daughters. God was in Liberia before I got there and God's been there since I left. And in those few short months, both *in* and *in spite* of me, God was working.

Let these confessions do what they can, as both admissions of guilt and acts of praise. God is making all things new – even the faith of this Sunday school superstar.

Chapter 3

In Search of a Raceless Gospel

Starlette McNeill

There's a well-known song often heard within the walls of Sunday school classrooms: "Jesus loves the little children / all the children of the world / red and yellow, black and white / all are precious in his sight / Jesus loves the little children of the world."[1]

But the truth is that this is not how Jesus loves children – or anybody, for that matter. Rather, this song speaks of how Christ's church loves young people and how the leaders of children and youth teach them to love themselves and others. We (the church and those of us who lead, teach, and minister in the church) teach young people to love conditionally or categorically. Consciously or unconsciously, after we pass out the cookies, the Bible story colouring books, and the crayons, we pass down to the children and youth of our sacred communities the traditions of race.

There is a reason I distrust race and call for its exclusion in the development and practice of the Christian faith. I can't be satisfied with simply the end of racism. I have a niece who's ten years old. When she was born, the women of the family gathered in my sister's hospital room. With the same mixture of excitement and concern as when they counted her fingers and toes, they inspected her ears. These women were

Starlette McNeill is Coordinator for the Center for Ministerial Leadership at the District of Columbia Baptist Convention in Washington, D.C. She is a graduate of Buffalo State College and Colgate Rochester Crozer Divinity School. Her blog, *The Daily Race*, seeks to create sacred space for the questions that arise in the practice of faith due to the social reality of race. She is married to John C. McNeill, Jr. and they have an amazing son, John C. McNeill, III.

trying to determine whether she would be light- or dark-skinned, because some African-Americans believe that the colour of a baby's ears at birth determines the skin colour of the child.

After the women had checked her ears, they breathed a sigh of relief, as if we had avoided a major health scare. They all agreed that she would be light-skinned. I sat in a corner of the room, staring in disbelief. It was as if I had witnessed a murder, the death of my niece's unique life and its gifts. Soon thereafter, the women began to discuss all of the hardships that this child would escape because she had avoided the compound curse of being "black and ugly." It was then that I decided that I would check my own ears and begin to examine the ways in which race was ruling my life and determining the outlook and outcome of the lives of others. There is so much more to my niece's life, and the lives of all children, than race. I began this journey in hopes of finding healthier ways of describing it. A living document, this chapter is part of the journey.

I can only speak out of my own experience. Thus, I have few anecdotes as intimate as that one to provide insight into how persons of other backgrounds demonstrate as deep a racial grounding. But I know they have that grounding, and I have experienced the ramifications of it all my life. I trust that readers can examine closely and deal honestly with their own experiences so as to see what damage racial structures both within and without have done to them and those around them.

Colouring Christianity

Historically the church has tended to accept race and agree with its conclusions regarding humanity while affirming the creation narrative in Genesis and claiming the believer's position as redeemed in Christ. Instead of challenging the use of race in society and ensuring that it finds no place in the kingdom of God, we have tended to create theories,[2] theologies, denominations, and worship services that support the social construct of race and its progeny. Winthrop D. Jordan wrote of this "fusion of religion and nationality" in *The White Man's Burden*, concluding that, "From the first, then, the concept embedded in the term *Christian* seems to have conveyed much of the idea and feeling of *we* against *they*: to be Christian was to be civilized rather than barbarous, English rather than African, white rather than black."[3] He goes on to say that by the early 1700s, "'Christianity' had somehow become intimately and explicitly linked with complexion."[4]

Today, we continue to place persons of different cultures into these social categories and thus incorporate racial formation (the shaping of a racial identity and perspective) into our teachings on Jesus Christ and his love. Though we may feel that children are too young to understand race and racialization, we sing about Jesus and we talk about race. We create distinctions, separating persons according to the social colouring of skin like loads of laundry – light and dark. But this does not depict the unconditional love of God. Instead, it depicts the way that race loves us. And as leaders of children and youth, it is vital for us to speak to this truth and do the difficult work of removing race from our faith.

It is only after we are able to acknowledge our participation in the work of race and commit to undermining its position within the church and uprooting it from our lives that we will be able to lead children and youth away from it. We must live into the new life and its reality that Christ gives us, a life outlined by Paul in 2 Corinthians:

> For the love of Christ urges us on, because we are convinced that one has died for all; therefore all have died. And he died for all, so that those who live might live no longer for themselves, but for him who died and was raised for them. From now on, therefore, we regard no one from a human point of view; even though we once knew Christ from a human point of view, we know him no longer in that way. So if anyone is in Christ, there is a new creation: everything old has passed away; see, everything has become new! All this is from God, who reconciled us to himself through Christ, and has given us the ministry of reconciliation.[5]

We must separate our faith from race and teach young people that racism, stereotyping, and prejudice are not part of God's plan for humanity and that they have no place in the practice of our faith. Because of the social construct of race, we love according to the social colouring of skin, from "a human point of view." But when we begin this sacred work of undoing and untangling, children and youth can begin to imagine their lives without race as evidence of new life in Christ.

Children don't come into the world with historical racial grudges, knowledge of white privilege, or a desire to benefit from it. Still, we continue to tell the story of race, play its roles, and attempt to couple it with the good news of Jesus Christ. The church draws colour lines when it uses race as an excuse for not worshipping with persons from other cultures or traditions, imitating society's segregation model. But young children are not naturally inclined to draw colour lines in the sandbox, unlike those who redlined[6] communities in years past. Children don't want to live or learn or love or play separately. Many children will talk to anyone they meet and will befriend strangers; this is why we tell them not to talk to them. And the games that young people play are often communal and inclusive. Perhaps we need a child to lead us down a path of inclusion and friendship without borders.[7]

Unfortunately, much like assumptions made due to race, we may assume that because we are able to identify ourselves and others racially we understand race. We may believe that we control its influence over us, that we can stop thinking racially whenever we want to, and that we are not prejudiced or racist. But we lose control over race when we allow it to define who we love, the manner in which we serve, and the nature of our fellowship with other believers. Sadly, the church has yet to comprehend the levels to which race has infiltrated its members, and the amount of resultant loss of prophetic vision and witness of Christ's love, redemption, and reconciliation to the world.

Coming to Terms

Due to these assumptions and the fact that no two perspectives, experiences, or resultant interpretations regarding race are the same, I find it necessary to define a few terms. This will, I hope, provide clarification as to my point of view regarding race, its progeny, and its impact on Christianity in the U.S.A. and beyond. Though I speak of Christianity in the U.S.A. because it is my religious and social context, the implications of these ideas have significance beyond the borders of my home country, as race and its pseudo-scientific findings have impacted countless societies and people groups throughout modern history.

Michael Omi and Howard Winant define race as "a concept which signifies and symbolizes social conflicts and interests referring to different types of human bodies."[8] Race has also traditionally been defined as a means by which human beings are divided according to physicality: size of lips, shape of eyes and nose, body type, and structure. I would add that race is a *social colouring* of skin, and its meanings are socially constructed in order to justify and maintain social distance, cultural conflicts, economic disparity, exploitation, oppression, and privilege – all of which are contrary to the work and ministry of Jesus Christ. I say "social colouring" because race is a means by which a society views its citizens. But it's not a given. Race isn't an inherent, predestined way of classifying human beings. There are no physically black/white/red/yellow/brown/beige people. These colour-coded terms speak to a racialized reality in which persons are assigned worth and subsequent purpose based on this skin colour code.

This is why I believe in the raceless life and the racelessness of Christ's gospel. However, racelessness should not be confused with colour-blindness or race-blindness, which suggests that persons disregard the characteristics associated with race. We don't need to lose our sight in order to see people differently. Instead, we need to lose race as a definition of human identity, a means by which to assign personal value and social worth. Racelessness is the belief that race is purely a social construct and not a part of God's divine plan for humanity. Consequently, it is not an expression of Christian identity, it should not define the Christian experience, and it should not be employed in the practice of the Christian faith. Racelessness says that racial bias shouldn't exist in our churches and that it is not a part of Christ's good news. And while I hold to this view of race, I do, however, affirm and respect *cultural distinctions* that exist throughout society and in the world. In so doing, I employ cultural designations like African-American, European-American, Native American, and Asian-American in order to link persons to a country of origin rather than a potential stereotype.

Racism is the conviction that natural physical differences among human beings determine cultural ability and subsequent social achievement; it also suggests that one's own race is superior and has an inherent right to rule others. It may even reference the systems and structures by which one either consciously or unconsciously leverages said superiority. Of course, neither this belief nor the systems constructed to facilitate it are supported by the gospel.

Omi and Winant are credited with the theory of *racial formation*, a term that refers to

> the socio-historical process by which racial categories are created, inhabited, transformed and destroyed.... [It is] a process of historically situated projects in which human bodies and social structures are represented and organized.... Racial formation [is linked] to the evolution of hegemony, the way in which society is organized and ruled. [Defining racial formation in these terms facilitates] understanding of a whole range of contemporary controversies and dilemmas involving race, including the nature of racism, the relationship of race to other forms of differences, inequalities and oppression such as sexism and nationalism and the dilemmas of racial identity today.[9]

The term *racial formation* is used to explain why people "see" one another in terms of race and the power or the lack thereof that is assigned to persons because of this way of seeing. We have no obligation to view racial formation as synonymous, tangential, corollary, or related in any way to spiritual formation, giving us no reason to enshrine it in the songs, stories, and teachings of our faith.

Knowing what these terms mean is important, but more important is our ability to redefine them. We need to know more about race as a whole, and not just its prejudices and stereotypes, in order to put race in its place, redefining it as a social construct and not allowing it to define us as racial beings. It is necessary that we learn more about *why* we define ourselves according to race as opposed to *how*. For me, it's not about who apologizes, forgives, or changes first, because the practice of racelessness, of letting go of an opportunity to lord over someone because of a social privilege or a past offence, is a part of being a disciple of Jesus Christ. We need to redefine the conditions by which we live for the sake of peace, not because it will prove that we were right or better than this person or that people group.

Children of God, Children of Colour?

While these terms have social meanings that must be acknowledged and understood, my core assertion is that Christians are not children of colour, but children of God. Our identity is not rooted in our flesh or its appendages but in God. John Calvin wrote that "there is no deep knowing of God without a deep knowing of self and no deep knowing of self without a deep knowing of God."[10] Our self-awareness and self-worth lie not in race, but in God. To suggest the contrary would imply that race is the creator of humanity.

While this is a radically different perspective on race to that which is commonly held, passing a raceless faith onto children and youth is possible. We simply cannot be both socially-coloured black/white/red/yellow/brown/beige *and* Christian. We can't be privileged, judgmental, and xenophobic because of the social colouring of skin and at the same time be "poor in spirit,"[11] gracious, and welcoming of the stranger because of our identity as a follower of Jesus. We can't be oppressed, angry, and revengeful because of the social colouring of skin and also be peaceful, forgiving, and "more than conquerors through him who loved us."[12] We must show young people these differences and lead them in choosing between believing in race and believing in Jesus Christ.

A racial identity is a social identity, created for the social, economic, and political advantage or disadvantage of another, calling us to serve our skin and the skin of others. A racialized life is one lived to, in, and for the flesh. This is why living racially does not complement the Christian faith. Racial identities are of this world. But we, as members of Christ's body, are not to conform to them.[13] Race informs us of how the world sees us, not how God sees us. Race looks at the social colouring of skin, the outward appearance. But God looks at the heart.[14]

The church's poor witness as the Body of Christ is evident when we profess to be disciples of Jesus but continue to live the same racialized lives that we led before following him. This falsely suggests, at least to me, that Jesus may be able to "conquer death, hell, and the grave,"[15] but when it comes to matters of race, Jesus has no power. It assumes that Jesus can't deliver us from race or its prejudices, that he can't free us of our hatreds nor heal us of its effects. Additionally, it seems to suggest that race can be baptized, that our racial identity is a part of our Christian identity, that our socially colour-coded bodies cannot and should not die with Christ. But I beg to differ. I agree with William Willimon who asks,

> What are we to do with a church that speaks to people on the basis of their gender or race, all the while baptizing them on the basis of Galatians 3:28?[16]

> In baptism, the text becomes Scripture for us, canon, laid on us as a new story that illumines our stories. In baptism, we are adopted into the people who answer to this story and are held accountable to its description of reality... "Scripture" suggests that authority has shifted from ourselves to Scripture's use of us... Baptism asserts that we meet and speak under an identity that challenges and endangers all other identities.[17]

Unfortunately, race continues to inform our understanding of scripture and influence our relationships with believers from other cultures. Instead of race being subjected to the power and authority of scripture, it has become the narrator of our faith. Race tells us what we are to believe and how we are to practise our faith. Race defines our faith. But our identity as followers of Jesus should, "challenge and endanger all other identities," including racial identity.

I imagine that some readers may become uncomfortable and even downright angry at what I am arguing. But I think that these reactions show the extent of the racialization of Christianity. It seems that it can be difficult or impossible for some people to imagine the church – or life itself – without race.

Helmut Thielicke wrote that "our understanding of freedom is threatened with disintegration because we do not know what 'we should become' because we have lost our sense of what we were intended to be."[18] We who call ourselves Christian do not know what Christ must be in us. This is why race is so appealing. It does the work of becoming for us though a prepackaged existence. But as Immanuel Kant reminds us, "You can, because you ought."[19] So we can break the seal of race because we ought to do so.

Despite trepidation, this new kind of life can begin with us and with the children and youth who we serve. Discipleship happens in relationship. Young people learn about the ministry and message of Jesus and the commitment of discipleship by watching other disciples. Unfortunately, they can also learn prejudice and stereotypes. But since we are human beings and not racial beings, such prejudices and stereotypes can be *unlearned*. Our sacred spaces may have a colour line drawn around them, but we can erase it by practising the boundless love and acceptance of Jesus Christ. We should not allow society to tell us and our young people who we can be seen with, who we can serve, and by whom we can be served. As children of God, and not children of colour, we are all family.[20]

Teaching What It Means to Be Family

This is how the raceless life is lived – as a family. In order to teach our children what it means to lay down race (and not just racism), we can start by looking at the words and actions of Jesus. He identified the members of his family not by their physical appearances but by their commitment to the will of God.[21] As believers, we must accept Christ's definition of family and the family members that he embraces.

Racelessness is a journey in truth-telling and self-confrontation. It requires spiritual discipline, obedience to the commandments of Christ, and faith in his proclamations. Racelessness is countercultural and counterintuitive. It goes against familial traditions and patterns of history. It is a step in another direction, a way not often taken. To live without race, we need to focus our eyes on Jesus as the solution instead of looking at others as the problem.

As leaders of children and youth, we need to deconstruct the perspectives and prejudices that are buried deep in our lives in order to have a better chance of passing a raceless gospel on to young people. Because if we do not take the beams out of our own eyes first, we will not be able to lead our children and youth with clear vision.

We can talk about race and what it means to us.
We can tell our stories about our relationships with race. We can ask questions like, "How did I meet race or how did I come to know it? How did I come to be known by a racial category?" This can be done privately

through the use of a journal or through the formation of a small group at one's church. The goal is to demystify race and in so doing, create a sacred space where real relationships can develop through honest conversations without the interruptions of what race tells us about each other.

We can challenge our relationship with race and its position in our lives.
We can question racial stereotypes and prejudices, asking questions such as, "What parts of my life do stereotypes/prejudices support or enhance? Why is race in my life in the first place? How did it get there? Who or what extended the invitation?" We can ask questions of ourselves and others; often, answers can be found in the form of questions. For some, it may help to make a list of ill feelings that are harboured because of race and next to each point write a scripture passage that affirms the new life that Christ calls us to. We can investigate and interrogate the traditions of race in our minds, families, neighbourhoods, and churches. In so doing, we reveal the superficiality of its position and loosen its grip on our identities and the practices of our faith.

We can form friendships across cultures.
We can ask ourselves, "Why can't I talk to *those* people, and who told me not to?" Ignorance breeds fear and fear breeds ignorance. We can give up colouring people in and, instead, let genuine relationships with others fill in the blanks. We must find our own voices. To avoid talking to persons of different cultures because race says so speaks to our commitment to live as disciples of race as opposed to being disciples of Jesus.

If we continue to be led by our prejudices and our perspectives continue to be misconstrued by our stereotypes; if we do not commit to teaching this raceless gospel and unlearning racism as a demonstration of our faith in the new kind of life that Jesus died for, we will fail to offer the children and youth of this generation and those to come a kind of Christianity that is truly new. Instead, we will extend to them more of the same old racially bound and socially constructed ways of being church apart from those who look and act differently than we do. We will teach them to live as the church before them lived, falsely believing that race-consciousness is synonymous with God-consciousness. Jesus' love for the little children and youth will continue to be divided by race, and the ministry of reconciliation will be lost.

The raceless gospel of Jesus Christ offers to us the opportunity for a new kind of Christianity and a new kind of life. By the grace of God and the power of the Holy Spirit, it will equip and empower young people to overturn the powers of race in the church. It won't happen all at once. But child by child, teen by teen, we can forge the kind of faith that Jesus imagined as he prayed that "they may be one, as we are one."[22]

Chapter 4

Welcoming Rainbow Kids

Melinda Melone

The Need and the Hope

When my sister heard that I was leading a workshop about LGBTQ (lesbian, gay, bisexual, transgender, queer/questioning) issues for the 2012 Children, Youth, and a New Kind of Christianity conference, she shared a photo on a social media site. It shows a big dog apparently protecting a little goat, with a caption reading, "Show Me Where the Bullies Are."

Many of us are all too aware of the issue of bullying and its connection to suicides, especially among gay, lesbian, and transgender youth. And unfortunately, many children and youth experience their own families and churches as "where the bullies are." This is particularly true of "rainbow kids," an umbrella term I use to describe all kinds of sexual minority and gender-variant children and teens, as well as children of LGBTQ parents and other children and youth who are friends, allies, or family members of LGBTQ folks. As more young people come out as gay at younger ages, as more gay and lesbian couples have children, and as more youth identify as bisexual, transgender, queer, or other sexual minority and gender-variant identity, practitioners in children's and youth ministry may be confronted with booming populations of rainbow kids.

Or we may not. Since some of the loudest bullying voices aimed against rainbow kids are claiming to speak for Christianity or the Bible

Melinda Melone is a follower of Jesus, a parent, a Montessori elementary teacher, and a children's ministry coordinator. She holds a master's degree in education from the University of California at Santa Cruz and one in American politics from Georgetown University. She is active in the Gay Christian Network Capital Cluster and Burgundy Crescent Volunteers.

(voices that have earned the church as a whole a disheartening reputation for being anti-gay[1]), many rainbow kids and their families avoid or leave churches in order to protect against the expected negative reactions of Christians. Recognizing this, Brian McLaren includes homosexuality as one of his "ten questions" to be addressed by a new kind of Christianity.[2]

As the children's ministry coordinator at a small, traditional church, and as a Montessori elementary teacher, I have the privilege of working with increasing numbers of rainbow kids in a variety of settings – so I see a growing need for churches to respond to them. I also made my college-age son an official rainbow kid by coming out at age 50 (I was a classic "late bloomer"). He took it in stride: far more important to him than having an out gay mom is the fact that his roommate is gay and many of his college friends are also part of their campus LGBTQ communities. So I have a few different windows into the lives of rainbow kids, and from what I'm seeing, I can say that, while more and more rainbow kids seem to discover that "it gets better,"[3] this isn't true for everyone. It doesn't always get better; bullying, harassment, and inhospitality toward rainbow kids continues to be the norm in some places. And, sadly, the church can be one of these places.

My hope is that those of us in the church, particularly those of us playing with new forms of Christianity, can put ourselves in the picture not as bullies or bystanders but as the big dogs, the defenders (rather than the attackers) of these particular "least of these." As a matter of justice, it's fitting that we who are Christian speak out against discrimination, harassment, and violence against anyone, including LGBTQ folks. As a matter of love, it is clear that followers of Jesus are called to grow in our ability to welcome everyone, no matter how uncomfortable they may make us. As a matter of humility before God, it is imperative that we move beyond both self-righteousness and the "ick" factor in dealing with brothers and sisters in Christ (as well as with members of those communities who may not count themselves as followers of Jesus) who identify as LGBTQ.

For those seeking new kinds of Christianity, there are particular opportunities to engage issues facing rainbow kids and their families. As more and more churches seek to move beyond traditional limits to generosity in doctrinal issues, there may be room to discuss sexual ethics that encompass new social realities, such as marriage equality and access to medical procedures for sexual transition. As traditional "right answers" give way to complex, creative, multilayered experiences of biblical narratives, there's room for new interpretations of the traditional "clobber passages"[4] in Genesis, Leviticus, Romans, 1 Corinthians, and 1 Timothy. And as new kinds of Christian churches work out their missional and communitarian ideals, they will certainly encounter rainbow kids and their families along the way.

If we want to step up as defenders and allies of rainbow kids, we can begin by making our churches and ministries more welcoming. And then we can explore advocating for rainbow kids in the wider community. There are many ways to do this. We can educate ourselves about the LGBTQ landscape and consider where we and our faith communities are located within this landscape. We can look at various approaches that may fit within our faith communities and begin with small steps. We can be open to learning from our own rainbow kids and their families, asking them to lead us to more inclusive and welcoming beliefs and practices while taking into consideration the challenges this will pose for other members of our communities. Most importantly, we can respond to the call to love across all of our differences and disagreements.

Notes on Language

One way to educate ourselves about the needs of rainbow kids in our communities is to look at language surrounding LGBTQ people and issues.

At first, it can seem like the "gay community" doesn't even know what to call itself. There is no single definitive set of letters to describe gender-variant and sexual minority communities. I'm using LGBTQ for now – but I also see GLBT, LGBT★QI, and other acronyms, including QUILTBAG, used more or less frequently. Many Americans are familiar with LGBT as an abbreviation for lesbian, gay, bisexual and transgender. I usually include Q (for queer and/or questioning) because I see and hear it used very frequently – particularly by youth – in my usual circles.[5] Letters in other acronyms may stand for two-spirited, intersex, unidentified, cisgender (opposite of transgender), asexual, allies, and so on – and new terms are continually developed.

I know that all this jargon may feel overwhelming. But it's no reason to give up – everybody's struggling with it. There's a funny bit in the Gay Christian Network musical *Straight to Heaven*,[6] in which a gay activist talks about building an annex to the community centre in order to accommodate even more letters on the sign![7]

Language can be a tricky thing. People want to be sure to use language and terms that aren't going to unintentionally insult LGBTQ folks. So churches seeking to become friends and advocates of rainbow kids need to be aware of language red flags from clichés, stereotypes, and (within Christian circles) "clobber passages." For example, the terms *abomination, sodomy,* and *sodomite* are generally considered (as well as perpetuating) inaccurate interpretations of Genesis and Leviticus. Clichéd phrases that can be unwelcoming include "love the sinner, hate the sin" (what about the planks in our own eyes?), and "homosexual (or gay) lifestyle/agenda" (there is no one gay lifestyle or agenda, any more than there is one straight lifestyle or agenda). Other disputed terms surround political issues, like "gay marriage" (the preferred term for advocates of the issue is "marriage equality"). And be aware of terms like *queer* and *dyke* that can be either badges of pride or offensive epithets, depending on who's saying them.

As with all language issues, members of these communities may disagree about the use of these words and phrases. So it's important to listen to how members of local LGBTQ communities refer to themselves and to show them respect by following their practices.

Within Christian contexts, language is often connected to theological viewpoints and traditions. For example, think of the terms "same sex attraction(s)" (SSA) and "sexual orientation." Christians who use the first term tend to be more conservative on this issue; they are often associated with "conversion therapy" or the "ex-gay" movement, and they may deny the existence of any innate, permanent homosexual orientation. They typically claim that identifying as homosexual is immoral and prohibited by scripture (as is any homosexual behaviour), and they often believe that people can choose not to act on their "attractions" and even be "healed" or "delivered" from them (as if being LGBTQ is an illness).[8]

Those who use the term "sexual orientation," tend to see it as an intrinsic, unchangeable part of one's identity. From this view, sexual orientation is something to be accepted and, at best, celebrated as a gift. They see orientation as much more than sexual desire; it's a complex set of biological and psychological factors, attitudes, strengths, and weaknesses. In this view, sexual orientation is seen as similar to other inherent personality traits or physical variations, so that being gay is just as morally neutral as being an introvert or extrovert, or being left-handed or right-handed.

The LGBTQ Landscape

In order to understand the experiences of the rainbow kids we serve, or hope to serve, we need to educate ourselves about local LGBTQ communities and the specific issues we face. Social contexts matter because they provide parameters for conversations within our churches and with members of our broader communities. We may live in a rural, suburban, exurban, or urban area, in the Bible belt or on the Left Coast, in locations that have seen recent legislative battles or those with highly publicized incidents of suicide, bullying, or violence. All of these factors will affect how we relate to local rainbow kids.

We also need to become aware of national and international debates and organizations that help shape our local communities. When the Supreme Court of the United States takes up marriage equality, when Westboro Baptist Church commits another egregious act of tragic ignorance, when the Ugandan Parliament tries to legislate the death penalty for sexual minorities, or when a local diocese is led by a lesbian bishop, our conversations surrounding and with our rainbow kids are changed.

As people of the church, we need to be especially aware of the positions of our own faith communities and of those around us. The church can be as complex, contradictory, and even dangerous for rainbow kids as the wider community (or more so), but it can also be a haven of love and affirmation. We need to take a long, deep look at our own faith communities and have honest and humble conversations about our own differences before attempting to take on the world outside our doorsteps. Many faith communities that are new to addressing rainbow kids may not even have useful language to discuss different perspectives on the issue. Other communities, particularly those in denominations and traditions where it's been a contentious issue for years, may have

MELINDA MELONE

well-defined positions yet be sick to death of arguing about them.

The Gay Christian Network (GCN) has helpfully articulated a spectrum of Christian attitudes surrounding LGBTQ folks. Here are "sides" of what they name the "Great Debate."[9]

- Side A: God blesses loving, Christ-centred relationships and marriages regardless of the genders/sexes of those involved.
- Side B: Being LGBTQ is not sinful in itself, but God calls gay and lesbian Christians to lifelong celibacy.[10]
- Side C: Undecided between sides A and B.
- Side X: Being anything but straight and cisgender is *not* okay. "Same sex attractions" are sinful, should be fought, and both they and gender dysphoria can be "healed."

These positions can be held by individuals, organizations, and faith communities. And many churches include members on several sides of the debate, which leads me to suggest that there is another "side" for faith communities:

- Side D: Don't ask, don't tell. If you're a LGBTQ member, don't "do" anything about it, in order to avoid conflict in the church.

From its inception, GCN has included members from across the "Great Debate."[11] It has always emphasized that our unity in Christ is more important than our diversity of opinions. Its founder, Justin Lee, is "Side A," yet regularly does speaking engagements with a friend, Ron Belgau, who is "Side B," in order to model how not to let the issue divide us.[12] The local GCN Bible study group that I attend has some members who identify as "A," some who are "B," and some who don't relate to or use the "sides" language at all.

Getting an honest, realistic picture of where one stands on this debate, and where one's faith community stands (if it has a stance at all), is a necessary prerequisite to any further work on the issue. For example, if a person's church falls into the "Side D" position or has simply never discussed the issue, that person will need to begin from a very different starting point than allies in churches with clearly defined beliefs or policies (whether "A," "B" or "X"), or if that person was in a church or denomination in the middle of a heated battle over the issue. Another way of locating ourselves in the LGBTQ landscape is to consider how we and our communities would respond to contact with rainbow kids and their families. For some of us, this contact is a daily or weekly experience. For others, it's unprecedented.

If a faith community is new to these issues, it may be helpful to start by considering the following possible scenarios:

1. Two men bring a four-year-old girl into a preschool class and both men sign the registration form as parents.
2. An eight-year-old biological boy always wants to be with the girls, refuses to use the boys' bathroom, and asks to be called by a girl's name.
3. A congregant's 17-year-old daughter brings her girlfriend to church with the approval of her parents.

Do we know how we and the members of our faith communities would respond in these situations? If not, it's important to consider how to respond to these scenarios in welcoming ways. Of course, the suggestions below aren't hard and fast rules – they're just possibilities to consider. And our community response depends a lot on where the community places itself on the "Side A" to "Side X" continuum.

In the first case, it would be helpful if Sunday school or preschool registration forms have more than one blank space for parents, and these spaces aren't labelled "mother" and "father." Churches can simply treat same-sex couples as they would any other new parents, although if a church has "family" or ungendered bathrooms it's important to point them out, as a man taking a little girl to a gendered bathroom can be problematic. We can avoid questions like "Who's the *real* dad?" or "Where's your mommy?" Other welcoming gestures can include having inclusive children's books on the shelves, avoiding making a big deal out of Mother's Day and Father's Day,[13] and using story illustrations in class that include a variety of family structures.

Responses in the second scenario might depend on how the parents are handling the child's behaviour. If they accept and support the child's desire to identify as a girl, their church and ministry leaders can follow their lead and direct all questions by adults back to the parents and all appropriate questions by children to the child. It's best to handle any inappropriate questions or comments by children gently but firmly ("That's a question for another time" or "Let's keep our comments kind and respectful").

If the parents ask leaders to ignore their child's requests, saying, "It's a phase," or, "He just wants attention," leaders can do their best to foster a gender-neutral environment. And they can avoid asking kids to choose teams, line up, or assign roles according to gender or allowing the children to do so of their own accord. Emphasizing non-traditional gender roles in story examples and applications for lessons is also helpful and, if possible, there should be access to a gender-neutral bathroom. In overnight activities or those requiring changes of clothes, it makes sense to ensure that children have privacy when appropriate and are not segregated by gender.

In the last example, we can treat the teenage couple as we would any other. If a church or youth group already has guidelines about discussions of controversial topics and PDA (public displays of affection), it can simply be consistent. But, afterwards, it helps to be prepared for questions from adults and teens, and direct them back to the parent (questions from adults) or the daughter (questions from peers). It also wouldn't hurt to make both the parents and youth aware, privately at first but publicly if necessary, that we're there to support them in any way we can.

Now What? First and Second Steps

As we embark on a journey of making our world more welcoming for rainbow kids, we must remember to *pray*. Pray hard, pray long, pray unceasingly. Pray for wisdom and humility, for opportunities to meet and listen to rainbow kids and their families, for direction and guidance in ministry, for inspiration for leaders at all levels (parish, nation, world), for protection for young people most at risk, and for grace for those who can help them. And we mustn't forget prayers of praise – they're restorative, and kind of fun, too!

Additional steps will vary widely according to our communities. But there are some low-risk secondary steps available to everyone, regardless of "sides" or locations in the landscape. These steps can lay a foundation for those new to LGBTQ communities and they can help faith communities and individuals who have been involved in these issues for some time continue building on foundations already there.

Observe

We can observe our communities through the eyes of rainbow kids. We can look around our churches, websites, and publications for signs of bias and exclusion, or affirmation and inclusion. We can explore photos, graphics, signs on bathrooms, meeting agendas, and budgets. We can listen to sermons, conversations over coffee, and small group discussions. Many well-meaning churches are simply unwelcoming due to a complete absence of LGBTQ members or welcoming signifiers.

Educate

We can educate ourselves. No matter how long we've been ministering with rainbow kids, there's always new information. Read, watch, lurk on websites, and enter discussions in the relative anonymity of message boards. Learn about national and local advocacy groups such as Parents and Friends of Lesbians and Gays, and the Gay, Lesbian and Straight Education Network.[14] Follow current legislative and judicial action on LGBTQ issues. Educating ourselves removes some of the burden of constantly educating everyone around them that rainbow kids and their families often carry.

Volunteer

We can volunteer in the local LGBTQ community. This can provide opportunities to serve and to get to know LGBTQ folks on their own terms. Perhaps by getting involved, we may be one of the first welcoming Christians they ever meet. Or perhaps we'll find vibrant Christian groups among our LGBTQ communities. If a town doesn't have an LGBTQ health centre, gay-affirming church, or other visibly out community centre, it's helpful to check with local and state/provincial chapters of national organizations. Some volunteering can even be done online or by phone.

MELINDA MELONE

And Further Steps: Models of Public Engagement

In addition to, in response to, or in preparation for welcoming rainbow kids and their families, we may feel called to consider other types of work as allies of and advocates for these young people. There are many ways to step up – but each person and church must act in ways that suit them best.

There are many factors we might want to consider before jumping in. We should be aware of any local or national history on LGBTQ issues – at church, community, provincial/state and denominational levels – as well as our faith community's history of dealing with conflict, because this issue will inevitably raise conflict. It helps to be aware of probable stakeholders in these potential conflicts. Children, teens, parents, teachers, elders, pastoral staff, more conservative congregants, and more progressive members all have competing interests and priorities.

All that said, we don't need to be afraid to jump in – or at least tiptoe in. We can keep praying, stay in touch with as many different perspectives as possible in order to anticipate conflict, and remind ourselves that it's okay to go slowly and start small. Here are some practices to consider as we wade into the water.

Service

One way to become more welcoming is through service projects in the rainbow community. This is suitable for groups that don't have a lot of (or any) out LGBTQ members, and have some expertise in service. Like any cross-cultural service, being active in a "not like us" community and serving its members can be educational for both groups. Consider participating in a local AIDSWalk, handing out water at a Pride Parade, or delivering meals to those living with AIDS/HIV. These sorts of projects are best done in conjunction with local organizations already serving the rainbow community.

Inclusion

For churches with a visible group of LGBTQ members, another type of work may be acknowledging them and raising their acceptance profile. If a church has learned to acknowledge blended families or differently-abled persons as integral and valued parts of the community, then there's precedent in this church for acknowledging and celebrating the gifts that come with diversity, including sexual diversity. This is also related to discussions a church may have already addressed, such as gender inclusive/neutral language and women in leadership. Are rainbow folks in visible leadership? Do public prayers and songs explicitly speak of issues that rainbow kids face? Are family events as welcoming and comfortable for rainbow families as they are other families? These sorts of questions matter.

Edutainment

I know of a church that sponsored a LGBTQ-themed film festival open to the public. Others support annual karaoke nights and drag shows; provide high-quality, fun childcare for local LGBTQ conferences; and run rainbow kids-sensitive vacation Bible school. If our faith communities have gifts in the arts, education, and media, there are countless ways to use these gifts to be more welcoming.

Dialogue toward Reconciliation

Another way to become known as a welcoming place for rainbow families is to host a series of public dialogues on issues within the local rainbow community such as marriage equality, adoption, and health care. Inviting local participants who disagree on these culture-war topics to come together in civil dialogue is risky, but can prove worthwhile if handled well. The goal of such discussions is not to change anyone's mind, but to build reconciling relationships across divides and promote civil public communication. Like sponsoring racial reconciliation workshops or abortion "common ground" discussions, this work requires trained and experienced facilitators and mediators.

Public Activism

If a person or church is really ambitious or has gifts and experience in public advocacy and handling the press, then that person or church might be ready for major public activism. There are all sorts of opportunities that faith communities can consider. They can begin city-wide or state/province-wide coalitions of welcoming churches and ministries. Another option is to throw public support behind marriage equality, adoption, or other rainbow family-related legislation. Or perhaps a church can organize a pro-rainbow kids lobbying trip to its capital city for local clergy.

Take It Easy, But Take It

I can imagine that some readers may be feeling overwhelmed or frustrated right now. Others may be on fire to jump right into a new ministry with rainbow kids. Either way, it's important to stop and think: Why are you interested in this work? Is this the latest issue of the month (not that there's anything wrong with that) or do you have a deeper call to this work? Not everyone in the church needs to work at equal levels on all issues of love and justice. But if you feel called to this work, go slowly. Take time to educate yourself; find allies; build deep relationships and ministries that can last. And if you're in the LGBTQ community and have been wounded by the church, take time to heal.

Rainbow kids in the church need ministry and support now more than ever, with so many social factors raising awareness of (and backlash against) issues within LGBTQ communities. So much is going on and so much needs to be done that the temptation to jump in and do everything at once is very real – as is the temptation to be overwhelmed and do nothing. No one needs to do and know everything right away. But if we're ready, we can do something. Rainbow kids need all the big dogs they can get. And the church needs a new reputation based on love, kindness, and radical inclusion.

Chapter 5

Rescripting Youth Education
Carl Stauffer

Violence continues to be a significant and powerful educational force that youth are routinely and systematically exposed to in the formal and informal spaces of everyday life all around the world. The text of violence saturates our cultures and permeates the enclaves of our homes, the hallways and playgrounds of our schools, the fibre of our communities, and policies of our nations. It is no respecter of class, race, or ethnic origin, and it surfaces in the dazzle of glitzy lights, fast money, and turf solidification of our urban centres, and in the squalor of the poverty-stricken rural peripheries of our societies. It erupts in the fissures of contesting ideologies and religions, in the struggle over scarce resources, and in the desperate scramble for identity recognition and validation. Whether in gang formations, crime syndicates, fraternities of suicide bombers, or posses of child combatants, the youth of this generation are on the frontlines of these rupturing, ever-morphing social constructions of violence.

In our desperate attempt to understand this "youth violence," we are apt to quickly fall prey to the symptomatic, totalizing narratives decrying this violence as originating from single source units of "cause and effect" rationalities such as computer games, male testosterone, anarchy and rebellion, permissive cultures, lack of mental health services, and the breakdown in law and order – all of which are the dominant modernist myths of explanation touted by our systems of media, governance,

**Carl Stauffer** is Assistant Professor of Justice and Development Studies at the Center for Justice and Peacebuilding at Eastern Mennonite University. He has worked in the fields of peace, justice, and reconciliation for 22 years and his work in restorative, transitional, and indigenous justice has taken him to 30 countries.

religion, justice, security, and education. While all of these elements provide plausible clarifications of the problem of violence, no one of them is a sufficient elucidation on its own. The violence equation is entirely too complex to be restrained by unitary explanations.

Unfortunately in predictable modernist form, the institutional response to this complex violence, whether in democracies or dictatorial states, is too frequently the application of force. Traditional organizational equilibrium demands this quelling of threatening expressions of opposition in order to maintain the status quo. The missing piece in all this is the marked inability of any efficient bureaucracy to effectually hear and actively listen to the voices from the margins; in this case, the youth.

Many youth on the margins of societies tell stories of living with extreme deprivation, loss, trauma, and perpetual states of fear. Theirs is a script of clashing justices, young persons destined to be born into "cultures of violence" that defy race, class, and socio-economic standing. Theirs is a script of being forced to fight wars from as young as seven years old; terrorizing wars that they could not have imagined on their own. Theirs is a script of protracted violence that forcibly drives whole communities to flee from their farms, neighbourhoods, and homes and strips them of their human dignity[1]; not just their human rights, but the dignity that connects them to ancestral identity, family, clan, and land. They make meaning through these scripts playing out in their desperate realities. Their stories are filled with deep relationships and broken isolation, of high hopes and shattered dreams, of cowardice and courage, of severe trauma and wounded healing, of life and death.

Social anthropologist and author Paul Richards, writing about the brutal 12-year civil war in Sierra Leone, offers a graphic characterization of the estimated 4,500 child soldiers who fought that terrorizing war, "marginalized belligerents trying to cut in on a conversation they have been left out of... Their violence trashes a rotten set, flapping in the breeze of a film epic in which they no longer believe."[2]

Collin's Story

Chills ran up and down my spine as I felt a thick, deep emotional cloud settle over the group. What was going on? This was a training simulation and yet it felt so real. I had facilitated this particular exercise on many occasions in different countries worldwide, but this time it was different. The sadness, the pain, the loss seemed to hit us all viscerally. The main character, a young man named Collin,[3] from a "coloured" township in South Africa, had captured our hearts, minds, and imaginations. We were fully immersed in the role-play. The grimacing expressions, the solemnly bowed heads, the tears flowing; it was as if all of us were re-living a trauma that we had never known.

As the facilitator, I had allowed the simulation to take its full course because of the powerful re-enactment that we were all drawn into. But it was 4:30 p.m. and time to close the second day of the workshop. What this meant was that there was no time left to debrief the learning from that experience – that would have to be saved for first thing the next morning. As we adjourned, I was determined to find out who this young man was. In fact, at that time I did not even know his name, although I had noticed his striking looks, his tight-knit hair in braided rows, and the gold chains on his neck and rings on his fingers – he looked like he came straight off the streets. He was not a registered participant of the training event. He had stepped into this community training of civil society leaders, pastors, social workers, and teachers to deliver a package to one of the participants. He was so struck by the language of restorative justice and reconciliation that he decided to sit in the back of the room and take in the workshop. No one bothered to introduce him to me.

When it came time to break into simulation groups, Collin joined the participant group that was acting out the role of the family of the perpetrator. In the simulation script, the culprit was a young man who had murdered a neighbour and friend in gang violence. Now the young offender was being released from prison and the two families were attempting to meet for the first time in years. To my chagrin, this group assigned Collin the lead role as the antagonist returning from prison and requesting to meet the family of his murder victim. So I took it upon myself to bring this young stranger up to speed on the training content and encouraged him to internalize his role and play with it as authentically as possible. I was dubious that this would work. But I was wrong. As he began to articulate his role in the killing, his apology to the family, and his remorse for the loss of a friend and brother, we were enthralled and felt the sacredness of that moment.

The next morning as we gathered to debrief, Collin introduced himself and told us his story. He was 23 years old at the time of this workshop. As a 16-year-old rising gang leader, he killed a rival gang leader and was sent to prison, where he served seven years of his sentence. He had been released just months before this training. While in prison, Collin had a personal transformation experience and decided to write a letter to the mother of his victim. He ended up writing a 17-page letter detailing how he had come to kill this woman's son, his apology, his remorse, and his desire to meet the mother when he was released from prison. Upon his release he made every effort to visit the mother of his victim, but because her home was located in "enemy" territory, he was refused the opportunity to meet with her by the protective, distrusting rival gang members. The reconciliation he had dreamed of in prison was denied him. Missing the encounter was deeply disappointing.

So when he stepped into the training workshop, he heard a language he had never had words for, a narrative that described his circumstances, his emotions, and his longings for a restored future. Collin shared how therapeutic this simulation had been for him and that he did not feel like he was "playing" a role; he felt he was the role. He found his script and his emotion inside himself. Collin knew, and we knew, that this was not a coincidence. The engagement that had just transpired was a serendipitous moment that was meant to function as a turning point in Collin's life, and the community participants involved in this training event played a pivotal role in his journey.

Following this workshop, I was able to build a relationship of trust with Collin, and I linked him to a group of 12 peacebuilding professionals (including myself) who had organized into a regional peace network that met on a quarterly basis. These dozen community leaders from all walks of life became his mentors and coaches. Collin was also trained in peacebuilding skills and became a youth trainer in his community.

Central to the learning that could be derived from this story is the realization that it wasn't until Collin had the opportunity to act out his reality in "real-time" that he truly understood what he had always imagined reconciliation could be like. It wasn't until that moment that he was able to start to put his shameful, violent past behind him; that he was free to start the trauma healing process and for the first time experience re-integrative meaning and balance in his life.

Collin's story is encoded with the vision and process that I suggest we use to "rescript" our youth educational systems (both inside and outside of the church), especially when dealing with scenarios of youth violence on both the domestic and international frontlines.

Rescripting Youth Education

Most of us who are products of the modern Western educational system would like to believe that the overarching aim of our educational enterprise is to transform the minds and hearts of our youth, the so-called "next generation" or "future leaders" (problematic as these terms may be). However, it is becoming increasingly clear that we are failing miserably in this noble educational goal. Our educational system is bankrupt and imploding.

I would submit that the present crisis in education is directly connected to the failure of the structure of our Western educational system (which is dutifully imitated around the world), caused in part by the legacy of historical colonialism, and in part by the fact that it remains founded on the relics of a modernist project of enlightenment. Paulo Freire characterized the western educational system by using the metaphor of a "banking system."[4] In this comparison, the learner is expected to be a docile, open receptacle (an empty account) waiting to be filled by the intellectual information at the initiation of the expert teacher (depositor). This banking analogy alleges that education is not only non-participatory and disempowering, but that it is also suspended in a knowledge vacuum, a liminal space devoid of the critical cultural, ethical, and moral contexts of analysis required for true learning and growth. The unidirectional educational flow is not only easily manipulated in order to maintain the status quo (which often consists of various forms of covert structural violence), it can be (and is often) utilized to reinforce overt repression and oppression perpetrated by socio-political and economical institutions of state and society. As playwright and activist Augusto Boal so succinctly put it, "When dialogue becomes a monologue, oppression ensues."[5]

With 44% of sub-Saharan Africa's population under the age of 15, and 30% of Asia and Latin America's population the same, the global youth bulge is a phenomena that we must contend with.[6] Relegating the current generation of postmoderns to the repository of "future leaders" has proven to be ineffectual, as this new generation of techno-innovators and constructivist communicators has made it clear that they are not only shaping the world, they are demanding recognition in this public role, and if that demand is not satisfied, they will obtain recognition through force (whether lethal or nonlethal).[7] We must increasingly configure our future educational models around the pillars of participatory and empowering formulations of pedagogy.[8] The youth of today are calling to become co-learners, co-teachers, and co-pilgrims with their adult counterparts in the educational process.

To rescript the educational process, we as educators will need to migrate from violence (the forceful imposition of "groupthink" and the elimination of any detractors) to nonviolence (the safe-space to explore divergent thinking in the context of mutual relationship). In order to elucidate this further, allow me to refer again to the context of Sierra Leone, although I would like to suggest that the context (a foreign country) is less important than the descriptive cycles of violence that have application to multiple sectors of my own society in North America.

Paul Richards eloquently frames his violence analysis on four critical process underpinnings (practice, performance, narrative, and cultural context) that give the vicious acts of Sierra Leone's horrific civil war new understanding and nuanced meaning with a postmodern twist.[9] For purposes of this chapter, where the core issue is how to reinvent Christian educational enterprises in order to fashion young peace builders, I would promulgate the following proposition: If, in a destructive sense, these four conceptions have assisted us to better comprehend how "violence-education" is effectively transmitted by mimesis (the generative process by which people imitate the behaviour of others in order to effect social change) from one generation to the next, then possibly the inverse is also true, that we can apply these same four notions as a basis for a constructive framework of peace education that will have a contagious effect[10] on this postmodern generation. To explore this idea further, I'll expound on the four critical process underpinnings cited above.

mimesis

Practice

A good description of "practice" is summed up in the common adage
that says, "The way is made, or the path is forged as we go." Put differently, the processes of knowing and learning occur in the midst of practice.
In the very activity of practice, knowledge is generated. It is in the essence of the action that the impulse of learning is discovered. In much of
the contemporary ideations of violence – which are increasingly being
carried out by youthful, non-state actors who often appear disorganized
and even random in their actions – there may be no overall scheme or
logical plan that is being followed, no calculating military generals in a
boardroom discussing strategy. Instead, different configurations of violence are enacted and, depending on the spectrum of responses, the next
counter-tactic is decided upon.

While this may feel unsettling as a mechanism of learning –
especially when applied to violence – it proves to be quite instructive as
a manner of educating for transformative ends (for example, The Action-
Reflection Learning Cycle[11]). The utilization of interpersonal and group
games, role-play, simulation, and social media in the educational environment is essential. This laboratory mode of practice-education allows for
"real-time'" experiences of physical, emotional, intellectual, and spiritual
impulses to be integrated into the learning process. Integrative learning
is especially important in the enterprise of peace education, as successful
peacebuilding interventions employ all aspects of our embodied selves.
Thus, in practice, meaning making occurs in the spontaneity of creative
action.

Performance

Performance differs from practice in that it is an orchestrated production
– it has a projected strategic outcome and it is developed with a particular message and audience in mind. Performance is the public culmina-
tion of the practice rehearsal – it is the gathering of the divergent pieces
of practice and putting them together in a unified whole. Through the
lens of dramaturgical studies,[12] sociological phenomena (social interactions such as conflict or violence) are analyzed using the theatrical and
literary categories of plot, script, actors, stage, audience, and props.[13] In
performative violence, the central aspects of analysis revolve around the

actors (those perpetrating and being harmed by the violence), the stage (the actual space, environment, or platform) where the violence is occurring, and the audience (the people most affected by the violence). If the performance is "successful," it will have elicited the desired reaction (shock, horror, sympathy, retaliation) required to give ample "voice" to the act of violence (for example, acts of suicide bombings, or mass public shootings).[14]

Lisa Schirch writes about the pivotal use of the arts (visual, performance, poetry, dance, and so on) in the process of building peace. The expressive arts provide symbolic channels through which unspoken or subconscious healing can occur.[15] Likewise, Catholic theologian and author William Cavanaugh works with the importance of ritual in peacemaking when he contrasts torture as a death-dealing ritual of violence, pain, and isolation with the Eucharist as a life-giving ritual of non-violence, healing, and community building.[16] In peace education, the power of performance lies in its repetitive function and its ability to bring to the surface the mysterious, hidden, and intuitive elements of conflict, justice, and reconciliation. Also, the use of performance benefits the peace education process by building collective unity through shared experiences of being, knowing, and feeling, and by providing a public forum to reach a larger mass of people with the message of peace. Future efforts at youth peace education would do well to maximize the use of performance, ritual, and the expressive arts in the learning repertoire.

Narrative

The study of narrative (narratology) concerns itself with the scripts we use to "socially construct our preferred realities."[17] We live by social scripts that form our identities, world views, and actions, which in turn inform the organizational structures, institutions, and networks that we create in society around us. Just as we are able to socially construct our reality through narrative, so we can de-construct our social reality if it becomes violent or destructive through the new narratives we choose to internalize.

John Winslade and Gerald Monk coined the term "narrative mediation"[18] to describe the process of using narration as an instrument of peace building. Their premise is that if we can assist antagonists to jointly deconstruct the "conflict-saturated stories" that drive their actions, then spaces open for reconstructing alternative stories of conflict transformation. As humans, we have been imbued with the generative impulse of speech, and just as God created the universe with the spoken word and God chose to use narrative (story and parable) as the primary medium of communication in the scriptures, so we create and make sense of our worlds with the narrative scripts by which we live. In short, how we speak about our realities matters because we live in, act upon, and love out of our stories about God, other human beings, and what we believe the world consists of.

With this in mind, Christian peace education must be fashioned by the narrative story of the Bible, and as faith educators we must find alternative "ways of knowing" that capture the imagination of this social media generation. Moving beyond dogma recitation and historical investigations into the sacred past, we need to discover attractive educational forays that invite a new generation of youth to step into a present-tense gospel experience, a living-faith story that remains seamless in its regenerative qualities as it moves from the past to the present and into the future.[19]

Cultural Context

For younger generations, culture and context are vital signposts of meaning. Again, our current reductionist educational paradigms are instructive. As the world of travel, the transfer of knowledge, and access to communication have become almost instantaneous, the reliance on "cultural essentialism" (rigid, stereotypical or generalist characterizations of different ethnic people groups) has become unacceptable. For postmodern youth, culture is no longer a fixed entity; it is a social construct that can be reinvented multiple times in one lifetime.

What this means for peace education is that the particularities of a conflict must be taken seriously. In his work on training across cultures, John Paul Lederach[20] masterfully contrasts the "prescriptive" and the "elicitive" models of education. He delineates a vital distinction between the prescriptive idea of "culture as technique" (a skill-set to be learned or mastered) and the elicitive idea of "culture as the seedbed of knowledge" (the basis of what we know and do in a particular context). In this way, the local, indigenous culture of knowing becomes foundational for effective youth peace education, instead of being seen as something that must be unlearned.

Our Challenge

Collin's story illustrates the transformative nature of what might be referred to as "emancipatory" education. For this young man, emancipatory education was realized in at least four ways. First, in practice, when he was drawn into a participatory and empowering training process. Second, in performance, when he acted out his reality in a simulated experience. Third, in narrative, when through the generative simulation experience he received a new narrative of redemption and hope. And finally, in context, where he was surrounded by an understanding community that could walk with him and, when appropriate, coach him as he struggled to live out the new narrative he now embraced. Eventually, Collin became a local neighbourhood trainer and served not only as a peace education resource to his own people, but also as a transformative challenge to the very culture of violence that had formed, taught, and mentored him in his youth. Collin's emancipation came through an "elicitive" and not a "prescriptive" process.

Collin's story is not only about gangsters or child soldiers in faraway places; it is about the same prescriptive cycles of violence that exist in our own context, in our own backyards. For, while we in North America may not be experiencing overt war, we are embedded in a society that has been bolstered by covert structural violence in every sector. In the educational sector, this prescriptive violence plays itself out at a systemic level as school bullies unleash on fellow students the very cycles of abuse heaped on them in their own homes; as homicidal youth, in one final performative act to get the attention and recognition that they have been deprived of all their lives, go on shooting sprees in schools; and as troubled youth are lost in the vortex of "zero tolerance" school discipline and an over-zealous law enforcement establishment enacting their "war on drugs" in the racial margins of society, leading to a phenomenon termed the "schools to prison pipeline"[21] which allows the U.S.A. to have the dubious honour of imprisoning the largest percentage of its population in the world.

These cycles of prescriptive violence need to be broken. In this chapter, I have advocated for a new framework of peace education for youth – one that will include at least the following four elicitive processes:

- just relationship practices and restorative paradigms (emphasizing harms, accountability, and healing as opposed to blame, shame, and punishment)[22]
- community-based approaches (where a shared learning community, as opposed to an individual teacher-student relationship, is the nucleus of the educational process)[23]
- opportunities-focused models (expanding freedoms, choices, and opportunities for youth to redirect a life trapped in cycles of violence)[24]
- culturally mediated interventions (using local, indigenous, and culturally appropriate knowledge systems as the channels for meaning-making).[25]

Our challenge to rescript youth education in this postmodern age must accomplish at least three great tasks. The new script must provide youth with embodied experiences of life reconstruction, capture their media-drenched imagination, and harness the energies that drive destructive impulses and transform them into redemptive passions. This mandate looms tall; however, it remains absolutely essential if we are to see our youth emerge out of the peripheries of violence and into the core of societal conflict transformation.

Chapter 6

God Moves Sideways

Samir Selmanović

For most of the history of their faith, Christians have experienced the world in a vertical manner. Apart from a few exceptions, we have conceived of the order of the universe in terms of what is up and what is down, who is higher and who is lower. Those of us seeking to understand the world and the spirituality of our children and youth have inherited this way of measuring reality. We are conditioned to rank everything vertically, from our empires, economies, companies, neighbourhoods, athletes, artists, churches, and pastors, to our circles of friends and our lovers. From pre-pre-Kindergarten to college and beyond, we have been taught that life movements of consequence are vertical.

My teenage daughters, on the other hand, have grown up in a horizontal world. Theirs is not so much an equal-opportunity world as it is a world that has tried the vertical and found it wanting. Their generation has found that bigger isn't necessarily better, and that those who have climbed the highest might not have the best views after all. They know that many valuable things in life, such as friendship, love, creativity, and life itself, move horizontally. Life is not about climbing to the top, but about walking the landscape.

It started with the movement of information, I suppose, but it goes

Samir Selmanović is an author, activist, leader, and lover. He is a founder and Executive Director of Faith House Manhattan, an interfaith "community of communities" that brings together Christians, Muslims, Jews, atheists, and others who seek to learn from one another's belief systems. He is author of *It's Really All About God* and he works as Director of Consulting for Get Storied, Inc.

way, way beyond that. At one time, God was managed and transformation was brokered to people. But the transformational power once curated by elders, pastors, and priests is now in civilian hands. It is there for everyone. What was sacred is now profane and encounters with God can happen anywhere and anytime. What was managed is now on the loose. What was once delivered from above now comes sideways. My daughters live in a horizontal world – and beautifully so.

Of course, the world is neither horizontal nor vertical; the world just is. But my daughters' eyes see the world in a way that I have not, and their hearts have formed accordingly. They are puzzled by how important the vertical dimension is to their parents and their parents' world. It is not that they don't care about growing and achieving – they do. But they expect life to happen in a plane where they live. It is life – daily ordinary life – that is the curator and ultimate arbiter of whatever we mean when we speak of faith.

As I think about what it means to live in a horizontal world, I wonder how we who work with children and youth can learn new ways of living, thinking, and being Christian in this world. As a consultant in community engagement and transformational storytelling, often working with faith-based organizations, I hear versions of this concern from people of many faiths – Hindus, Muslims, Jews, and others. We live in a disruptive age where those of us from a vertical world find ourselves over-linked, over-exposed, and over-friended. We are forced to reconstitute our identity for new ways of connecting. Our sense of identity faces an evolutionary challenge. And to religious groups, nothing can be more important than identity.

It is not only that we see the world in a vertical way. We monotheists conceived a vertical God. Angels ascend, and God comes down to us. We in turn descend to the world, the object of our love, in order to improve it (by being relevant, missional, or countercultural).

But we have from our children and youth an unspoken invitation to de-verticalize God, to learn about their world, to give up truncated versions of the divine – idols – and turn to the whole God of the Bible. I will share five observations about how we might get in touch with a horizontal God and help our young people know God in today's horizontal world.

Strangers Bring Revelation

From beginning to end, the Bible carries an obsession with strangers and hospitality that goes beyond the cultural conventions of the Middle East at the time. We are called to sacrifice our comfort, possessions, and even our safety in order to accommodate strangers. We see that instead of speaking down a holy chain of command, God moves sideways in the Bible, visiting God's people through strangers, especially at defining moments of this grand faith story. Let me offer two examples, although there are dozens to choose from.

In the book of Genesis, we read about Abraham, the very first believer. In chapter 14, we learn that Melchizedek encounters this first believer and blesses him. Melchizedek is a stranger who appears only once in the story, but in a critical role. He ordains Abraham (who was still going by Abram at the time). Melchizedek, the High Priest, makes Abraham legit. But where did Melchizedek come from? Who ordained him? What were his holy texts? What holy rituals did he practice? Which seminary did he go to? Which denomination was he part of? Who financed and endorsed his priestly education? What liturgy did he use to bless Abraham? We don't know. All we know is that he was God's. His time, space, authority, life, people, practices, and texts were not ours, but were nevertheless God's. God showed up sideways in Melchizedek, just as God showed up sideways to Abraham to announce Sarah's pregnancy at a time when Abraham had given up on a solution from God above.

Fast forward to another formative and somewhat parallel text in the New Testament: the birth narrative of Jesus. Here too, are the issues of first believers, blessing, authority, and legitimacy. After Jesus' birth, wise men from the East – nobody knows how many there were – come to honour him. Although we know they were astrologers, we don't know much else about them. What were their texts, rituals, and ethics? For all we know, they never became Jews or Christians. But they too were God's. Besides legitimizing Jesus as the one, they bring gifts to him, which were the very first gifts to the fledgling Christian movement, a movement that at this point consisted of Jesus' family. The worldwide Christian church of today was first funded by pagans. They were the first donors, the first folks to put an offering into a church basket, so to speak. While everyone was looking at the sky for signs, God visited Jesus and his family through the strangers, entering the story sideways.

These two examples of how God moves through strangers are not curious incidents. In fact, John 1:11 says that Jesus came to his own people and they did not recognize him. He came into this world as a stranger and suffered as a stranger. At the end of the gospel narratives, Jesus appears once again on the road to Emmaus and, as a stranger, offers Eucharist.

The notion that God moves through strangers offers two lessons to those who are willing to consider faith in a horizontal world. First, without the stranger, we cannot know ourselves. Strangers see what we cannot see. They say what we cannot say. They think what we cannot think. In the church, we tend to look to texts, theologians, and magistrates to better understand and know our faith and our community. But in our disruptive age in which worlds collide, we need people from other religions to help us understand ourselves. They can advise us, bless us, provoke us, love us, disrupt us, and upset us. Teaching this to our children and youth and practicing it with them will help them to be *expectant* of revelation. Once the side door to God is open, the whirlwind of faith that animated so many of our faith mothers and fathers will blow in.

Second, without strangers we cannot know God. In Muslim cultures it is said that you must accept a stranger, because if you don't, you may be rejecting an angel of God. Strangers are not made in our image, but they are made in God's image. Through the human other, we experience divine otherness. The human other and divine other are connected. The otherness of God becomes more bearable as we accept the otherness of people coming to us. Hospitality is deeply important in Christian theology, and it isn't just about Christian manners. Christ's life depended on our ability to cope with otherness. And perhaps this generation's "practicing the presence of God" could be supplemented with "practicing the presence of God *in the other,*" both now and in coming generations.

In her book *Men in Dark Times,* Hannah Arendt says that "political questions are far too serious to be left to the politicians."[1] I imagine God thinking that Christianity is too important to leave to Christians. We need the other to know our own faith.

In light of this, I often tell Christians that when we meet people who are strangers and who are other – those who order their lives through horoscopes, who practice another religion, who come from another country, who have a different gender identity from us, who see the world differently from how we see it – we should be open to hearing what they have to teach us. Mission is a two-way street. We evangelize not only in order to give good news but also in order to receive. Good news always gets better.

Furthermore, our children and youth are strangers to us. They come from a horizontal world and they bring fresh eyes to Christianity. They can see what we cannot see, they can say what we cannot say, they can think what we cannot think, and they can do what we cannot do. We who call ourselves teachers also have to be taught, and children and youth have much to contribute to our own faith journeys.

Part Is Better than the Whole

Some of the best stories, novels, television shows, and screenplays have heroes on a journey to get what they want. And when they get what they want, they realize that what they wanted isn't what they actually need, or still want.

So it has been with Christianity. We fought so hard to be at the top, in everything from wars to apologetics to institutions. We aspired to be the only, to be everything for everybody. Yet once we achieved any semblance of this – whether through Constantine's edict of Milan or local matters or even in our personal lives – we realized that this isn't what we need in order to be faithful disciples of Jesus. We wanted religious supremacy, but what we need and what is called for is to be a part of the whole.

Jesus' call to come and enter the kingdom of God means that we are to come and learn to be part of something larger than ourselves. This is difficult. It's much more challenging to learn to be part of a whole than it is to learn to be in charge. Because in being part of a whole, we need to go through a Copernican revolution all over again; we need to move from the self to the community. Other stories don't exist simply to serve our story. Other people don't exist to be a control group for a cosmic experiment to prove that following Jesus is the best.

I am convinced that the kingdom of God that Jesus spoke about isn't made up of Christians. It's made up of human beings. Christians are only a part of God's kingdom. We are called to learn to be great human beings, and to do that together with those who are not in our image.

God's kingdom is a kingdom of interdependence.

And this interdependence isn't something that we give in to or surrender to. Interdependence has always sustained us and the world in which we live. We read in the Bible that God built interdependence into the world. From the beginning, there was day and night, light and darkness, female and male, spirit and matter, sea and earth, electron and proton, individual and community, finite and infinite. As Christian people, we are called to live with the other with gratitude. We are called to thank the other for not only offering us new perspectives on ourselves but for providing a balance and thus giving us meaning.

The good news of Jesus is not that we will be on top. It is that we do not need to be on top, that there is joy in being a part of something larger than ourselves. We will realize that being a part of the whole is the greatest calling a sentient being can have. Interdependence affirms and protects our particularity. In a horizontal world, we are Christians because we know how to have genuine, dynamic, two-way, life-giving relationships with those around us.

Children today are sensing the interdependent nature of existence more than we have done in recent generations. So, instead of positioning Christianity as a player in a zero-sum game, we can use Christian faith and the teachings of Jesus to help children and youth connect with the people around them. We do not help them connect with others in spite of their Christian identity, but because of it. The act of connecting with the other becomes a deepening of Christian identity. Christian faith can be strengthened through authentic encounters with the other. To do this, we need to help our children and youth internalize a reflexive response to the teaching of the kingdom of God, which is generosity. God is greater than Christianity. Our Christian faith can help us see ourselves as a part of the whole. We are not *It*. The kingdom of God is *It*. And that is a reason to celebrate!

Boundaries Are Connections

We live in a world where identity is defined by boundaries – walls, fences, and other screens are used to separate who is in from who is out. Boundaries are necessary for identities. In the past, cities were surrounded by walls to protect them from outsider attack. Boundaries kept outsiders on the outside. But today, strong cities are connected cities; connected through highways, Wi-Fi, airports, and in countless other ways. The boundaries of our identities do not have to be obstacles; they can be connections.

All this is difficult for us to unlearn, learn, and manage. Those of us who are vertical Christians may have a hard time conceiving of boundaries as points of connection. We have particular beliefs, practices, and rituals that distinguish us from others and give us a precious sense of identity. At the very same time we feel that God, goodness, and grace are also present in the other. We are one, but we are not the same, as Bono puts it.

This is bewildering.

A Sufi imam gently observes my state of heart every time I visit her. Once I told her that I felt we were all one yet we were all different, and I didn't know what to do with this feeling. I thought I was verbalizing something negative about myself, as if as a Christian I wasn't supposed to feel this way. How was I supposed to hold my Christian identity in this moment? It was a struggle of identity amidst an overdose of diversity. My Sufi friend said that I was bewildered and that this bewilderment is an important aspect of spiritual growth. When we are in positions of bewilderment, we are expanding and deepening. It is a hard work, but I have carried her words in my heart ever since she offered them to me – and a bewilderment of diversity has become easier to bear.

People often ask me what will happen to our Christian identity if we conceive of it as having multiple connections rather than clearly delineated separators. The call to the humility of seeing God, goodness, and grace in the other is often perceived to be at the expense of a strong identity. Many people see identity and humility as opposites and believe they can't have a strong identity that is at one and the same time humble.

In actuality, Christianity professes that humility *is* our identity. When we are humble, we affirm our identity. Receiving from others is our identity. Brian McLaren calls this a strong-benevolent identity.[2] When we possess these identities, we see value in protecting each other's stories. We protect each other's dignity of difference instead of colonizing others into what we want them to be. In the kingdom of God, we can afford to be generous this way. In fact, we can't afford not to do this. God is sovereign outside of the boundaries that our human minds, traditions, and hearts have created.

All of this makes me wonder about the horizontal world of our children and youth. Are they bewildered by diversity and by connections to others? Or is this a vertical person's burden? We need to have continuous conversations about identity with youth and help them form identities of passion wrapped up in humility. We also need to teach them to regularly withdraw into our Christian tradition, language, and meanings, and dwell there deeply. The truth is that only people who have gone deep enough into their own well and drunk can grasp that God is the underground water that sustains all wells.

Shallow roots and big walls go together. Young people need to learn that stepping out and learning from the other is an act of strengthening their Christian identity. Through connections, they can deepen their roots and tear down their walls. Plants with deep roots can survive in an open space. And an open space, a space where an uncontrollable wind blows, deepens one's roots.

It Is in Receiving that We Give

I've heard countless Christians talk about the importance of loving and caring for the world. But the curious thing is that Christians are often not perceived as loving and caring and giving, even though we do care and love and give with our budgets, time, and actions. How then is it possible that so many people perceive Christians as not loving?

This question burdened me to no end until it dawned on me that the main reason why loving people are perceived as unloving is because they don't know how to receive. A giver is in a position of power, so being the one who always gives and always loves easily leads us into a position of power. Christians may know how to meet needs in the world, but we don't know how to be in need of the world. And as long as we don't need the world, the world will not need us. It is in receiving that we acknowledge that there is good in other people. It is in receiving that we show that others have something of value to give to us. Through receiving we concede the presence of God in the other.

There is emptiness in all of us, an emptiness that existed in the world before the fall. If we want to live as part of an interdependent world, we need to remember that interdependence does not mean that "they" depend and "we" provide; that "they" receive and "we" give. In an interdependent world, we all give and we all receive. This is a tipping point for a new kind of Christianity – to have a community, text, and theology that is able to receive. Imagine a theology that is always growing and deepening through receiving what God can bring into it sideways, which God has always done!

Receiving is crucial for those who serve in ministry with children and youth. Youth pastors depend on mentors, pastors, and youth to make their ministries work. Children's ministers require teachers, donors, and volunteers in order to form children into faithful disciples. We need to become comfortable with listing our needs and asking other people to help us, to give us what we need. When we show that we are dependent creatures and when we demonstrate openness to receiving from others, we teach young people the value of living in an interdependent world and we induct them into God's interdependent kingdom.

When I was a pastor, I achieved much more by receiving and being served than by giving and serving people. After all, there is much joy and love in receiving. We love to receive recipes from our grandmothers; we love to receive forgiveness from our children; we love to receive advice from friends; and we love to receive blessings from non-Christians. Learning to receive is part of what it means to follow Jesus, for he was a person who was able to receive all the time.

Death Interrupts Theology, and So Does Life

Many people believe that theology makes ultimate statements about death and life. But the truth is that death and life make ultimate statements about theology. They interrupt our preconceived notions of how we interpret holy texts, sacred practices, and what it means to be a spiritual being. If we read our holy texts in the presence of the other, we come to interpret the meaning of the text in light of the other who lives next to us. We used to read texts about pagans, women, slaves, and other marginalized people in one way, but life changed us and our theologies have changed in the process. And now the lived reality of living with people who have sexual orientations that are "other" to us helps us to reinterpret our beliefs. Life wins. Theology always has to give in to life. It's just a matter of time.

Through this process of reading our faith in light of what life and death teach us, we speak back to our religions. It's like a love relationship. We have our beloved and we embrace our beloved. But we also fight with our beloved. At times, we can't stand our beloved. We are silent to our beloved. We want to change our beloved. Our beloved wants to change us. So our relationship with our own religion is a dynamic relationship, and one we need our children and young people to form. We need to teach them to fight with their religion as two lovers fight with one another, and to change and be changed by their religion in light of life.

Sherpa in a Horizontal World

Many Christians of my generation hold to a vertical religion and a vertical God, but live in a world that is increasingly horizontal. One option is to keep on living as we have been doing and hope that the world will come full circle back to us and our vertical perspectives, perhaps by passing on our vertical faith to younger generations.

But I believe that a better option is to learn *to be with our children and youth* in their horizontal world. In such a world, God continuously shows up sideways, like God did in biblical times. In their horizontal world, there are blessings we know not of. In their world, there are things we need to learn to save our own lives. Only when we learn to be blessed and learn again will we be invited to teach.

God comes sideways. And our children and youth can be our Sherpa guides through the digital, over-connected, over-clicked, and over-friended kingdom of God that is at hand.

Cultivating a New Imagination

Imagine for a moment now

Just how this world would change.

Upside-down, inside-out

Dramatically rearranged

If we took the time to ask what

God would like to see

And listened closely to the way

God wants this world to be…

Let's ask God,

Tell me what you wish for, tell me what you'd like

Tell me what you dream of in the middle of the night

Tell me what you hope for, what do you desire?

I want to know just what it is that sets your heart on fire.

-Bryan Moyer Suderman[1]

Chapter 7

Reason for Hope

Ivy Beckwith

Several years ago I had the privilege of speaking at a children's ministry conference sponsored by the Willow Creek Association. The conference was held at Willow Creek Community Church in Barrington, Illinois. It was lunchtime and conferees were streaming into the large common area where lunch was being served. I'd positioned myself on a staircase so that I overlooked that space and I watched many of the thousand or so participants. And as I was watching them, a thought occurred to me: With all these people (plus countless more across the country and beyond) dedicating their lives and careers to the spiritual nurture of young people in churches, how come we aren't seeing amazing changes for the good in both the church and the world? Where is the discernible difference in our world because of the hard work these people are doing?

We've all heard about the studies that speak to these questions. There is the recent research from the Barna Group delineating six reasons why young Christians leave the church.[1] There's the recent Pew research on Millennials showing that many members of this generation who had a childhood faith or church affiliation now describe themselves as unaffiliated.[2] And I'm sure that many readers are familiar with the highly-talked-about conclusion from the National Study of Youth and Religion (led by Christian Smith), which says that many teens and young adults

Ivy Beckwith is Director of Educational Ministries at Rutgers Presbyterian Church in Manhattan. She is a speaker, consultant, and author of several books, including *Postmodern Children's Ministry*, *Formational Children's Ministry*, and *Children's Ministry in the Way of Jesus* (with David Csinos). She holds degrees in English and religious education and has held educational positions in churches throughout the United States.

believe in Moral Therapeutic Deism, a faith bearing little relationship to the gospel; a faith that is all about living a good life so that one can get to heaven; a faith that calls on God when sticky, thorny problems arise in one's life.[3]

So, after so many decades of devotion to children's and youth ministries, so many decades of the proliferation of conferences on how to do children's and youth ministry better, so many decades of creating resource upon resource to teach the Bible in creative and age-appropriate ways, so many decades of churches spending copious amounts of money on their spaces for children and youth, why are results so dreary? Why are we seeing young people unplug from church or form shallow versions of faith that don't resemble the gospel of Jesus Christ? Shouldn't these younger generations have benefitted most from all this attention to ministry with children and youth?

I think if we dig a little deeper into the research, we might uncover some answers. The Barna Group found that the number two reason why young people leave the church is that they experience Christianity in their church as shallow, boring, and irrelevant to their lives and the world. Overall, they felt that God is missing.[4] The Pew Forum research suggests that Millennials find the church to be hypocritical.[5] And the latest research from the National Study of Youth and Religion found that "any notion of the responsibilities of a common humanity, a transcendent call to protect the life and dignity of one's neighbor, or a moral responsibility to seek the common good was almost entirely absent among the [18- to 23-year-old] respondents. Most emerging adults in America have extremely modest to no expectations for ways society or the world can be changed for the better."[6] Emerging adults have tenuous concepts of the common good, those concepts that tend to motivate people to put one another's interests ahead of their own or influence one another's behaviour for the common good. Those who do continue to see faith as important believe that "once one has gotten belief in God figured out... and...feels confident about going to heaven...there is really not much more to think about or pay attention to."[7]

Where's Our Imagination?

The problem, I believe, is that in the scramble to get the biggest, best, shiniest, hippest, and most fun ministry for children and youth on the block, our churches have utterly failed to offer our children and youth an alternative vision of the world and how to live in it. We have failed to offer them an alternate reality to what they encounter every day. We have not given them the ability to imagine and envision alternatives to their current personal, social, and cultural situations. We have failed to offer them Jesus' vision of good Samaritans, prodigal-welcoming fathers, elaborate parties offered to the poorest of the poor, and tiny mustard seeds that grow into mighty trees. And we have failed to offer them a vision of hope for the future. We have failed to give them a kingdom vision of *shalom* that helps them to see life with God and God's people as it was meant to be. Jesus said the kingdom is here. N.T. Wright puts it this way: "Suppose the world's way of empire is all wrong. Suppose there's a different way. And suppose that Jesus, in his life, death, and resurrection has brought it about."[8] We seem not to have helped our children and youth suppose this vision in any meaningful and lasting way.

I believe that these failures have resulted from a lack of imagination among those of us who minister with children and youth. If we can't envision and imagine and live in the world Jesus talked about, then we can't pass this vision on to our children and get them excited about it. Many of us, despite years of church-going, Bible studies, and seminary education, lack imagination to live any differently than the culture around us – and our children see this. Because we often live like everyone else, because we don't always (or often) live into the peculiar way of Jesus, we have failed to capture young people's imaginations, to mystify them by God's love.

Let me give you an example. A few years ago, I served a church in Connecticut that was smack in the middle of one of the wealthiest zip codes in the United States. Residents of this town include the CEO of a national television network, hedge fund managers, bankers, news anchorman Brian Williams, and musician Harry Connick, Jr. Several leaders of this church worked on Wall Street and were present or former CEOs or lawyers related to the financial industry or corporate America. Even the church's senior minister had been a hot-shot corporate litigator in a former career. So when the financial meltdown of 2007–2008 occurred, these church leaders were running scared, worried that we would not meet our promised pledge income and thus end the year with a deficit.

The first Monday night of each month was committee meeting night. Prior to these meetings, all of our church trustees, deacons, committee members, and ministerial staff would gather in our fellowship hall for a short devotional led by one of the pastors. One Monday night during these perilous financial times I was tapped to lead this devotional. I chose to tell these titans of finance – many of whom could write a personal cheque to cover any shortfall the church might encounter – the story of George Müller.

George Müller was a 19th-century British reformer who built and ran orphanages in London for abandoned children. I'm fascinated that he never asked for money for these orphanages. He didn't have a development department or a stewardship chairman. When he needed money or help, he simply prayed. This is the story I told that night.

> On one particular morning, the larders were empty at the orphanage. The children sat at their tables with empty plates and cups. Müller asked them to pray for their daily bread. Just then there was a knock at the door. It was a baker offering loaves of bread that he had baked extra. But they still needed milk. At that moment, a milk wagon broke down outside the orphanage. In order to fix the wagon, the milkman needed to unload the milk. So he offered it to Müller and the orphans. Miraculously, God provided for their needs. They prayed, and milk and bread appeared.

Now, I'm still not quite sure what I expected from the folks gathered in that Connecticut church. I guess that in optimistic naïveté I had imagined them all applauding the story and acknowledging joyfully that, of course, God would provide all of the church's needs. And didn't we all need to be more like George Müller and trust in God's promises? But I got nothing. There was absolutely no response to this story of God's miraculous provision. In fact, I sensed that they thought I was a little crazy for even suggesting that this story had anything to do with us and our church and what we should be doing. And I also got the impression that telling this story had diminished me in their eyes. They simply could not imagine a world where God could be counted on to act this way. They could not imagine themselves counting on God in this way. That evening, I saw a remarkable lack of imagination about a world in which God has promised to provide for our needs in the same way God cares for the birds of the air and the lilies of the field.

Fear and Loathing in the Church

What is behind this lack of imagination? Why is it that the people of God can have such difficulty imagining an alternative narrative for our life together, a new way of living that captivates our children and youth? What keeps us from inhabiting what Walter Brueggemann calls the "prophetic imagination,"[9] the ability to envisage an alternative to current personal and social situations?

I think one reason is fear. I think we are afraid of what this sort of imagination may mean for us, the changes it would demand. I think we are afraid of the work and sacrifice it would take to implement such vision. And this fear is paralyzing, so we maintain the status quo and celebrate small victories and glimpses of grace rather than being bold in how we imagine the kingdom. And I think we are afraid that we'll blow it, that we'll get it wrong. But this fear means we refuse to take God at God's word.

I was leading a Bible study on 1 John with a group of women at a church in Minnesota. We were looking at chapter 2 and we came upon the passage in which the apostle writes: "Whoever does the will of God lives forever."[10] I asked these women how they would live their lives differently if they truly believed that they would live forever. The response from them was much the same as that which I received from the financial world's movers and shakers in that fellowship hall in Connecticut. They didn't seem able even to begin to embrace the question, let alone formulate an answer. And even though exhortations to "be not afraid" and to "trust God" wind their way through the New Testament, Jesus-followers are some of the most fearful people I know. Depending on where we stand on the theological spectrum we might be afraid of culture, science, or people who are different from us; we may be fearful of evangelical churches or mainline churches or emerging churches. And this fear blocks our ability to imagine what is not visible. We (and I use this word intentionally to include myself in this) need to be continually reminded that Jesus said that "the time has come. The kingdom of God has come near. Repent and believe the good news."[11]

I am indebted to Walter Brueggemann for offering a second reason for our lack of a "prophetic imagination." He said that the church has been numbed by consumer satiation. Self-preoccupation and consumerism deny a lively communal imagination that can resist a mindless humanity of despairing conformity. Brueggemann calls for faith communities to refuse "to live inside an alien, numbing imagination"[12] and to instead embrace the very imagination of God. He argues that the contemporary American church is so largely enculturated to the American ethos of consumerism that it has little power to believe or act other than according to this status quo.

Over the past year, I have been doing a lot of thinking about selfishness. In our culture, I see it everywhere I turn. I see it on the New York City subway when people by the doors won't cede space to those trying to enter or exit the train. I see it in people who don't pick up their dog's poop. I see it in the people who think dogs should be banned because some people don't pick up their dog's poop. I see it in churches that have trouble staffing ministries for children and youth (and let's not think the children don't pick up on this selfishness and hypocrisy in the church). I see it in debates over taxes, the role of government, and economic fairness. And I see it in myself when I walk past a homeless man on the street asking me to buy him a slice of pizza and rationalize my reluctance by saying to myself that it would be foolish to dig through my wallet standing in the middle of a busy New York City sidewalk.

But if the first question we ask about everything is ultimately about our own interests and desires (how will this affect *me* and *my* needs and wants?), without any consideration of others, then we're never going to see beyond our own noses and perhaps those of our nearest and dearest. We'll never see beyond fulfilling our own needs, wants, and desires, and staving off our own fears. We'll never begin to imagine how we can live into God's narrative of *shalom* – life as it was meant to be – when it means we need to change and give up things in order for God's kingdom to be manifest for all people. Imagining another way means we may have to give up our life in order to find it. This is difficult and scary. But the lives of our children and youth just might depend on it.

Dreaming God's *Shalom*

So an important first question (okay, maybe a first couple of questions) we need to ask ourselves is this: Do we truly believe what God promises us? Do we really believe that there *is* another way; an alternative, better narrative for the way we live now? This was essentially the question I was asking when I told the story of George Müller's faith and when I spoke with those Minnesota women about what living a life that will not end might look like. Do we really believe that God is for us? We can't envision a new way if we don't believe it is possible. And if all we have to offer our children and youth is "same old, same old," why should they stick with us and follow what we *say*, but perhaps don't *do*? And if we do believe that God is doing and will do a new thing, then we must be brave enough to acknowledge that in a consuming society such as ours an alternative consciousness is difficult to sustain. We must acknowledge that we must be ever-vigilant in pursuing and enacting God's vision of *shalom*. We must be aware that God's vision for the world isn't the popular vision. So as we pursue God's *shalom*, God's kingdom reality, there will be people who will not like us – and some of these people may be members of our churches. As Brueggemann says, "passion as the capacity and readiness to care, to suffer, to die, and to feel is the enemy of imperial reality."[13]

Brueggemann states that a prophetic imagination requires a tension between a criticized present and an energizing future.[14] To help young people have such an imagination, we need to deconstruct what is happening in our world here and now. But deconstruction is not enough. We need to put something better into place. We need to reconstruct the world in ways that are imagination-capturing and passion-generating for younger generations now and to come. Brueggemann calls this "engaging in futuring fantasy."[15] I might call it dreaming: taking the words of God and of Jesus about the way we were created to live and visioning what that might look like in our own lives and in the world around us. But Brueggemann reminds us that imagination goes hand-in-hand with (and even comes before) implementation: "Our culture is competent to implement almost anything and to imagine almost nothing."[16] I think this caution is especially important for the church, for we're often really good at developing and implementing programs for this problem and that issue. We see a problem or a need or a self-marketing opportunity and we create a program to address it. We're proven that we're competent, but we don't seem to be very imaginative.

Part of this future fantasy, this dreaming an alternate future, is contained in articulating what it means to hope. Brueggemann defines hope as the refusal to accept the reality which is the majority opinion.[17] He says that hope is a decision against despair.[18] A person can't have imagination without hope. And hope comes with feelings. Hope, even though it's a wonderfully good thing, comes with anguish, pain, and tears, as well as happiness and freedom. It pushes us out of our numbness, because with hope we begin to see the difference between the way things are and the way things could be, the way they were meant to be. Without the feelings (even the harsh, not-so-pleasant feelings) that hope allows, our imaginations are stunted and numbed.

So the task of the prophetic imagination is to evoke an alternative community that knows it is about doing different things in different ways from the culture-at-large. The prophetic imagination seeks to penetrate despair so that new feelings can be named and embraced. And it seeks to stun people out of business-as-usual into believing that a different way is possible. The prophetic imagination infects God's people – including (dare I say especially?) children and youth – with the hope of the kingdom of God. It turns our mourning into dancing. It lives out the words of the Psalmist that joy comes in the morning.[19]

Thy Kingdom Come

My premise throughout this chapter has been that, looking at the big picture, the Christian church in the West is losing its children and youth. I believe this is so because we (again, and throughout this chapter, I include myself in this *we*) have lacked the imagination to offer them an alternative vision of reality, a reality in which God's people live unselfishly in the joy of the already present kingdom of God.

That's my deconstruction, my criticized present. But I don't want to wrap up this chapter without some hint of where to look for an energized future. So let me share three stories of where I've seen glimpses of the prophetic imagination, where I've seen people living, being, and acting as if the kingdom has already come.

Illuminating the Imagination

A few years ago I was at Princeton Theological Seminary for their annual Forum on Youth Ministry. All of the workshops, seminars, and presentations revolved around the arts and creativity. There was an amazing presentation on the Saint John's Bible, the illuminated Bible spearheaded by Saint John's Abbey in Collegeville, Minnesota. Attendees learned about the ink used in the making of this Bible, the calligraphy, and the genesis of the artwork. I was entranced!

But the thing about the production of this Bible that captured my imagination above all else was the illumination of the Psalms. As the committee and artists who worked on the Saint John's Bible approached the Psalms, they decided that they didn't want to use pictures to illustrate the Hebrew poetry. So they recorded monks at the abbey chanting the particular Psalms chosen for this Bible, loaded those recordings onto a computer, and translated the chanting into a digital voice print. That digital voice print was then incorporated into the illustration of each particular Psalm. I thought this was amazing enough! But they went one step further. Running vertically on the same pages are digital voice prints of Jewish, Muslim, Buddhist, Hindu, Taoist, and Aboriginal worshippers praying. In those pages, I saw a glimpse of that alternative vision of life, a glimpse of the kingdom of God.

"Kick off Your Sunday Shoes"

The original version of the film *Footloose* was released in 1984. The film is about a young man (played by Kevin Bacon) who moves to a small town where, mostly through the efforts of a local church pastor, dancing has been banned. The film chronicles this young man's rebellious and clandestine efforts to bring dancing back to the town. Eventually the local minister relents and permission to dance is again granted to the town. The young people celebrate by having a dance. The movie ends with a scene of all the young people in town arriving at the dance and then dancing their collective hearts out or, as the title song of the movie states, kicking off their Sunday shoes. It is one of the most energizing and joyful clips of film I have ever seen.

I have a friend who absolutely loves this movie. A while back, as we sat in his living room after watching this final scene for the umpteenth time, he turned to me and said, "Why can't church be like that?" That question has stayed with me for years. Can it be that the last scene of *Footloose* is a picture of the kingdom of God?

Jumping into the Kingdom

The 2011–2012 theatre season brought a revival of the musical *Godspell* to Broadway. In January 2012 I took the middle school and high school kids from my church to see it one Friday evening. It was winsome and delightful and energizing and I'd forgotten how much the good news of Matthew's Gospel is quoted word for word throughout the play. It's a Bible study live on stage.

This version of the musical made use of trap doors in the stage floor in order to create biblical settings like the Jordan River for the scene depicting Jesus' baptism. Toward the end of the show, these trap doors were opened to reveal trampolines below – one for each cast member. The music segued into "We Beseech Thee" and the cast members sang the song jumping up and down on the trampolines, spinning and dancing and leaping. I sat in my seat absolutely transfixed by the sheer joy on that stage, and all I could think was "the kingdom of God is like this."

Plato once said that "poetry is nearer to vital truth than history." It's no mystery to me why totalitarian regimes crack down first on the poets and artists in a society. These are the people who tell truth in an imagination-capturing way. And when imaginations are roused and dreams are sparked, revolutions become possible.

As we work to lose our numbness, to recover our imagination around what a true life of loving God and following Jesus looks like and how we can share this life with children and youth, perhaps we should first turn to poets and artists for our inspiration. Wherever we look for our inspiration, it is vital that we recover our imagination for walking in the way of Jesus, an imagination that spurs hope in our lives, in the church, and in the world, a hope that children and youth find dazzling and infectious, a hope that allows them to imagine living in new ways as part of the church universal. As the Christian philosopher Teilhard de Chardin said, "The future belongs to those who give the next generation reason for hope."

Chapter 8

Expanding Children's Imaginations for Peace

Amy Gingerich and Rebecca Seiling

Six-year-old Eden has two favourite stories from the Bible: the story of Cain and Abel and the story of David and Goliath. She pages through her story Bible to find them, poring over the pictures and reading the stories aloud, word by word. Why do these stories interest her? Eden says that she enjoys the action and the messages that small people (like David) can make a difference and people (like Cain) can be angry.

Each of these stories depicts anger and violence of some of the worst kinds and we both struggle with how to introduce these texts to children. In many Bible stories, God's ways are mysterious, God's people make awful mistakes, and there is no clear winner or loser.

The two of us are currently working to develop a new Sunday school

Amy Gingerich is Director of Media at MennoMedia, an agency of Mennonite Church USA and Mennonite Church Canada that produces faith-based print, video, radio, and web materials with ideas for living out the faith from a Mennonite perspective. She works from her home outside Cleveland, Ohio.

Rebecca Seiling has worked extensively with children and youth as a teacher, youth pastor, camp worker, and writer. Her children's writing includes *Plant a Seed of Peace*, *Don't Be Afraid*, and curricula for *Gather 'Round* and MennoMedia. She blogs about faith and family at hearthstrings.ca. Rebecca lives with her family in Waterloo, Ontario.

curriculum that highlights God's way of peace.[1] And as we explore and reflect on how to teach children about peace, we are left wondering what to do with violent texts in the Bible. How should we lift up stories of peace – from the Bible, from our faith tradition (Mennonite), from Christian history, and from around the world? What tools do our children get from the church for living in a changing and sometimes violent world?

The Bible is the living text of our people. The scriptures contain stories that we can learn from and live by. As parents, educators, and writers, we know that the stories we tell matter. The verses, rhymes, fairy tales, songs, and slogans that we repeat to our children help them to form frameworks for looking at the world. Stories from the Bible and from traditions and histories in the church can help children expand their imaginations for peace.

A Broad View of *Shalom*

Theologically, we locate ourselves as members of the Anabaptist tradition, specifically the Mennonite church. And in terms of how we identify our faith as followers of Jesus Christ, we believe that the sword and violence are outside the perfection of Christ[2] and outside God's desire for humanity.

The Hebrew word *shalom* has deeper meanings than those we get from common English translations. In many instances, *shalom* is translated as *peace*. While this Hebrew word certainly refers to the absence of warfare between two entities, it also encompasses right relationship, well-being, welfare, wholeness, and safety. It is an ideal lifted up in the Bible that encapsulates all of life.[3] "It is clear that the creator God intends that the world should be whole, safe, prosperous, peaceable, just, fruitful, and productive, that is, the world should be marked in every part by *shalom*."[4] If this vision of *shalom* is for all life, it is also for all ages and all of humanity. All people are created in God's good image. All of us need to experience nurture, mutuality, equality, and respect in relationships; for when we feel known and loved by God and have a sense of self-worth, we are better empowered to give of ourselves and make peace.

One of the reasons we believe in the importance of teaching peace to children is that we believe that human beings are created in God's good image[5] and that God created us to be in relationship with one another and not isolated from other people.[6] God sensed Adam's loneliness and created Eve to be a partner with him. Together, Adam and Eve were naked and unashamed, suggesting they were vulnerable, trusting, and peaceful with one another. This image of humanity gives us a glimpse of God's broad view of *shalom*, an image that we want to impart to young people.

The Bible as a Resource for Peace

Genesis 1 and 2 are excellent starting points for teaching peace to children, to remind them over and over about being created in God's good image. This is an important, foundational message to convey to people of all ages because they are empowered to make peace when they sense that they are known, loved, and cherished by God and when they have a sense of self-worth and value. These Genesis passages also challenge us to see God's image even in our worst enemies.

In the gospels, we see that Jesus modelled a path toward peace as he welcomed outsiders, re-interpreted scripture, challenged assumptions, and confronted conflict. Children, therefore, should not be taught that peace simply refers to the *absence* of conflict. Rather, they need to hear stories of boldness or directness like those that we find in the words and actions of Jesus. For example, in Matthew 18:15–20, Jesus outlined a method for resolving conflicts and told his followers to "go and correct" another rather than not responding or letting resentment build up.

Boldness and directness in confronting conflicts take courage, but young people – especially older children and youth – are able to take responsibility for conflicts in which they are involved. It is neither helpful nor biblically sound to teach that "Jesus would not want you to argue." Arguments happen, people disagree, conflicts erupt. They are inevitable aspects of life in our world. So instead, we can help children own a sense of responsibility for their actions; for when they understand how their actions affect others, it can help eliminate their sense of powerlessness. It is out of this feeling of powerlessness that children often first act out to get attention.

It is not easy for children – or adults, for that matter – to act as peacemakers when life does not seem fair. Children readily understand that life is not always fair. "He took my toy; it is not fair" or "Why should I have to help set the table when she doesn't have to?" or "Why did he get the promotion I deserved?" are phrases to which many can relate. But one of the reasons we teach peace to children is because we trust in a God of justice, a God who is at work to restore balance in our unbalanced world.[7] The first shall be last. The last shall be first. God's warm embrace has room for everyone.

We also teach peace to children because we want to raise a generation of disciples who are willing to extend forgiveness and reconciliation. No one wants to live in a world where children are shot in schools, where we live in fear of our neighbours, where the violence in video games becomes the reality on the streets. Instead, we look to stories of forgiveness like that in Genesis of Joseph forgiving his brothers. As a person with great power in Egypt, Joseph could have had his brothers thrown in prison, killed, or simply sent home without the food and aid that they so badly needed. They had sold him into slavery and separated him from his family. But the biblical account shows a Joseph who ultimately resists the temptation of vengeance and instead embraces a desire to restore right relationship, find wholeness, and seek *shalom*.

True, there are many passages in the Bible that depict vengeance and violence, showing that *shalom* is not present. But we can see these stories of God's people more as descriptive, cautionary tales rather than prescriptive examples for us to follow. The story of Cain and Abel in Genesis 4 describes a tragic relationship between brothers – one we are surely not called to emulate. Such passages do not serve to legitimize violence, but rather point to the problems associated with a violent way. This is one approach to understanding and teaching the Bible, and it does not resolve the issue of violence in scripture. However, our communities of faith are called to engage in Bible study together – young and old alike – to wrestle with passages that are problematic because of their violence.

Peace Heroes from Church History

While it is a rich and varied resource for teaching peace to children, the Bible isn't our only resource. Throughout history, there have been many examples of people living out commitments to peace and choosing to live in a different way. These people were inspired by the nonviolent model of Jesus. One example is the story of Preacher Peter, who lived in a small town in Switzerland in the 1700s. Preacher Peter was not a particularly popular pastor. Some of his views about baptism and peace-making made him not just unpopular, but downright despised.

One night, Peter was just nodding off to sleep when he heard a noise outside. What could it be? Peter lit a lantern and went out to investigate. The sounds were coming from his roof! He looked up and saw two men stealing the thatch from his roof. They were ruining his home!

Peter prayed to God: *What should I do?*

We wonder what we would do if we were in this situation. Would we shout angry threats? Call the police? Take them to court? Run from the house?

This is what Peter did that night.

He went back into the house, woke his wife and told her of a plan he had devised. A little while later, Peter went outside. He called up to the men, "We have prepared a meal for you! Come! Eat!"

The men weren't quite sure what to do. They looked at each other, and, after a few minutes, they climbed down.

Peter and his wife welcomed them to a table filled with food. A fire was burning and the candles were lit. Peter prayed a blessing over the food and the four of them gathered around the table to eat. The men gazed speechless at their plates, then quietly ate what they had been served.

After they finished, the men went back outside. Again, Peter heard noises coming from the roof. He stepped outside. He looked up and was surprised at what he saw. The men were busy repairing the damage they had done.[8]

This story illustrates that peace is possible. Creative ways of resolving conflict are within our reach. In fact, they are woven deep into the fabric of Christian tradition. But sometimes we lack the imagination to forge new paths. Telling children stories like this one about Preacher Peter helps to nurture their imaginations toward the way of peace.

Motivation and Method

Our *motivation* for teaching peace to children comes from the belief that peace is the will of God, that Jesus taught and lived the way of peace, and that his followers also work to be peacemakers.[9] We believe that this is part of what it means to be a disciple and also part of what it means to disciple others.

And we believe that the good news of Jesus is about peace – that is part of our theology. Practically and pedagogically, we've found that telling stories of peace and lifting up stories about specific peacemakers are among the best ways to help children – and people of all ages – learn to make peace and to weave peace deep within their own emerging theologies.

The stories we tell matter to our theologies because stories shape, form, and transform us as a people of God. Stories of peace inspire children's imaginations to wander in different directions: to imagine peace; to pursue the love of strangers; to follow Jesus, especially during difficult times. Some of the stories we tell about peace can and should be from the Bible, but they should also be about other times in history, contemporary events, circumstances, and heroes. This range of stories can help children recognize that peace is attainable today and it isn't something that's only from the Bible.

The more that children hear adults tell stories about peace and then watch adults model peacemaking in their lives, the more they will remember and understand that peace is not just a *method* for resolving conflict or the absence of conflict. They will know that the *motivation* for making peace comes directly from what it means to follow God.[10]

It is important to define the terms *method* and *motivation* and what they mean in terms of peacemaking. A *method* is a way of resolving conflict – a mechanism to use. There are countless programs out there about how to teach peace and methods of nonviolence to children. Children today often know about peer mediation programs and how to use "I feel" statements to express their emotions. They might have used art programs to resolve conflict or a stoplight approach where they stop and think about their words before moving forward together with a plan of action. These programs all teach appropriate ways to resolve conflict. They are proven *methods*.

But if a peaceful method that a child uses to solve a problem does not work, she will move on and try out another method, one that may not foster *shalom*. For example, if talking it out did not work the first time for Farah on the playground, she might try it a second time. But if she does not feel successful with those results she may ask her older brother, Adam, to step in with angry words or flying fists.

Motivations are deep convictions – those things that undergird all of our thoughts and actions. Motivations form a person's framework for looking at the world. The stories we tell matter because they help form our motivations and the motivations of the young people with whom we share these stories.

In describing *methods* and *motivations* in this way, the two are set up as *practices* and *beliefs,* and we propose that we need to have solid beliefs – or motivations – in place to be able to sustain the practice of making peace and teaching peace to children. We don't need to have all our beliefs and motivations figured out before we work for peace. In fact, practicing peacemaking can help to form our motivations; as our beliefs about peace shape our practices for making peace, so do our practices for making peace shape our beliefs about peace. But for peacemaking to be sustained as a practice in the life of a child, motivation matters.

It is often said that the place to begin to create a peaceful world is with our self: our attitudes, our word choices, our tone of voice, our behaviours. How we understand God and how we read the Bible will influence the motivations in ourselves and in our children, motivations that can, in turn, lead them to practice peace creatively and boldly in their everyday lives.

Transformed, Renewed Minds

In Romans 12, Paul writes about transformation, saying that for peace to be part of our motivation and framework, we must first be transformed by God:

> Do not be conformed to this world, but be transformed by the renewing of your minds, so that you may discern what is the will of God – what is good and acceptable and perfect… If it is possible, so far as it depends on you, live peaceably with all.[11]

This text calls us to be transformed. It dares us to imagine life very differently to that of today's prevailing narrative, a narrative in which one's individual rights are glorified above all else. Paul's words call us to understand and embrace God's wide vision of *shalom* – a vision in which fighting, hatred, and selfishness are replaced by well-being, harmony, and wholeness.

In light of this, we dream of raising up a generation of transformed young people who can imagine a world where God's peace and justice reign; who understand that ours is a God of justice, a God who is far from nonchalant about injustice in our neighbourhoods, a God who is at work to restore balance to our unbalanced world. We dream of cultivating generations of young people who press beyond retributive urges to extend forgiveness and reconciliation, as Joseph did to his brothers in Genesis.

Telling stories to children about peace and about peacemakers can help make this dream come true. Stories like that of Preacher Peter can help them to be transformed to live into God's vision of *shalom*. Many stories that children hear today help them to imagine violence. The church is called to help them imagine peace and equip them with tools for waging peace. Preacher Peter acted with unflinching discipleship because he had been transformed by the gospel of peace. His motivations were in order because he was committed to Jesus' way of peace. He had dared to imagine another way. This is the kind of story worth sharing with children.

Teaching Peace

There are countless ways to help young people be transformed by God's dream for peace. Perhaps the most basic way is simply to tell stories. Find anthologies about peace heroes, then share them with children. Books such as *Plant a Seed of Peace*[12] and *Walking with Jesus*[13] tell stories about people from various eras and countries who have followed Christ's way of peace.

As we think about how to share the gospel of peace, we need to remember that peace comes in all shapes and sizes – from the impossible-sounding adventure of Preacher Peter to a simple story of a young child, who when asked what peace feels like to her, draws a picture of Grandma giving her a cookie. Peace comes through simple acts like sharing a meal with those we might see as our enemies. It comes by responding in love when it would be easy to lash out in hatred. By enacting peace in large and small ways, children will understand that peace is something they can experience right now in many different ways.

Another idea is to ask children to use their imaginations and senses to think in new ways about peace. Give them paper, crayons or markers, and lots of room to use their minds. Ask them to imagine through questions such as: What does peace look like? What does peace sound like? What does peace feel like? Then create a book together about what it means to taste, touch, breathe, listen for, and look for peace.

And let's not forget to let a little child lead us! Children can help us to imagine and live into a new world. They have ideas of how to make a difference in our world, from helping out at a local social service agency to collecting food for the food bank. Adults can empower children by giving them the tools they need to put their faith into action. And we can allow children's visions of peace to speak prophetically to the adults in their faith community. Try setting up a children's art gallery inside or outside the church building with their visions of peace, or encouraging children to create dramatic pieces that can be incorporated into worship services.

We can also try working together to create a "dare to make peace" list, looking to the Bible for examples of radical peacemaking. Such a list might look like this:

Dare to make peace
- Make a snack and share it with your enemy (Isaac and the wells, Genesis 26:1–5, 16–32).
- Hug your brother, even if he's done something to make you mad (Esau with Jacob, Genesis 33:1–20).
- Forgive your sister, even if her words or actions hurt you long ago (Joseph with his brothers, Genesis 50:15–21).
- Speak up, even when you don't feel confident (Moses, Exodus 4:10).
- Bring a snack to people who look like they're going to fight each other (Abigail averting a war, 1 Samuel 25:1–35).
- Allow your faith to move mountains and do other things that seem impossible (Matthew 17:20).

- Have a party for someone whose life has been transformed (prodigal son, Luke 15:11–32).
- Ask someone who is standing all alone to play with you (Jesus with Zacchaeus, Luke 19:1–10).
- Meet someone at the water fountain and talk, even though you may be from different countries (Jesus with Samaritan woman, John 4:1–42).
- Welcome a stranger to your home (Romans 12).

There are many ways to make peace, such as hospitality, doing something unusual and unexpected, forgiving, including others, being welcoming, and showing courage. In the list we've shared, scripture references are placed alongside each idea, connecting each point to biblical passages and showing children that the Bible can give them tools and ideas for responding to events in peaceful, life-giving ways. Think together of other ideas of how people, young and old, can respond to injustice and seek peace in our time. Engage in Bible study that calls young people to action, and find ways to act together.

Start Small

In our hurting world, it's easy to become overwhelmed with the violence around us and around young people. And when we're overwhelmed with violence, we may feel helpless, like we can't do anything about it. But sometimes peace begins with a tiny bit of faith that allows us to imagine creative responses to trying situations, and to use our stories as examples of another way.

Great peacemakers started with a little faith. How can we encourage our children to do the same? Peaceful change can come through the small actions of small people. In *Plant a Seed of Peace*, Rebecca encourages us to make peace in little ways, using the faith that we have, no matter how great or small it may be. The following poem, taken from this book, calls us to empower our children to bring forth a world where peace is pursued.

If you would have faith as small as a seed
A tiny amount, it's all that you need
Your faith could move mountains, or buildings, or trees,
It could move them for miles, to the oceans or seas.
The size of your faith doesn't matter at all
Whether it's big or whether it's small.
You might say, "Look at me, now what can I do?
I'm too small to matter. God must've called you."
But you can be brave, and you can be wise
Your faith can change things, no matter the size.
So start out real small, small is all that you need,
Now get your faith working, and plant a small seed.[14]

Chapter 9

Nurturing an Imaginative, Inquiring Spirit

Susan Burt

We live in exciting times, times that are variously described as postmodern, postcolonial, post-Christendom, peri-emergent, liminal, and transitional. This is a restless time of radical change of all kinds – cultural, political, social, spiritual, environmental. Inundated with information about global climate change, environmental catastrophes, and economic crises, people are looking to build a better world – from the grassroots up. New ways of being in the world, in community, with each other, and with the environment are emerging. Within the Christian faith, where there are concerns for diminishing numbers and the relevancy of faith and church for new generations, we are motivated by an emerging vision that embraces search and meaning rather than certainty; questions rather than answers.

"There is a new story emerging in consciousness, one that evokes awe, wonder, and reverence as it expands our notion of God."[1] The power of imagination to take us to this place of awe, wonder, and reverence is

Susan Burt is Managing Editor of *Seasons of the Spirit,* an international, ecumenical, and lectionary-based Christian education and worship resource. She has served as the Australian editor of *The Whole People of God* and has worked in children's ministry for the Uniting Church in Australia. Susan lives in Adelaide, South Australia, where she is a member of the Christ Church Uniting Church, a theologically progressive community that seeks to celebrate the best of the old with the possibility of the new.

captured beautifully by a young child in the opening scene of *Gratitude*, a short film by Louie Schwartzberg.

> When I watch TV, it's just some show that you just…pretend. But when you explore, you get more imagination than you already had, and when you get more imagination, it makes you want to go deeper in so you can get more and see beautifuller things. Like…if it's a path it could lead you to a beach or something, and it could be beautiful…[2]

Imagination, not passive engagement, opens the world to this young girl, takes her deeper into it, and leads her to things not yet discovered. How might imagination in children be awakened, nurtured, and nourished so they "enter imaginatively into scripture, experiencing the message that transcends the printed words"?[3]

The human imagination is awakened, nurtured, and nourished in many ways: when we play and explore; when we practice hospitality, stillness and silence, care and compassion; when we observe or participate in the arts (literature, music, visual art, dance, drama); and when we enter the world of the story and the world view of the storyteller. While much can be said about any of these ways, I set my gaze on how we might nurture the imagination of young people by breathing new life into familiar stories. As we consider the power of imagination and story to build and liberate, or destroy and oppress, we are reminded that words, images, didactic teaching, and closed answers can stifle, diminish, shut down, and impoverish imaginative, inquiring spirits and bring harm rather than life and good news. When we learn to use our imaginations, we experience new life in the old stories of our faith.

When did a story provoke your enquiry, engage your senses, stir your imagination, take you deeper into something "beautifuller"? What made it so? When was enquiry suppressed, senses dulled, imagination wounded, paralyzed, or diminished? What made it so?

I was once asked to exegete Mark 7:24–30 and Matthew 15:21–28, which tell the story of Jesus' encounter with the Syrophoenician/Canaanite woman. My first reaction to this request reminded me how this story had impacted my childhood emotions; how it had shut down, silenced, and diminished my imaginative, inquiring spirit.

When I was a child, I did not like the story and I did not want to spend time with it. My life experience of being on the receiving end of name-calling shaped how I imagined this story. To me, calling the woman a dog made Jesus seem mean and uncaring. How different my first experience of this story would have been if the questions and wonderings it raised in me were welcomed, and if I had been encouraged to focus not only on Jesus, but also on the woman and her actions and words, her power and tenacity. Instead I had been boxed in by barriers and boundaries set by poor attempts at didactic teaching, teaching that had distilled everything down to one meaning, providing an answer, and closing the text to the imagination. We all enter story from the known – our life experience – and it takes skill, care, and understanding to help us move into the unknown, uncover new truths, and recognize how our own life experiences/stories intersect and connect with the stories of our faith.

It is crucial that those of us who seek to nurture young imaginations frame our questions so they don't suggest there is a right or wrong answer. Questions or wondering that might be offered for the story of the Syrophonecian woman might include: What surprised you about that story? I wonder why Jesus changed his mind? I wonder what gave the woman such power to speak? I wonder what the woman's expression was? I wonder how she sounded? I wonder what the disciples said to Jesus after the woman left? What do you think the disciples learned that day? I wonder what Jesus learned? I wonder what the woman said to her friends, to her daughter? I wonder what the daughter said and thought? *[handwritten: wondering Qs]*

Without encouragement to wander around the story, to wonder, to pull back the layers and look, children can be led on a straight, narrow, and soul-stifling path. But stories are not straight and narrow paths.

A story is like a labyrinth into which we step and move at whatever pace we choose; listening, wondering, questioning, reflecting, circling back and then forward as we discover new truths. We reach the centre, wait, and find meaning for ourselves in a particular time and place. As we travel back to engage in the world, we find praxis changes as well, influenced by our engagement with the story. The story becomes our own, and we live it. But the story does not remain the same, for we will enter the labyrinth again and the story will speak to us in new ways. Like ripples of water, a story is not contained. Drop a pebble into water and ripples move out and out and out. There are circles within a circle, stories within a story.

Jewish tradition says that the Torah is written "black fire on white fire." The black fire refers to the words, the writing; the white fire refers to the space, the gaps between the words, what is not written. Some say that what the writer does not say matters more than what is written. Words are limited and fixed; they might be dissected, discussed, highlighted, defined. But others believe that an "aha moment" is more likely to come when what is between the words – what is in the spaces and silences – is questioned and imagined.[4] In these moments, the fires give heat and light, warming the spirit and illuminating the imagination.

The Bible is full of characters who seem to exist within the gaps of the written word. They want and need a voice. They want to be embodied and liberated. They want their stories told.

Drawing Fresh Water from Old Wells

A child once asked a storyteller, "Every time you tell us a story, you have to put it inside your own head first, don't you?" Wise words. There are no shortcuts in educating children in matters of faith, in sharing stories with them. First and foremost, the storyteller needs to experience the story, to exercise and nurture her or his own imaginative spirit.

But how do we do this? How do we experience a story through our own imagination so that we can in turn offer the gift of the story to young people? The following process of hearing, wondering, and imagining can help to move the story out of literalism, factuality, certainty, and fixed answers and into the realm of the imagination.

1. Prepare.
- Read the text (the "black fire").
- Let go of any preconceived ideas or notions about the text. Try to hear it as if for the first time.
- Look for as much context as possible: geographical setting, characters, symbols/objects that are keys to the story (for example, the stone at the tomb, the water jars at the wedding, the loaves and fish in the story of a multitude fed). Look for who is at the

centre of the story, keeping in mind that the centre will shift as the story progresses. This is the "known" part of the story and it prepares us to imagine the "unknown."

2. Move about in the gaps, the spaces between the words, in the silences, and bring questions and wonderings to the text, such as:
- What's going on in the world of the story? What anxieties seem present in the story?
- What's going on in the world of the storyteller or writer?
- What anxieties seem present in this world?
- What special knowledge does this text require (back-story, words, phrases, proper names, theology) in order to enter the story?
- What is missing from the story? What has the storyteller or writer not included? Why might the storyteller or writer be silent on these matters?
- What details are missing?
- Who gets to speak? Who does not? Why?
- What are the characters thinking? What are they feeling?
- What hovers and lives beneath, around, and behind the words on the page, waiting to be discovered, waiting to break free, waiting to be liberated?
- What questions arise when considering "the other" – people of differing backgrounds, cultures, socio-economic statuses, abilities, ages, stages, orientations?

3. Consider what's going on in the lives of children who will interact with this text.
- Imagine what might emerge in their lives through interaction with it.
- How will the story be told so young people enter into it and engage all their senses as they also imagine it?

Jesus offers us a pattern for nurturing the inquiring, imaginative spirit in the story of his encounter with a lawyer who asks, "What must I do to inherit eternal life?"

"What do you think?" Jesus asks.

The lawyer offers a response. "Good answer," replies Jesus, which prompts yet another question from the lawyer: "Who is my neighbour?" Jesus tells a story, a story that sparks imagination and takes those present (and those of us reading today) deeper. The lawyer might have entered that story as any one of the characters – priest, Levite, injured one, innkeeper, Samaritan, even the one at home who is waiting for the traveller to return. I imagine that the story continued to unfold for the lawyer as more questions bubbled up and led to something deeper. But for now, Jesus asks, "Who do you think is the neighbour?"

Jesus facilitates a discovery that goes beyond the set lines or boundaries, and with a simple commission says, "Go and do the same." We can only imagine where the lawyer went from there, and we can only imagine to what extent he embraced "the other" as neighbour. He leaves the story, and we enter it.

As New Stories Take Shape

This is how narrative works. It allows us to move in and out in different roles and thereby learn what it means to walk in another's shoes and gain perspective. However, narrative is not the only way to tell, engage, and enter a story. The Bible offers many examples of ways to enter a story of our faith imaginatively; ways we might share, tell, and embody these stories as we nurture the imaginative, enquiring spirit in young people.

Stories are observed.

In Mark 12:41–44, we read that Jesus sits down opposite the treasury box and watches. A widow comes out of the shadows and gives all she has. While her action might demonstrate sacrificial love, it also exposes the oppressive nature of a system that takes all she has to live on. The temple and scribes have abdicated their responsibilities to care for the widows and instead "devour their houses" (Mark 12:40). A story of injustice and oppression is played out right there in the temple. It reminds us that the "hidden curriculum" is our own story, how we live our faith. Children learn about faith from observing our living and lived faith. As people called to the ministry of educating in matters of faith, we are called to be advocates and prophets, challenging any behaviour that is not life-giving.

Stories are ritualized.

Jesus broke bread, shared it, and said, "Remember me." Key faith stories are ritualized, embodied, imagined, and remembered at various times in the church year. For example: red vestments, flowers, invitations to wear red, calls to worship in many languages, bubbles and balloons on Pentecost; putting away our alleluias at the beginning of Lent and releasing them on Easter Day; removing elements and items from the Communion table and covering the worship furniture with black on Good Friday; and transforming worship space with flowers and open windows on Easter Sunday. These rituals embody the stories we hold dear.

Stories are sung and danced.

Through imagination, we hear Miriam and the women of Israel breaking into song after the people cross the Jordan. We see David dancing uninhibitedly as the Ark of the Covenant is brought home into the city. However, the power of liturgical song or interpretative dance to move us into a deeper experience of the story can be limited by our preconceived notions that such movement is for professionals or people with training in dance. Lindsay McLaughlin shares this story by way of encouraging us to move beyond this thinking:

> The elderly woman in the seventh pew slowly, hesitantly, lifted her left arm. The gesture was tentative, but the expression on her face was intent. She was absorbed in the drama unfolding before her, that of the death of Lazarus and the desperate pleas from his sisters to his dear friend Jesus to come to his side.

> It was Lent, and the church was making an extra effort to make the scripture readings meaningful and alive. In this instance, dancers were interpreting the words as they were read, using simple, clear movements that the congregation could "echo" (mirror, really) from their seats. Standing on the wide step before the altar, caught up in the synthesis of the gestures I was making and the anguish and fearsome joy of the story, I faced the people in the pews. It was evident that by using more than just their ears, those in the church that morning were accessing the story and its meaning at a

deeper, inner level. I had only to glance at the woman in front of me to confirm this.[5]

Stories are painted.
It is well documented how Rembrandt's painting, *The Return of the Prodigal Son*, impacted the life of Henri Nouwen, provoking inquiry, engaging his senses, stirring his imagination.[6] He imagined himself as each of the characters in the painting, and the story was born again, and again, and again. It set him on his path toward ministry with the L'Arche community in Toronto. Nouwen calls us to stir the imagination through visual art.

We can invite reflection on an art image by saying something as simple as, "I wonder why the artist chose these colours." We can continue by asking people to place themselves in the painting and explore where they find themselves in the story it evokes. If children ask about the story of the painting, we can suggest that they make up their own story from what they see. We can encourage them to notice their inner thoughts. As the viewers think about the artwork closely, they begin to separate their personal responses to the art from the artist's intentions. In this, they recognize many layers of the art: their personal responses, the artist's story, and the places where the artist's story and their stories intersect.

Stories are acted or pantomimed.
Stories are invitations to share the emotions, thoughts, feelings, and choices of the characters. They are invitations to experience where the story connects and intersects with our own lives.

Interpretive play, role-playing, and improvisation offer opportunity to include both "black fire" and "white fire" characters. They can include nonhuman characters, places, and objects (the donkey that carried Jesus into Jerusalem, the tree that helped Zacchaeus to see). We can begin with a question or activity that connects with our own lives, and then move into the story by setting the scene. Is it by the sea/lake, wilderness, in a home, on the road, in a garden? We might describe the view, but also the context (the community, what happened before this story), and ask what the young people see in this setting.

For example, sharing the story of Zacchaeus might begin by asking about young people's experiences of meals. A brief conversation about meals or unexpected guests prepares them to hear the story of Zacchaeus from a point of view other than his height and enter the story from an identified life experience. Having set a focus, the story from the Gospel of Luke might then be introduced as a story about a meal that changed relationships and the way people saw things. We might say something about the gospel storyteller wanting to give an "orderly account" about Jesus of Nazareth, a devout Jewish man, an itinerant preacher, a teacher who welcomed the outcast and marginalized, bringing them from the periphery to the centre.

Setting the scene/context might include a comment about the gospel's theme of journey, with Jesus teaching and healing as he travels with his disciples toward Jerusalem. In this story, we join Jesus and the disciples as they enter Jericho, the last town before Jerusalem. We might offer words about tax collectors and what it meant to be a chief tax collector, providing background that does not have people assume Zacchaeus was a deceitful thief. As we read Luke 19:1–4, we might invite people to imagine they are Zacchaeus and ask them to consider why they want to see Jesus. As we move to Luke 19:5, we might invite them to imagine they are Jesus and ask them to wonder why they must stay at Zacchaeus' house. We might invite young people to imagine they are Zacchaeus again and to reflect on what is he thinking and feeling. Moving forward to verse 6, we might invite them to imagine they are a person in the crowd – what are they thinking and feeling? Reading verses 7 and 8, we might ask what the young people are thinking and feeling now and what they would want to say to Zacchaeus. And the list of characters in whose sandals we can imagine ourselves goes on and on – Zacchaeus' family, servants, friends... After imagining the scene, the characters, and the conversation, the interpretative play or role-play might end with verses 9 and 10 read in unison.

Another practice is to invite a child to sit in a "character" chair within the circle. He or she then role-plays the story character as the group asks questions like, "What would you (in your role) like to say about the situation?" Alternatively, the young people might ask questions of a character. Or children can divide into pairs and choose to be two characters of a story and engage in dialogue in their roles.

After an interpretative role-play or meditation, it is important to have a way for children to step out of their roles and become themselves again. This can be done by debriefing and inviting their thoughts about the story and what the community might have learned that day. We may ask the group to imagine Zacchaeus meeting with the other tax collectors later that week and wonder what they may have talked about.

Stories are poetic.

Stories engage all our senses. Consider how the unspoken action of a woman pouring out perfumed oil enlivens senses. As one teacher was discussing the anointing at Bethany (Mark 14:3–9) with a group of which I was part, he brought a small bottle of pure nard, opened it, and handed it around. The aroma filled the room, overwhelmed us, jolted awake our senses. We experienced and truly sensed the extravagance of a gift that filled the room and touched everyone. While senses can be engaged by introducing aromas, tastes, sights, and sounds, we can also describe the environment and setting of the story and help the listener engage all senses as he or she imagines the scene. We can describe some sights, sounds, smells, tastes, and textures, or ask children to imagine what they see, hear, smell, taste, and touch in this story.

Stories are imagined.

Prophets imagined a highway through the wilderness, predator and prey together, and a child leading the parade toward God's reign of justice, peace, and love. Sometimes we need do no more than present a story to young people and invite them to imagine it into being. What do they see, hear, and feel? What do they smell and taste? When we imagine in this way, we begin to live the vision. God-given, Christ-motivated imagination catapults us into practices and creative acts that transform and build the world. Imagination, as displayed in the prophetic vision of Isaiah, will lead to acts of peace, justice, and mutual respect.

The Journey Within

In entering a story, each person will find herself or himself at a different place on the path, and the different points on the path will invite exploration. Different truths are revealed at different times for different people and in different ways. "Imagination," said the young child in the film *Gratitude*, "could lead you to a beach or something and it could be beautiful…"

For some, the path will lead beyond the beach, perhaps to an island. Others will stop before the beach, at a sand dune. And some may settle on the beach with shells that are waiting to share their stories.

The challenge for each of us, in our different contexts, is how we travel that pathway with children. Do we hurry them along to a destination, or do we stop, explore, take side-tracks, and scratch and crawl under the bushes? How do we travel the pathway with young people? Do we allow them to take risks, to go to the edges, explore, find their own way home? Or do we haul them back to what we think is a "safe" theology?

As companions on the path that leads children to something "beautifuller," do the words we choose leave opportunities for more than one response, depending on where people are on their journeys? If they do, we extend an invitation for explorations that can lead to a new understanding and faith growth. Open-ended questions provide openings for us to see anew how God is in the world and to imagine new ways of being in the world. As we gather around story we might ask and discuss questions and wonderings such as these: The Bible does not tell us what happened next in the story – I wonder what the older brother did next? I wonder what the ten who were cured of leprosy said when they arrived home? I wonder if the disciples did as Jesus asked? What questions does this story raise for you? What truths did you discover in this story? What do you think it reveals about who God is? …about who Jesus is? What does this story/vision suggest about the way we might live as disciples following in the way of Jesus?

In an interview about her book *Hunwick's Egg*, Australian children's writer Mem Fox was asked what children might feel about Hunwick's relationship with the egg. "Whatever they want to feel," she said. "Sad, happy, full of hope, comforted, or encouraged. The beauty of this story is that children will take from it whatever they need, depending on their own loneliness and when they read it, or their own friendships, or their need for good friends in their lives."[7]

Young people will take from a story whatever they need. That should be enough for us, as well.

An animated cartoon by Australian cartoonist, poet, and philosopher

SUSAN BURT

Michael Leunig depicts a lonely figure sitting on a simple stool and holding a book titled "Book of Butterflies." As the character leafs through the book, it slowly begins to come alive and literally take flight. The room brightens as the illustrations in the book fill with colour, and the butterflies are liberated from the page. Butterflies fill the room, delighting the reader. How might this be an image of the stories of our faith? How will the word be liberated for new generations and new kinds of Christianity?

May we journey also with a vision that will bring us into something "beautifuller."

Chapter 10

Girls and God When Everything's Changing

Joyce Ann Mercer and Dori Grinenko Baker

We listen to girls. Whether through one-on-one holy listening, life-journey conversations, or small girlfriend theology story circles, we listen to girls. We hear their stories and support them as they make meaning – theological meaning – out of their experiences in life, in relationships, in the world that God created and loves.

We've been doing this for 20 years. We see the need for more listeners to join us on this journey, now more than ever. And we believe that

Joyce Ann Mercer is Professor of Practical Theology at Virginia Theological Seminary in Alexandria, Virginia. She completed her Ph.D. at Emory University, focusing on issues of faith, gender, and violence in the lives of adolescent girls. She is the author of *Welcoming Children*, *Lives to Offer* (with Dori Baker), and *Girl Talk, God Talk*.

Dori Grinenko Baker is Scholar-in-Residence for the Fund for Theological Education, where she helps cultivate practices that support the next generation of pastoral leaders for the church and the world. She also serves as Director of Spiritual Life at Sweet Briar College. She is the author of *The Barefoot Way*, *Lives to Offer* (with Joyce Ann Mercer), and *Doing Girlfriend Theology*, and she is the editor of *Greenhouses of Hope*. Dori completed her Ph.D. in religious studies at Northwestern University and lives in southern Virginia with her husband and two teenage daughters.

new kinds of Christianity offer spaces and opportunities to honour the voices of girls.

The girls we listen to affirm again and again the beauty and necessity of a particular kind of space – safe, challenging, free of demands to "perform" being a girl, space that uplifts the souls of girls. Boys need space too. We've spent lots of time wondering with male colleagues, students, and partners what boys need from the church today. But the place where our passions overlap is in creating particular kinds of spaces with girls, spaces that tend and nurture the souls of girls. Our vision for children, youth, and a new kind of Christianity is one in which there is – in church, whatever form it takes – a particular, peculiar, soul-expanding, out-of-the ordinary kind of space that listens to girls, hears their inchoate yearnings, and helps them hold on to the image of God within them. We wonder if church might be one of the few places in our world where this space can be created.

Dori came out of seminary happily infused with the liberatory Christianities – womanist theology, mujerista theology, and Asian-feminist theology – that were bubbling up in the late 1980s and early 1990s from oppressed peoples, mostly from the global south. Almost giddy with her newfound knowledge, she skipped into her first appointment as a United Methodist pastor, set loose on the world to hear the voices of the voiceless in a middle class suburb of Chicago. She was not in the midst of widespread economic oppression, and she wondered if she'd "been itinerated" to the wrong place.

That was until she started paying attention to girls. Girls were cutting themselves. Girls were starving. Girls were isolating themselves from the people who wanted to support them. Girls were checking out and going on antidepressants at alarming rates. Girls were going underground, and she followed them.

Joyce entered graduate school after several years of ministry with teens who were drug-addicted, sexually abused, in trouble with the law, and runaways. She began thinking about what happens in the transition from girlhood to the teen years. She wondered how new theological expressions might help girls in the midst of violence. So she began her research with girls, designing a process for listening to life stories, helping them imagine life as a river. Where are the places where the river flows smoothly and gently? Where are the rocks – points where dangerous rapids threaten? What events in a girl's life cause the river to turn in a whole new direction?[1]

She began to interview girls one-on-one, plunging into the depths and complexities of their stories, many of which had never been voiced before. One girl described the experience of her "River of Life" conversation this way: "No one has ever listened to me like this before who wasn't being paid to."

Girlspace

We call this holy listening.

In this kind of listening – when all else is still and a girl tells the truth of her life out loud to a trusted person – a girl actually finds herself saying some things she's never said before, naming parts of herself she hadn't previously known.

About the same time that Joyce was interviewing girls, Dori was setting up listening circles in which a girl would tell a story from her life, out loud, to a group of girls and a few adult women.[2] Beneath uniforms that ranged from from goth to Barbie doll, she experienced shy souls who actually loved to come out of hiding. She experienced highly emotional creatures with highly connecting brains ready to make unlikely friendships when they weren't being watched by boys, dads, moms, and, perhaps most importantly, girls whom they perceived to be in the "in crowd" – a group always shifting like quicksand and into which no girl ever has permanent membership.

Most of the stories that girls shared were hard, tragic, filled with grief. Time after time, upon coming up out of a circle of holy listening, girls told Dori that they had shared a story they'd never told before. The girls relished the opportunity to name God for themselves and entertain nontraditional images of the divine. Up until this point, girls had learned that church was some place to bring their fixed-up selves, not their broken selves. Girlfriend theology seemed a welcomed intervention.

Cat,[3] a 16-year-old, told a story about the slow ways in which her father withdrew emotionally when she became a teenager. At the end of the group's reflection on her story, she said, "Talking here felt different – totally different. I have my Granny. Granny listens to me with ears open wide… But to have people I haven't known listen to me – now that was pretty cool, to not have to say, 'Well, I'm sorry for the way I feel.'"

May, another girl in the circle, interrupted her at this point, saying "Don't ever say that to anybody! I think!"

To which Cat responded: "I'm glad you all didn't say, 'Well, you're wrong in feeling that way,' because that's what I've been told. I am living in this box."

Girls today need more willing listeners than the occasional granny. They need to be reminded how to gather ranks occasionally, sit still for a while, and set themselves apart from the many voices telling them who they should be while they hear one another into their own deep wisdom. We connect this to the ancient Christian practice of building community and we name it *girlspace*.

By the time Dori's daughter was three, she knew how to circle up her Barbies (Dori tried to keep them out of the house, really she did!) for a session of girlfriend theology, complete with glasses of cold refreshing water, a candle for centring, and dark chocolate, well, just because.

Vampires and Chai Lattés

Our world is full of stories telling girls who they're *supposed* to be. The message is spoken through the 98-pound woman with perfect complexion and teeth staring at her from the poster on the bus, telling her what she should look like.

It's echoed by the panties at Victoria's Secret, marketed to her at age 11.

It's reinforced in the fact that she can't go for a walk alone safely, almost anywhere.

It's chimed through the infatuation with a vampire – someone who sucks out all of life's energy – as the most desirable lover. And a werewolf as a close second.

We listen appreciatively to girls and hear the desires for connection, for spiritual wholeness, and for romance embedded in such fantasy fiction such as the *Twilight* series.[4] Sometimes we hear girls critiquing these cultural forms.

Hope, 16 years old and active in her Unitarian Universalist church, offered this critical reading of Bella, the female protagonist in the *Twilight* series:

Look at what girls and women do in these books. They fall down a lot. [Bella is portrayed as excessively clumsy and "needing a lot of looking after."] They are either totally incompetent like Renée [Bella's mother], or they are completely wild and out of control like Victoria [the vengeful redheaded female vampire who is the primary villain]. Some of my friends think Bella is so liberated and independent because she goes off on her own and lives with her dad more like an adult than a kid. But look at what she does when she gets there – she cooks for him and waits on him, while he comes in and puts his feet up in front of the TV! And she gets all suicidal over being separated from Edward. How liberated is that if she can't go on living without him? Yuk.

Several other girls in this circle of holy listening also critiqued Bella, calling her "annoying" and "shallow," and saying she does "not really have a very interesting life." They disdain her singular focus on her relationship with Edward, the vampire boyfriend.

As these girls tell us, there's not just one single interpretation on a vampire tale – and there's no single story of girlhood. There are multiple narratives. But when the stories are in conflict with each other, the journey gets difficult. Conflicting narratives of girlhood say at the same time, don't have sex, but be sexy; and, you can be anything, but first of all, be attractive.

Kayla, a 13-year-old, once told Joyce, "I can do or be anything I want to" – but then she went on to describe the pull to spend time overfocused on appearance, celebrities, and fantasies of romantic relationships. She continued, "It's not like I think that's a *good thing*, being obsessed with hot movie stars, clothes, and makeup. But it's like I can't help it, it's what *feels* more important even if it's not what I think in my mind."

The ability of a girl to speak a counter-narrative – to strike out in a new interpretation of *Twilight*, or the Bible, or what she wants in an intimate relationship, or how she wants to offer her life to the world – is fostered by the wild, unfettered mash-up of practices we are talking about here. This mash-up includes holy listening, girlspace, girltalk, godtalk, girlfriend theology, horseback rides, moonlit canoe adventures with women ages 15–55, working side-by-side in an urban garden. It includes any place where girls and women meet to share and shape the ways they offer their lives to the world God loves.

Let us describe one young woman as she came to her counter-narrative. Addie was 17 years old when she joined Dori and two of her friends for a session of girlfriend theology in a cozy tea shop.

Dori and her friends set down their chai and listened, riveted, as Addie told about a day during her volunteer service trip to Tanzania when she had been given the task of listening to the stories of orphans. On the specific day that she was describing, Addie was listening to the story of Michael, whom she had befriended. Michael began to sob as he told about watching his father beat his mother to death with a plank when he learned that she was HIV positive. Afterward, his father disappeared, but Michael and his brother found him six days later. He had killed himself out of remorse.

Addie described Michael's weeping "as the sound of something made to be whole shattering in a million pieces on the ground." She held him till the sobbing stopped, waited until his heartbeat returned to normal, and after a while, he was ready to go back to his friends on the playground. As he stepped out the door, he looked back and smiled, saying to her, "Tomorrow, Auntie, we play!"

When Addie was done telling her story, Dori and her friends honoured its substance with silence before sharing their feelings and moving into wondering where God is in the story. Dori suggested that maybe God was like Addie, holding us when we are broken. And Addie looked at her, then shook her head. "No, no. God was like Michael. God was broken. God was suffering."

Later, when they wondered where the "aha! moments" were in the story, Addie said, "I have learned that if I want to know God, if I want to feel close to God, I must go to where there is broken-heartedness in the world."

She also said this: "God was also in the last moment, when Michael looked back at me, smiling. It was just like the disciples going to the tomb on Easter morning. I expected to find death. But I found new life. That's the Easter story retold before my eyes."[5]

Listening to the Voices of Real Girls

Our lives of listening have shown us what a privilege it is to be present to catch newborn images of God when they slide out, all slippery and new. We have learned that, as Judith Siqueira says, our lives are like pens with which God is writing fifth gospels.[6] But we are left wondering: if a girl has a flash of knowing about the nature of God and who she is supposed to be in light of that, and she never gives it voice – if no one is there to catch it, hold it up with her, look at it long enough to make sure that it's real – might it be as if it never happened? Might it be more likely to slip away? Might it be just an ephemeral epiphany that never really matters?

Joyce vividly remembers a moment as a sixth-grade girl when she was asked to give a presentation on her favourite flower. She did some research and found out that the strawberry is vaguely related to the rose. So she decided to be creative and give her report on strawberries. She wrote the heck out of that report, thinking long and hard about how to present it. Her mom helped her dip strawberries in chocolate, one for each person in the class. And she practised and practised her presentation.

Overwhelmed with excitement, she gave her presentation to the sixth-grade class at Bensley Elementary School. At the end, there was a long pause, after which the teacher said, "Joyce, it's all very nice, but first of all you were supposed to talk about a flower, not a fruit. Also, it sounds like you copied it out of a book – too many big words, too perfectly spoken to be your own."

Stunned, she listened to some other girls stammer through their presentations. Joyce came back the next day and mumbled out a report about daisies in which she was not the least bit interested. "That's more like it," was her teacher's response. "That sounds like a real girl's voice."

Until that moment, Joyce had thought *her* voice was a real girl's voice.

She didn't learn much about flowers that day. What she did learn was that creativity, desire, and joy were not supposed to come to school with her. Do we send these messages to girls in church?

What Joyce also learned was that to have a "real girl's voice," she would have to pretend lack of competence and intelligence. She would have to do violence to her own true, strong self – what sociologist Pierre Bourdieu called "symbolic violence"[7] – a kind of violence that is done to girls and women through almost unconscious societal patterns that shape understandings about what it means to be a girl. To perform "being a girl" she would need to look anywhere but within her own deep well of wisdom.

This symbolic violence still happens to girls. But the voices of violence are louder, harsher, and more invasive today, because they exist in the limitless realm of cyberspace.

The "am I pretty/am I ugly" craze on YouTube, where the Internet functions as a diary and the audience numbers five million, is a new risk for girls. Girls starving for validation post video clips of themselves and ask viewers to comment on whether they are pretty or ugly. This trend has gone viral, with girls inviting random strangers to decide their value based on appearance.

Will new kinds of Christianity offer alternative communities that help girls know their own true worth? Will we listen to girls? What would church look like if it decided to consistently offer girlspace?

The girls we have worked with help us imagine a new kind of Christianity – one not just for girls, but for all people. They have shared images and ideas for what Christianity and church can look like in our world.

We didn't just make up holy listening with girls! Its echoes are heard throughout Christian scripture and theology. And the work's been done for us. Careful retrievals, reworkings, and re-imaginings that overcome centuries of interpreting texts in ways that are hostile to women and girls already exist. The flourishing of girls and women and the roles they play in the flourishing of God's *shalom* have always been part of God's prophetic Word. We see it in the story of Ruth and Naomi. We see it in Esther's story, full of courage. It's in Miriam's ecstatic song after crossing over the Red Sea. And it's in the unnamed slave girl who tells Naaman how to be healed from leprosy. We see it in Shiphrah and Puah, those rule-breaking midwives, and in the women disciples who came first to the empty tomb.

But this vision of God's *shalom* in which girls and women flourish grew dim throughout the years that followed. Again and again it went underground. But it was never completely eclipsed. Bold prophetic voices always emerged: Jaretta Lee, Sojourner Truth, St. Catherine of Siena, Letty Russell, Rosemary Radford Ruether, Georgia Harkness, St. Teresa of Avila, Antoinette Brown, Alice Walker, Dorothy Day,

Marian Wright Edelman, and Katie Cannon, to name just a few.

We are hopeful today. A new church is emerging. We are the minds and bodies, souls and selves God has chosen to create it. The flourishing of girls needs to be part of our prophetic imagination at this moment when everything "church" is changing.

Jesus listened to women and girls. He created girlspace. Will we go and do likewise?

Chapter 11

Missional Youth Ministry

Todd Hobart

I met Javier[1] a couple of years into working as a youth coordinator at St. Matthew Lutheran Church near Seattle, Washington. This church ran a before-school and after-school program for several years, and Javier was an occasional visitor. Sometimes he would come by with other students during non-program hours, either to talk for a bit or to see about getting into the cookies and pastries that were always left over.

On one of my Mondays off, I received an urgent email regarding Javier's family. I had never spoken with his mother in person, but a couple of weeks earlier I had worked with her on trying to get some money for a relative's burial. This request was more urgent: Javier's father had died, and his mom wanted someone to come and say a prayer at the memorial service the next day. I accepted with some trepidation, as I had only a passing relationship with Javier and did not know anything about his family or the circumstances under which his father had died.

Tuesdays are always busy days with the after-school program, and so I was 20 minutes late to the memorial service. It was in a part of town that I had never visited before. Upon entering the funeral home, I was unprepared for the sights, smells, and dinginess that greeted me. Children ran noisily through the aisles as Javier's mom bravely acted the part of funeral director for the memorial service. The body of Javier's father lay fully

Todd Hobart is Life Stage Youth Coordinator at St. Matthew Lutheran Church in Renton, Washington. He leads before-school and after-school programs for middle school students which serve over 500 students each year through a unique church/public school partnership. Todd graduated from Luther Seminary in 2009 with a Ph.D. in Congregational Mission and Leadership.

visible on a slab in front of the assembled group. My hastily-thrown-on sweater easily made me the most overdressed in the group.

After a somewhat awkward introduction to Javier's mother, I took my seat among those assembled to pay their respects. I offered my prayer after a few invitations failed to attract anyone else. It was a simple prayer, said in the most difficult of circumstances. I was very uncomfortable, but I was also not the one who had just lost a father or an ex-husband. I had a short conversation with Javier and his mom after the service, and then made my way home. A few days later, I saw Javier at our before-school breakfast and spoke with him about his grieving process and what it had been like for me years earlier to suddenly lose a family member.

I have seen Javier a few times since then, but less frequently since he was expelled from the local middle school. I consider it a great privilege to have been able to be present in that moment for him and his family, and to offer some words of comfort. Occasionally I wonder, Why me? Why my church? Why was I the only "religious professional" present at that service? Surely they must have had *some* connection, at *some* church. Was I really *it* for that family?

I believe the catalyst that allowed that connection and that moment at that memorial service to take place was my church's commitment to missional youth ministry. It is this type of ministry that allows the church to be involved in the lives of students in the greater community outside the church, in sometimes significant ways like the case of Javier, or in smaller ways such as the school programs. Before diving into missional church, missional theology, and missional youth ministry, I'd like to share some research results.

Job Postings Research

After being immersed in my church's commitment to missional youth ministry for several years, I began to wonder how other congregations viewed youth in their communities and neighbourhoods. To get a broad perspective on this question, I researched job postings for full-time, part-time, and volunteer church youth workers on seven different websites[2] over a three-month period. I wondered if congregations attribute any value to the youth in the wider community in and of themselves. Do the problems and needs of youth in a church's neighbourhood, town, or city matter to local congregations? To answer these questions, I searched each job posting for any mention of community youth and then analyzed the data in order to discover any themes in the many postings.

Over three months, I culled from the seven websites some 427 different job postings in 40 different denominations. In 49% of the posts, community youth were not mentioned at all, 27% mentioned community youth in some way, and in 24% it was unclear if the post was talking about youth in the surrounding community. Of the 27% that mentioned community youth, qualitative analysis revealed clusters around four distinct themes.

The first theme involved *building relationships with unchurched students*. Language in the job posting emphasized contacting students at school and getting involved in school activities. Job applicants were advised to develop relationships with educators. Meeting students on their own turf was a strong part of this theme, whether at school or at other places where youth tend to hang out.

The second theme involved *bringing youth into the church*. Language in the job postings spoke about developing programs to reach youth, and promoting these programs in the community. Churches and employers seemed to hope that youth programs would grow through outreach, which often involved inviting unchurched teens into the ministry and teaching youth in the church to engage unchurched teens. The purpose of all of this work appeared to be primarily about numerical growth in the church youth program.

The third and most common theme involved *reaching "lost youth."* It's interesting to notice the forceful language used in many of the postings: "Penetrate high school campuses with the Gospel"; "Impact youth with the Gospel message"; "Promote an aggressive outreach program." These phrases demonstrate an intentional (and sometimes forceful) approach to evangelism, to making non-Christian teens into Christian teens. Additional emphases from this category involved evangelizing lost youth, reaching unsaved youth, winning youth to Christ, and presenting opportunities for students to make a decision for Jesus.

Before moving on to the final theme, it is helpful to take a step back and consider what this research might teach us. Of all the job descriptions that I analyzed, nearly half did not mention youth in the wider community or neighbourhood at all when elaborating job requirements for prospective church volunteers or employees. Though I couldn't determine this with certainty, it seemed likely that many of these churches had little vision or interest in community youth, for these youth were not mentioned to the person likely to put the most time into youth ministry in the church. Of the 27% that did mention community youth, the language in those job postings mostly focused on either bringing those youth into the church to grow the youth ministry or evangelizing these teens.

The fourth theme evident in the job postings I surveyed involved *caring about community youth*. This care was provided regardless of membership in or involvement with the church. Job postings in this category spoke about helping students experience God's welcome, and helping the wider community to raise well-rounded and flourishing kids. Job postings told applicants that they would need to identify the needs of community youth and work with and for these young people. In this category, the youth program is for youth in the wider community and a worthy goal would be to mutually integrate church and community life. This fourth theme comes closest to what I am identifying as missional youth ministry.

Missional

The missional church conversation has advanced significantly through the years since Darrell Guder edited the 1998 book *Missional Church*.[3] There are now many resources available that discuss this important term so there is no need to reproduce here a fully-formed missional theology.[4] However, the key question I want to address in this chapter involves the relationship of missional theology with youth ministry. How does the missional church conversation of the past 15 years impact the practice of youth ministry today? This chapter will add to other voices in this discussion.[5]

One of the groundbreaking insights of the missional church conversation is the idea that mission first and foremost involves the activity of the Triune God in redeeming and restoring the world. The *mission* in *missional church* is God's. The church enters into God's activity, participating with God in the ongoing redemption and restoration of the fallen creation. Mission is not an activity that the church dreams up or undertakes on its own, but one that occurs as the church discerns where God is active and moving and then participates in that mission through the leading and empowering of the Spirit of God.

When it comes to youth ministry, churches need to ask themselves if they really believe that God is active and working in the lives of youth in their surrounding community. If churches believe that God is doing something in the lives of youth and families in their neighbourhood, they need to ask how they can participate in what God is doing. What needs are churches being led to address? How can churches be a part of God's redemptive mission in the lives of young people?

As my research into youth ministry job postings showed, it seems as if much youth ministry is focused inwardly on students who are already a part of the church. This research also suggests that churches that aren't entirely focused on their own youth are seeking in some way to benefit from community youth, either by adding them to the church or by converting them. There seems to be little (if any) interest in the needs and personhood of youth in the wider community unless there is some benefit for the church.

I propose that missional youth ministry involves looking at community youth and their needs without first seeking the benefit of the church. After all, if mission is primarily an activity of the Triune God and secondarily an activity of the church, it behooves churches to look outside themselves to see what God is up to among youth in their communities. No doubt they would also learn something as they themselves are converted in the presence of the youth who appear "other" to them. A church isn't meant to cannibalize its neighbourhood or wider community, consuming others to meet its own needs; it exists to pour its life out, participating in Jesus' mission of freely giving his life on behalf of others.

Along the way, no doubt some youth will be converted. Some will join the church as they catch a glimpse of what God is doing in the world and then want to be a part of it. But I believe that these are secondary concerns that take a backseat to discerning and participating in what God is doing in the world. After all, the message of the gospel involves the life of the community of Christ and its work participating in God's mission. That is the context for telling the story of Jesus and of God's redeeming work in the world.

Glimpses of Missional Youth Ministry

After learning about the small percentage of churches that seemed to be engaging in a missional type of youth ministry, I began to seek out churches to visit in person, churches that could provide some further insight into this kind of ministry. Aside from the congregation where I serve, I discovered ministries in three other Lutheran churches in the state of Washington that seemed to offer glimpses of missional youth ministry in action. I share the stories in the hope that they will inspire you as much as they did me.

Unwind (Grace Lutheran Church)

Unwind is an after-school program for high school students in a wealthy suburb north of Seattle, Washington. Four students from the existing youth ministry at Grace Lutheran Church started the program in the fall of 2009 and other students found the program through word of mouth. There is no advertising for the program at local schools.

The students meet in a designated youth room at the church. In the 2011–2012 school year there were from seven to 15 students attending the program, which runs from 2:00 to 5:00 p.m. every Wednesday throughout the school year. In this affluent community, youth tend to suffer from what Pamela Couture calls "the poverty of tenuous connections,"[6] rather than material poverty. Their families have money and material resources, but teens too often lack meaningful relationships. Thus, Unwind is highly relational and emphasizes friendships – with fellow students as well as with adult volunteers. During their time at Unwind, students usually choose to talk about their lives with other students and with the adults who are present. They also do homework or occasionally play video games.

Unwind makes no attempt to formally evangelize the students, though the youth are welcome to participate in youth group or other church activities, should they choose to do so. Following the program, the students often share in a meal together. A church youth group meets at 6:00 p.m. in the same room, so occasionally some of the same students from Unwind will stay for the youth group gathering.

Grace Lutheran Church has a saying that shows the theological vision behind its programs, including Unwind: "All means all." Everyone is welcome. Every expression of diversity is welcome. For this church, this vision most often comes up in its service to the homeless in its community. But it is also meaningful in its other ministries. The slogan indicates that all students in the community are valued for who they are – whether or not they call Grace Lutheran Church their home.

Yummy Mondays (Cedar Inlet Lutheran Church)
Cedar Inlet Lutheran Church is located on a quiet residential street across from the local high school in a small town about 50 kilometres north of Seattle. Their Yummy Mondays program began in September of 2007. The current coordinator of the program is an unpaid volunteer from the congregation who has helped with many high-level church projects, often relating to youth or children.

The current program averages about 60 students each week, although as many as 80 may show up on a Monday afternoon. School gets out early on Mondays (at 1:30 p.m.) and there are no programs or activities for students at the school until 2:30 p.m. Cedar Inlet Lutheran Church responded to the need to fill this gap by creating a drop-in program. Students enter the fellowship hall and immediately have a chance to have a drink or some snacks. They can then remain at tables and chat while enjoying their food, or they can head outside to an adjacent patio with a basketball hoop, or go to the high school youth room where they can shoot pool, play Ping-Pong, or sit on the couches and chat.

The purpose of the program is to provide a safe place for students to hang out and eat some food. "Preaching" is not allowed, and this has been the practice for so long that it's difficult for volunteers to remember the origin of this rule. Students do, however, see printed materials for church events that are left out on the tables or on a bulletin board. They can take part in the activities if they wish, but there's no pressure to participate. One of the remarkable aspects of this program is its persistence without a paid director. This would be a difficult feat for many churches and it shows how deeply the idea of missional ministry with students is embedded in the DNA of Cedar Inlet Lutheran Church.

Before-School and After-School Programs (St. Matthew Lutheran Church)
St. Matthew Lutheran Church is located in a diverse suburb immediately bordering Seattle to its south. In the fall of 2006, this church began an after-school program on Tuesdays from 2:30–4:00 p.m. in partnership with the middle school across the street. The school promotes upcoming program activities and supports the program with discipline and transportation issues. St. Matthew Lutheran Church secures funding for the program and provides weekly activities and volunteers.

The program offers a main activity that changes each week, for example, taekwondo, dance, or a fiesta. Age-appropriate video games are always available to the students, as well as an outdoor activity like basketball or soccer. In 2007 the church added a before-school breakfast on Fridays, when classes begin 90 minutes later than usual. This program provides students with a breakfast of apple juice and pancakes. All before-school and after-school activities are provided free.

The after-school program began with six middle school students and grew steadily over the next several years until now when it averages 100 students each Tuesday. The breakfast program likewise grew and now feeds about 75 students each Friday morning. For several years, the before-school and after-school programs drew over 500 different students each year, which represented about 40% of the population of the middle school.

St. Matthew Lutheran Church envisions itself as "a church where you don't have to be good enough to go," and the before-school and after-school programs are a natural outgrowth of this philosophy. These programs exist alongside other innovative missional ministries of this church, including a downtown café and pub that serves the local community.

Shalom Neighborhood Center
Shalom Neighborhood Center (SNC) is located in a historically impoverished and dangerous urban neighbourhood in Tacoma, Washington, that was well known in the 1980s and 1990s for its gang activity. SNC began as an initiative of Shalom Lutheran Church under the leadership of a long-standing pastor. SNC has been active since the fall of 2001, when $1.5 million was raised to renovate the church, purchase and move a nearby residence, and construct a multi-purpose area that includes office and classroom space, and a gym.

SNC began with immediate credibility because of the community care that Shalom Lutheran Church had always extended. The pastor walked the neighbourhood, visited homes, invited folks to church activities, heard prayers, and responded to needs that came up, and the community came to know that this church cared about them and their needs.

SNC employs eight full-time and several part-time staff members, along with seven AmeriCorps volunteers. These staff and volunteers serve 60 high school students, 33 middle school students, and 40 elementary school students. SNC runs after-school classes to help students develop skills that increase the possibility of academic success. It also offers after-school tutoring for students. It has helped about 65 students graduate from high school and eight students graduate from college.

The director of SNC also wishes students to graduate with an ethic of service, a desire to be in community with others, and a capacity to care for the community around them. He believes that "if we just help the kids become middle class...they are still going to be unhappy...unsatisfied." SNC is rooted in the ongoing outreach to the community by Shalom Lutheran Church. The goal is for students to encounter Christ "in a presence sort of way" through the activities provided by SNC.

The church invites students to participate in church activities, but it is done softly. There's some crossover from the high school students who participate at the centre and those who participate in the church youth group, as the youth group meets on Wednesday evenings after the SNC tutoring is done and some students hang around.

The centre's director believes that churches don't need a building to do the sort of work that SNC is doing. One volunteer contributed this advice: "Get to know your community. Walk the neighbourhood for 20 years and then come back and we'll talk."

Going Missional with Youth Ministry

How can churches participate in God's mission in their own communities and neighbourhoods? Most churches are not conveniently located across the street from a public school like three of those about which I shared. What is possible for other churches? How can they practice missional youth ministry?

A first idea to keep in mind is that context is critical. Grace Lutheran Church, Cedar Inlet Lutheran Church, and St. Matthew Lutheran Church all took advantage of their strategic locations near public schools. Shalom Neighborhood Center built upon the work that its long-time pastor had already done in the community. Each missional ministry functions significantly differently from the others because each addresses needs that are specific to its own context.

For folks who are thinking about starting a ministry or program like one of the ones mentioned, first think about what needs exist in the surrounding community. Is there primarily a need for educational support or tutoring? Do students need a safe, fun alternative to being on their own after school? Some churches may be well-positioned to address other recreational, fitness, or mental health needs for youth. Whatever the needs, they can be discovered by being attentive to a church's context. Part of this process naturally involves listening to those in the community. No doubt there are many people in the neighbourhood (teachers, educators, counsellors, coaches, and so on) who are in a position to understand the needs of youth in a particular community. It can be fruitful to look for potential partnerships through these conversations. No one needs to go it alone.

Partnering with others in the community increases a congregation's credibility. It is also challenging to participate in the give-and-take process with other community groups and organizations, so partnerships can help remind churches that the mission ultimately belongs to God. Just as churches participate in God's mission of redemption and restoration, so also do other community groups and organizations, though they likely will not use the same language. However, this realization can offer congregations humility as they understand themselves as a small but crucial part of what God is doing in the world.

Finally, a sense of missional imagination and Spirit-led discernment ought to permeate this entire process. After all, it is God's mission in which churches are participating. These ministries are not things that churches dream up in order to feel better about themselves or simply to do something good in the wider community. Ultimately, these ministries exist to be a part of what God is doing in the world. That is where the excitement and energy of these ministries come from. As a church participates in God's mission, it gains new perspectives into God's heart and into the ways in which God turns mission on its head, so that the churches that start serving discover that they are being stretched and served and shaped into something entirely new.

Javier is one of many youth with whom I have had the privilege of ministering through the missional youth ministry initiatives at my church. Some youth I know for only a short time, as the inconsistencies and fragility of their home lives eventually catch up with them and they move away. But I'm able to stay in contact with others for years. A missional view of youth ministry understands that God is already at work in the lives of youth and the neighbourhood around them, and that the church is privileged to join with God in that work. So whether I know a young person for a week, a month, or several years, I can try to join God in what God is doing in that person's life.

What does the future hold for Javier and other young people like him? I may not know for sure, but I am convinced that congregations have an opportunity to be a part of the answer to this question. Engaging in missional youth ministry means searching for this answer together with Javier and the other young people in the community as the church participates together with God in mission.

Chapter 12

Beauty in Brokenness:
One Family's Story of Serving Children and Youth through United Compassionate Action

Steve Park and Mary Park

The police tape stretched over the sidewalk near our rented ministry house across from Potomac Gardens, a public-housing complex that accommodates over 250 very-low-income families in southeast Washington, D.C., just 12 blocks from the U.S. Capitol. Someone on our block had been stabbed and possibly killed. The ambulance had parked directly in front of our house, its lights swirling frantically as the paramedics tended to the victim. Onlookers peeked to see what was happening, who was hurt. For most of our neighbours, it was just another day near Potomac Gardens.

But the story didn't end there, with those bright ambulance lights and the screeching sirens. Yes, violence (and the threat of violence) had become part of life for residents here and also for us, as we have committed our lives to serving Potomac Gardens and its families, and living in a low-income neighbourhood to lead an urban ministry called Little

Mary and Steve Park are Deputy Director and Executive Director of the non-profit Little Lights, serving the Potomac Gardens housing project in Washington, D.C. Their most recent united action in the community is called the Clean Green Team, which provides job training in landscaping maintenance and part-time employment through a contract with D.C. Housing Authority. Mary and Steve are married to each other and have two children, Dylan and Kayla.

Lights. But there was hope and light in the midst of the darkness that evening. A parent who lived in Potomac Gardens told us later that Tyra, a four-year-old girl, saw the ambulance in front of our house and heard rumours that Steve was the victim. The little girl had urgently and spontaneously gathered her friends in the courtyard in front of the apartment and formed a prayer circle – right in the middle of the housing project. Tyra began to pray that our family would be all right. With the faith of a child, she was waging a fight of hope and compassion against the forces of despair and indifference. She was fighting for us!

In the gospels, Jesus' passion for the marginalized and the poor is perfectly clear. According to Matthew 25, Jesus had the audacity to state how important and precious the poor were to him and to God. "Whatever you did for the least of these, my kin, you did for me," he declared. "And whatever you did not do for the least of these, you did not do for me." There are many like Tyra who hold out hope for a God who acts and who cares. Will we as Christians be the hands and feet of Christ to his kindred who cry out for someone to care?

As we contemplate what God is doing in our time, creating new visions of what Christianity can be, we believe that we must look in unexpected places if we are to remain true to the one we follow. We are obliged to search the shadows and sometimes to close our eyes and listen for the sounds of stress and strain.[1] Jesus says our new kinship is with those most spitefully regarded, most easily overlooked, the weak, the voiceless, the loud and obnoxious, even the hostile. This includes people of an ethnic or ideological background that is different from our own, perhaps immigrant communities, perhaps those separated from us by socioeconomics or religion.

We are both first-generation Korean immigrants to the United States and together we live and serve in a predominantly African-American community, seeking leadership from within this community. Many of the youth who grew up in the program we lead now work with us to help lead younger kids. We not only want to provide services *to* the residents, but seek genuine fellowship *with* community members. Does that make us new monastics, seeking solidarity with cities across the globe? Maybe. Are we evidence of God moving in the immigrant church to give new life to the broader church? Perhaps. Are we part of the new face of the civil rights movement in the 21st century? We leave that and similar questions for others to decide. What we recognize in our story is the need for new eyes to see how God works in seemingly intentionally unfamiliar ways.

Our Stories

Not in Steve's wildest fantasies did he imagine that he would start and spend most of his adult life running an urban ministry for children, youth, and families in public housing complexes in southeast Washington, D.C. As an atheist at Boston University in the early 1990s, he remembers repeatedly arguing with his Jewish roommate, unable to comprehend why any "intelligent" person could believe in God. At that time, Steve thought a lot more about clubbing and partying than about how he could serve people in need. He didn't even want to have children of his own, much less spend time caring for other people's kids.

The downward spiral which led to Steve's conversion to Christianity began when his friend convinced him to try a drug called ecstasy while on vacation. He got hooked and the two of them began dropping ecstasy a couple of times a week. During one of those times, Steve experienced something that he can only describe as supernatural and utterly terrifying. He became completely overwhelmed by fear. This fear, which was really a fear of evil, was the most intense thing he'd ever experienced, and it didn't seem to wear off over time. It felt like a living nightmare. Steve was humbled to realize that he was completely lost and needed help.

Then Steve read M. Scott Peck's *The Road Less Traveled*,[2] a book that seemed to point him in a different direction. The first line of the book, "Life is difficult," caught his attention because he had grown up on a steady diet of pop and youth culture that heralded the messages that life should be easy and always fun. Yet he knew at the deepest place in him that something was terribly wrong and getting out of it was not going to be easy.

The Road Less Traveled gave a bottom-line recommendation: learn how to experience grace through therapy. Steve was desperate enough to heed this advice and found a therapist. It was on the therapist's couch that he risked vulnerability. It was in the therapist's office that he shared for the first time that he was lonely and truly afraid. But he struggled to find any sense of hope.

On New Year's Eve 1993, Steve took a leap of faith and told his sister, who had gone through a serious depression in college, that he was losing the will to live. His sister did not say a single word, but embraced him with such tenderness that he broke down weeping. For the first time, Steve felt truly understood and accepted. Compassion filled his heart and he knew that he would never see the world in the same way again. He realized that he was not alone in his pain, that the whole world was hurting, and that people were (literally and figuratively) dying from a lack of compassion.

A few months later, Steve began thumbing through the pages of Huston Smith's book *The World's Religions*,[3] learning the basics about Islam, Buddhism, and other religions. But it was the chapter that outlined Christianity that captured his attention. It helped Steve understand the person of Jesus for the first time. He realized that Jesus was radical, that he hung around with tax collectors, lepers, prostitutes, and the poor. Jesus loved the rejects! He lived his life out of compassion, serving people and ultimately giving his life in sacrifice for others – including a reject like Steve.

Steve was overwhelmed by this Jesus, and he remembers falling to his knees and repenting of selfishness and self-centredness. At that very moment, he made a commitment to follow this beautiful Jesus.

As God was turning his life upside down, God introduced Steve to some amazing children in a low-income community. His parents had opened a taekwondo studio and Steve began to help manage the business. He met kids enrolled in the dojo as well as other children from the neighbourhood who walked by.

Steve fell in love with the kids who came to the dojo. He saw in them an openness and innocence that persevered despite the fact that they had been through a great deal at a young age. One of these children was Tyrone, a young boy who towered over his seventh-grade peers. Tyrone participated in a summer day camp that Steve had started with a neighbour. Steve realized during the camp that Tyrone could not read a simple Dr. Seuss book, even though he was in the seventh grade. It broke Steve's heart to think about the challenges that Tyrone would face as he grew into adulthood without knowing how to read.

Sadly, Tyrone's illiteracy was not uncommon. Steve began getting to know other children who were several grade levels behind in their school work. Seeing this great need in the community, Steve felt called to start a tutoring and Bible study program for the children he was meeting and building relationships with through his involvement in his parents' business. He knew that Jesus truly cared for these children and that they were in need of Christ's love and compassion. In Washington D.C., one of the wealthiest and most powerful cities in America, Steve discovered that there were children who were suffering greatly from poverty and neglect. There were churches on every block, but Steve saw little concern and too few caring relationships for these children.

So, with no experience and a few hundred dollars collected from a yard sale, "Little Lights" launched inside Steve's parents' business as a Christian tutoring ministry in 1995. Since that time, it has seen several thousand volunteers and a thousand students become involved in ministry together.

Mary's story is a little less dramatic, but it is woven with commitment to God's calling to serve those in need and to practise racial reconciliation. Mary grew up in church, even though her parents didn't come to faith until much later in life. Although she attended a Korean church with her family regularly, messages about Jesus' call to radical discipleship or God's love for the poor were hard to come by. But through involvement in a Korean Christian fellowship during college, Mary made a commitment to follow Jesus, and began a gradual journey of discipleship. She decided to pursue counselling and received her master's degree from Teachers College at Columbia University, thinking that this was the direction she was headed in life. She was committed to following Jesus, but still felt unsure about God's vision for her life beyond her career.

When she met Steve, who by this time had already started Little Lights, Mary was incredibly intrigued by this Korean-American guy who didn't seem to care about making a good income by becoming a lawyer or a doctor or starting a lucrative business in a low-income neighbourhood. Mary had moved to the Washington, D.C. suburbs for a pace of life that was slower than that of Manhattan. While looking for work, she decided to volunteer at the Little Lights summer day camp in 1998. While working with the children, Mary had a life-changing experience. She saw first-hand the way that God works through young people.

During that first summer, Mary was disrespected by some campers who argued constantly with one another. She took a moment to sit by herself, wondering why she was even doing this difficult work. She felt overwhelmed and underqualified to minister with these kids. At that moment, a gentle child named Ladarius, who was nine years old, sat down next to her. He put his arms around her and told her that he was happy that she was there as a camp counsellor. This small act of kindness boosted Mary's spirits. It was just the encouragement she needed to keep going that day and throughout the summer. Ladarius showed her that God's grace sometimes comes when we least expect it – and sometimes it comes from unexpected sources.

United Compassionate Action in Action

When Steve was an atheist, one of the things that made it easy for him to discredit or disregard Christianity was the deep racial segregation in the church. Steve wondered how Christians could claim that their God is loving when it was evident that they couldn't even get along with Christians who were from different cultures, races, and traditions. Then Steve learned that Jesus, on the other hand, had radical love for all people. Jesus befriended those on the margins and those rejected by others. In John 17, Jesus specifically prays for unity in the Body of Christ, stating that unity and our love for one another is the essence of evangelism, of preaching and living out the good news. Upon his conversion, Steve knew that true grace must be enacted and not just preached.

This compelling and beautiful vision of Jesus prompted Steve to move into a low-income, mostly African-American community to do ministry not only as a job, but a way of life. Our children now attend the local after-school programs and sing in the gospel choir with other children in our neighbourhood. Intentional, voluntary desegregation has proven rich and meaningful for our whole family.

Our family centre is (and has always been) a place where people come together. We hire teenagers from the neighbourhood to help run after-school programs, and for most of them Little Lights is their first job. It has been thrilling to get to know teens and young adults who are motivated and excited to work and give back to their community. These young people show genuine care and heartfelt compassion to the elementary and middle school students they support.

We are also committed to recruiting volunteers from churches that lie across divisions that exist in the world and mar God's plan for radical and messy diversity. Volunteers come from all sorts of racial and cultural backgrounds, denominations, and theological traditions. This coming together across divisions is a value that we hold tightly.

We are very relational and spend a great deal of time just "being in" the community. We are committed to relationships more than programs. Relationship as program focus can be difficult to pin down and describe to people. While our family centre helps adults search for jobs and write resumes, it is also a place of conversation and relationship-building. People sometimes come by simply to talk for hours with our associate director or with one of our young staff members from Potomac Gardens. It was this intentional coming together over and over – as a family, as program participants, as volunteers – that made room for us to begin to act compassionately together.

One summer day a few years ago, Mary received a call from one of the residents of Potomac Gardens, who told her that the stepfather of one of our students was critically wounded in a stabbing that took place in the student's home. By the time Mary was able to go to the family's apartment, the police and ambulance had already left, but the student's mother was inside and overwhelmed by the recent turn of events. The pools of blood on the floor and splatters of blood on the walls made Mary feel nauseated, but she tried to act calm. She felt as though she had to help this mother and this family, so she and a couple of camp counsellors volunteered to clean up the blood. She knew that this was a place where Jesus would be.

Several hours and countless sponges and towels later, the team finished cleaning the apartment. It was a humbling experience. Mary had dedicated many hours toward receiving her master's degree and she dreamed of having her own counselling practice in an office furnished with beautiful hardwood furniture – and here she was on her knees, with a bucket in one hand and a sponge in the other, cleaning pools of blood that had poured from a man she had never met. But she sensed God's presence with her.

Urban ministry comes with a whole slew of ups and downs, highs and lows. We've learned to be flexible and expect curveballs from all directions. We're constantly reminding ourselves and one another to look for the beauty in the places and the people we serve. And if we have eyes to see, we find beauty all around.

We make every effort to provide high-quality programs for our youth, and there is certainly no easy recipe or formula. It is a day-in, day-out commitment of our staff and youth leaders to be solid role models of a compassionate faith. It means setting and embracing high standards, and expecting the students to respect staff and other students. It means following through with consequences and practicing tough love when necessary. Compassionate cannot mean wimpy.

We also expect our staff to pray consistently for the children and to develop meaningful relationships with the students so that they are able to speak into their lives. We challenge our students daily to treat others with love and respect, even when they don't always see adults or peers in their community doing the same. It is a daily battle to keep standards for attitude and behaviour high because doing so is often very tiring. Yet, over time, students and staff catch on. Grant funders often remark about the great attitudes of our middle and high school students when they visit! We are amazed also at how hospitable our students are to volunteers and visiting groups who come from outside the community and who usually look completely different from them. While our staff and volunteers try to model grace and respect to the students, we constantly find ourselves learning from the children and youth around us what true grace and respect looks like.

Being in One Another's Lives

For those who desire to cultivate a community of united compassionate action through ministry with children or youth, there are a few things we've learned along the way that may be helpful on your journey.

Think Win-Win-Win

Over the years, we've seen our share of suburban churches or groups that want to go to an inner city to work with low-income communities. From our experience, a fair number of them tend to think about outreach primarily as an "experience" for their own congregation or youth group. But sustainable and impactful action is not found only by thinking of ourselves and what "our people" will get out of it. It's far better to find a good partner who specializes in ministry with communities in need of help and find ways to serve the existing organization. A key to a successful relationship as a suburban outside partner is to lighten the burden of the urban partner. Urban ministries often lack sufficient resources to meet the demands of their communities, so hosting an outside partner can easily become one more burden to bear unless the outside partner is sensitive to their needs.

Churches, youth groups, and ministries that aren't already involved in inner city work do well to think in terms of ministering and serving a long-term partner organization who will do the work day in and day out. This is far more productive and helpful than just wanting to get an experience for one's own congregation or group members. Opportunities to directly serve low-income populations should be a part of a larger strategy to help long-term organizations sustain the work they already do.[4] When churches and groups partner with existing organizations in respectful ways, all parties involved can benefit from compassionate action that is truly united.

Pray to See as Christ Sees

A common complaint among underserved residents about outside service providers or volunteers is paternalism. Nobody wants to be viewed as a project to "be fixed." As Christians, we are called to see our neighbours through the eyes of Christ, and one way to do this is to pray to have eyes to see them in this way. Those whom we serve may have particular needs, but these needs do not constitute their entire identity as persons. They are children of God, and if we are unable or unwilling to see the beauty in those we serve, we dehumanize the very people we are trying to help. Prayer not only helps us see our neighbours in Christ-like ways; it also helps us realize our own brokenness, spiritual poverty, and dependence on God, keeping us humble in our efforts to serve. Arrogant service can be more damaging than no service at all.

Get Educated and Get Educating

One way to pursue united compassionate action is to invite people who have the mission of empowering the underserved and the marginalized to come and speak to children and youth. Alternatively, we can show documentaries and videos on issues of social justice, racial reconciliation, and poverty. The devastation and suffering in inner cities is very real. For example, just before the turn of the millennium, the probability of a young black male in Washington, D.C., being murdered before reaching age 45 was 8.47%. By comparison, the death rate for American soldiers serving in the military during the World War II was 2.5%, and during the Vietnam War, 1.2%.[5] We can set an example for students and be passionate learners on issues that affect inner cities so they can see that this is not simply part of a curriculum, but a value held by disciples of Jesus.

Be Realistic

Inner city poverty is complex. Its causes are multiple and its roots run deep into history and spirituality. A common mistake that we've seen many outside groups make is thinking that a one-time evangelistic event or a week-long service project will "fix" people and neighbourhoods. This is unrealistic. A more realistic approach is to listen to long-term urban ministers and ask them what will help not only for the short-term, but also long-term. The battle for the futures and lives of people living in urban poverty requires persistent and long-term commitment. It is not advisable to underestimate either the challenge at hand or what God can do when people truly surrender their lives in service to God.

Finding Beauty in Brokenness

We believe in the gospel of Jesus. For us, one of the essential aspects of the gospel is seeing beauty within brokenness. It is easy for Christians (and others) to come into an inner city or a place like Potomac Gardens and see only problems. After all, the problems that plague an inner city are often quite visible: drug dealers hanging out in the doorways, litter strewn on the ground, graffiti on the walls of shops and homes. The gospel calls us to see beyond the problems in our world. The gospel calls us to see all people as bearers of the image of God.

We believe that Christians are called to be the healing hands and feet of Jesus in our beautiful but broken world. But this work is not easy. Serving God and the young people that God so loves in a challenging community like Potomac Gardens requires eyes to see beyond problems and pain. We've seen too many well-meaning people come to fix things and then leave when the problems they hoped to fix don't get resolved quickly or in ways they had expected.

Being able to see beauty in brokenness has been crucial for our lives and our commitment to united compassionate action with young people. We suspect that one reason we've been able to sustain being in this type of ministry for so many years is that we see beauty when we walk into Potomac Gardens and greet residents and receive hugs from children in the community. We are more apt to sense God's presence in Potomac Gardens than in a pew.

Take the story of Nakisha. This five-year-old girl came from a very poor family and lived with eight other females – sisters, mothers, aunts, and cousins. When Steve went to visit her family at their home, he was shocked to see that there was no furniture in the living room, only a bucket to catch the water leaking through the ceiling from the floor above. There was a bed in the bedroom, but no sheets or pillows.

To make things worse, Nakisha was picked on by other kids, including those in her own family, because she was not the prettiest, strongest, or the most quick-witted of girls. But she had a big heart.

Just before Christmas one year, this young girl came up to Steve at one of Little Lights' programs. With one hand behind her back, she said in a shy voice, "I have something for you, Mr. Steve."

"What is it, Nakisha?" he asked. Nakisha reached out her hand and in the middle of her five-year-old palm was a shiny quarter.

"Merry Christmas, Mr. Steve," she said with a big smile that was missing two front teeth. Steve gave her a big thanks and a huge hug.

That quarter may have been the only money this young child had to her name. Most kids her age, including us when we were children, would have bought candy at the corner store. But with a generosity that surpasses all understanding, Nakisha chose to give this quarter away. She wanted to express her love in a gesture that made her not just a recipient of our good deeds, but a co-labourer in the compassion Jesus calls us to live in with one another.

We fell in love with Jesus because he lived a life of radical compassion for people, and he was willing to sacrifice his life for others. We gave up past dreams to follow this call into the inner city to serve Jesus in his hunger and nakedness. And in the process, we have found abundant life and beauty – more than any we thought we were giving up.

Infiltrating the World

Now you've gone and done it
You chose to take the plunge
You've decided who you'll follow
And declared to everyone
That you're pledging your allegiance
Enlisting in the cause
Of the one who was crucified
Infiltrating the world with the love of God.

So welcome to the body
The body of our Lord
This ragtag band of misfits
Yearning for a world restored
Healing and broken
Full of hope and deeply flawed
Sent into our neighbourhood
Infiltrating the world with the love of God.

I pray that you'll be strengthened
For all that lies ahead
And I pray we'll pay attention
To what the Spirit says
As we're not-so-secret agents
In the ancient urgent cause
Of the one who died and rose again
Infiltrating the world with the love of God.

-Bryan Moyer Suderman[1]

Chapter 13

Personal Jesus, Public Faith:
Cultivating a Generation of
Young Public Theologians

Almeda M. Wright

You are my personal Jesus, without you where would I be…
So glad I know you… 'Cuz he's a friend of mine
I talk to you all the time… He's always been by my side…
If ever there is a problem, You always open the door…
And you're my personal, personal Jesus.[1]

Gospel artist Tonéx, popular during the late 1990s, penned these lines in a song entitled "Personal Jesus." He proclaimed to the entire world his love for, faith in, and relationship with a "personal Jesus." But Tonéx wasn't the first (or last) to write a song about a personal Jesus (Johnny Cash, among others, also has). His song offers an example of the religious language and paradigm that permeates much of American Christianity (and Christianity in other parts of the world), including that of the ethnically diverse youth with whom I work as well as the specifically African-American youth I have researched over the last decade.

Almeda M. Wright is Assistant Professor of Religion and Youth Ministry at Pfeiffer University. Her research focuses on African-American religion, adolescent spiritual development, and the intersections of religion and public life. Her publications include *Children, Youth, and Spirituality in a Troubling World* (edited with Mary Elizabeth Moore) and an issue of *Practical Matters*.

The concept of a personal Jesus also permeates my own background. When I was growing up, an emphasis was placed on having a "personal relationship with Christ," which meant having a personal and individual commitment to Christ that was not mediated by one's parents or friends. The religious language affirmed a concept that in order to be "saved," one had to fully commit to Christ for one's self.

In the decades since I was a youth and since Tonéx penned his love song to Jesus, the idea of a personal Jesus hasn't gone away. Instead, it persists in religious communities and in the popular theology and culture of many contemporary Christians. Heartfelt ballads and tongue-in-cheek expressions such as the mobile app that lets people download their own personal Jesus – in White, Black, Asian, or Celtic editions[2] – manifest this.

What do we make of the language of a personal Jesus? How do we make sense of the variety of expressions and sincere calls to develop a personal relationship with Jesus Christ? I must first acknowledge the many youth workers and pastors I have encountered who said things to me like, "If only I could get youth to love on Jesus and know Jesus for themselves, things would be really good." Like many other youth pastors, they struggle with and still have a desire to help youth grow in their personal understandings of Jesus and in their relationship to the divine. And I understand this fully. However, over the course of my time in youth ministry and doing research with young people, I have found that there's something inherently limiting in our discussions of a personal Jesus and the ways we translate this Jesus into our daily lives.

A Snapshot of Youth and Personal Jesus
Research Survey and Interview Findings

I have had the privilege of working with the Youth Theological Initiative (YTI)[3] hosted at Emory University's Candler School of Theology (Atlanta, Georgia), and doing research over the course of three summers. Since its formation in 1993, YTI has "served as a center for research into the religious practices and faith perspectives of youth"[4] and has offered a space to explore forms of liberative pedagogy in theological education and social criticism with youth. My research there serves as a starting point for my discussion of personal Jesus, public faith, and how we can cultivate a generation of public theologians.

Each summer, my colleagues and I explored the religious experiences and views of young people, and some of the ways that youth were thinking about the world around them. Using open-ended questions, we asked the youth to describe their hometowns, friends, families, schools, and churches and to include things they were excited about and things that concerned them. Through a series of short answer and Likert scale questions, we explored with each youth the theological perspectives of their religious communities and their understandings of God. We also surveyed youth regarding their concepts of "making a difference in the world" and asked them about their experiences while working in their communities and observing others there.

Of course, the data generated from this research do not represent all young people in the United States; it was a very "self-selective" group. Overall, group members were academically high-achieving and from an array of religious communities (with the largest representation among moderate mainline denominations and a smaller representation of evangelical or conservative denominations). In many ways this group of young people represents the "best and brightest" of mainline Protestant youth. They are leaders in their youth groups, curious about their faith and the world around them, and already on paths toward "greatness" (broadly defined).

Youth Communal Concerns
In describing their hometowns, schools, and primary groups of friends, the youth named an array of concerns. For example, in questions about their hometowns, 35% of the youth named violence or gangs as an issue of concern; 25% talked about different groups (races, classes, ethnicities, or religious groups) as being divided or segregated; and 16% specified concerns about racism. Depending on the specifics of their communities, youth also named concerns about illegal immigration, poor educational systems, environmental justice, natural disasters, poverty, sexually transmitted diseases, and teenage pregnancy. Youth were aware both of the things that made their communities great and of problems that existed.

ALMEDA M. WRIGHT

God's Activity in Personal Lives, the Community, the World,
and Government

Given the theological nature of the YTI summer academy, it was not surprising that most of the youth articulated a strong interest in their religious communities. Over 80% described themselves as regularly or very involved in a religious community. However, even in this group, some youth struggled to articulate what the core of their Christian faith was, or what the essential teachings of their church are. Their responses were peppered with answers of "I'm not sure" or "I don't know."[5] However, most of the young people surveyed and interviewed were very clear in their understandings of how God works in their individual lives. For example, when we asked them to describe a time when they felt the presence of God in their lives, 86% chose to answer the question, and of these respondents, only one person described not knowing or not being able to talk about a time when he experienced the presence of God.[6] The overwhelming majority of the youth surveyed were able to name an experience of God's presence in their lives. The overarching theme was that the young people felt God blessing them.

However, the vast majority of young people surveyed and interviewed were less certain about God's role or work in their communities, the world, or government. For example, most youth were vague in their responses to questions such as, "What does your church see as God's work in the world?" Some replied that "God wanted them to be light in darkness." Others spoke more generally about "helping others." These responses were typically peppered with "I don't know" or "I guess."

The responses became more complex and more uncertain when the youth were asked to relay the way they saw God working in government or politics. One young woman interviewed responded:

> I don't know if I see him [God] working in my community. I don't know if he's in the government. It's really obnoxious because our forefathers were all Christian and they created this country or the Pledge of Allegiance wouldn't have "under God" in it or our dollar bills wouldn't say "In God We Trust." And it's really, really sad because [the president] is a Christian (at least that's what he claims) and he has people fighting in a war that we don't even know what

we're fighting over anymore... Our society does not think that God is in the government because of the Sean Bell case, or simple cases where people have been shot and killed by the police and there is nothing you can do about it. I think that people give up that God is there. And that's probably why I'm on the fence whether he is there or not. I think he is but people don't pay attention.[7]

This complexity and uncertainty about God's role in their communities and government is not particularly surprising, as it parallels ongoing debates among adults and scholars of religion regarding the role that religion should or should not play in public life.

Youth Communal Involvement
In addition to naming things they were concerned about, all of the youth surveyed and interviewed were very involved in community service and other forms of communal involvement. Of course, some students attended schools that required a certain number of hours of community service. But even with this requirement, many said that they completed the requisite hours and more. The majority of youth spoke of being involved in community service as normative for youth, or something which all young people were doing.

In the survey, we asked youth to check the types of activities they were currently involved with in their communities. The most popular was recycling, with two-thirds of the youth recycling or pushing their families to recycle. The next popular was peer tutoring, at 48%. However, a much smaller percentage of youth were involved in civic or political issues.

The Challenge of Disconnection and Fragmentation
Collectively, this snapshot of Christian teens shows that 100% of the young people named some issue in their schools, communities, or core groups of friends that they were concerned about and wanted to see changed, 98% of the youth described a positive experience of God's presence in their lives, and 100% were involved in some way in their communities. While the young people were able to name concerns in their

communities and were involved in their communities in many ways, it is also important to note that most of the ways that young people were involved in their communities didn't address or relate directly to things that they were worried about. Perhaps by working on a problem, it no longer seemed like a major concern to them. However, this disconnection may point to a larger problem among youth (and people in general): young people do not feel empowered to participate in ameliorating the things that are really concerning them. In other words, the interviews and survey responses do not demonstrate a clear connection between communal concerns, understandings of God, and actions. The young people's concerns about their communities and their personal experiences of God do not translate into reflective and focused action in the world.

But why not? Why is their understanding of a personal experience with God not connected to, or integrated with, their concerns about the community, their understanding of how God works or should work in the world, or their actions in the world?

Several theories in youth and spirituality research are useful in reflecting on this disconnection. A full explication of this research is beyond the scope of this chapter, but I will point to some key findings.

Parallel trends emerged in the findings of Christian Smith and Melinda Lundquist Denton in their book *Soul Searching*. They note a trend among American adolescents toward "moralistic therapeutic deism," a simplistic religious view that includes a belief in God and focuses mostly on "feeling good, happy, safe, at peace," but does not stretch to a more complex sense of faith that also calls for passionate commitments or engagement.[8] Smith and Denton's research also argues that the majority of American teens understand God as cosmic butler and divine therapist, and religion as something that helps them become a nice and happy person. Thus, their findings indicate that the religion or spirituality of the majority of American teens does not tend toward engaged and intentional religious reflection and action. Religion is primarily understood as something that helps oneself, rather than something that changes a person or transforms larger issues.[9]

Similarly, Evelyn Parker's theory of fragmented or fractured spirituality underscores the trend of adolescents in the United States to disconnect or fragment significant areas of their lives from their religious experiences. Fragmented spirituality, as defined by Parker, is one in which a person's deeply held religious beliefs are kept separate from critical issues or areas of their life, such as a belief in a personally transformative and protective God and experiences of racism where one never names God as working to end racism.[10] In her interviews with youth in the Chicago area, Parker found the ways that youth described their understandings of God working in their lives contrasted starkly with the ways they described problems in their community. Many of the most hopeful and involved youth articulated no hope that changes could ever happen in certain areas (such as racism) and saw themselves as powerless to make a difference.

It is important to note that fragmented spirituality and "moralistic therapeutic deism" are not limited to adolescents – they reflect trends in the larger adult society as well. For example, a possible catalyst for disconnection could emerge from trends toward a privatization of religion and religious practice. Sociologist of religion José Casanova argues that privatization took place because religious beliefs became subjective in the face of pluralism or "alternative interpretations of life" and institutional religion became largely de-politicized "as a result of a functional differentiation of society."[11] These theories point to how many segments of modern society expect and encourage religious institutions and communities to remain separate from and not influence the public sphere. However, Casanova's discussion of the differentiation of modern (and postmodern) institutions does not presume that structural differentiation requires religion to be privatized – or even for people to fragment or compartmentalize the realms where they expect God, religion, or the church to have a stake. Instead, his larger work gives case studies of public faith.[12]

Looking at the role of Christian engagement in the public sphere, religious historian Mark Toulouse also pushes beyond a simple explanation of a separation of religion and the public sphere. His work outlines four ways that American Christianity and public life relate to one another.[13]

Both Casanova and Toulouse offer historical background for the religious context of differentiation of public and private, religious and secular institutions. But they also push us to think about how religious people and communities engage in public life.

ALMEDA M. WRIGHT

However, there remains a lack of research investigating public and private religious life in terms of how youth might be empowered to become involved in the public sphere. In turn, an equally important question persists, even in light of trends within larger bodies of research and American society: How do we help young people "reconnect" these disconnected areas of their lives? For example, even though all of the youth participants at YTI are active in their communities (engaged in some type of volunteer service), their motivations were not explicitly or clearly connected to their faith. Therefore, in order to help youth connect their understanding of a personal Jesus with a more public faith, I argue that a broader understanding of the Godhead (beyond a personal Jesus) must be put in place alongside a reorientation toward a public theology.

From Personal Jesus to Cooperative God

In the theological understandings of young people and popular Christianity, the centrality of a personal and beneficent God remains. As noted, all of the youth surveyed and interviewed at YTI described a time when they "experienced the presence" of God in their lives. They were very articulate about God moving in their individual lives, and some explicitly named God as a very powerful force propelling them toward personal success. At the same time, they showed a great deal of ambiguity and uncertainty in their understandings of God's work in their communities, the world, and politics.

In spite of the limitations and ambiguities in their discussions of God, I don't think that youth should get rid of their understandings of God's goodness and presence in their lives – they need to keep seeing God as spiritually powerful and concerned about their lives. In many ways, this is the most operative element in each of the interviews. And this understanding of God is also the most prevalent in the religious lives of youth within the larger body of research on youth religion.[14] However, responding to the disconnections and the resultant fragmented spirituality pushes us to explore strategies for expanding upon teens' understandings of a blessing, loving, and sometimes powerful God.

On one hand, the most obvious corrective includes pushing youth to embrace a vision of God as wonderfully good and all powerful in all areas of young people's lives and to affirm the miracle-working, transformative power of a God that does all things well. And for many Christian youth, a naïve belief in a wonderfully-good and all-powerful God is already operative. However, a blind embrace of the goodness and power of God conflicts with their lived realities, even if only on a subconscious level. Instead, I affirm that adolescents need to adopt a more complex understanding of God, beyond one of God being good and powerful.

What is required is an expansion of their understandings of what God does so that it includes a view that God may not always operate in miraculous or instantaneous ways. This is not an attempt to downplay or lessen the *power* of God. Instead, I argue that if the only understanding youth have of God is one in which God is all-powerful and all-good and only operates in the miraculous and instantaneous, then youth will constantly have to apologize or regroup when their lived realities and dehumanizing experiences call this image of God into question. A closer read of biblical texts, for example, in the narratives of Hagar and of Jesus Christ, reveals images of a God that does not always (or even most often) step in and miraculously change societal structures of oppression. The biblical narratives, however, present tremendous models and examples of human beings who are strengthened to survive, persist, endure, and work for change in the face of injustice.

In other words, youth have to learn that a personal Jesus is not a genie in a bottle. A relationship with Jesus does not mean that they have someone who can fix all of their problems miraculously and instantaneously. Their (and our) understanding of God and human work in the face of struggles has to expand.

Many theologians offer helpful correctives to counter the idea of passively waiting on the miraculous intervention or gift of God. Delores Williams in particular emphasizes the role of human agency and initiative in the struggles toward liberation. Essentially, she posits a model of active cooperation with God and pushes us to reconnect with "the [Christian] community's belief in God's presence in the struggle," even if or when the struggle persists and requires great endurance.[15] Similarly, womanist theologian Monica Coleman argues that salvation is an ongoing activity and we are called to live in "cooperation with God for the social transformation of the world."[16]

Expanding youth's understandings of God also requires conceiving of a God that calls youth to participate, cooperate, and act with God. I intentionally describe this as an "expansion" and not an introduction of the idea of youth cooperation with God, for many youth named an understanding that God calls them to work for change or to respond to things that concern them in their communities. Thus, I am simply asserting that we need to make this understanding of God – the one that calls and expects our active participation – normative, and not simply focus on the God that blesses us or rules over us.

Reorientation toward a Public Theology

Public theology can help us think about spirituality that empowers youth to connect their understanding of God as personally concerned and significant with an understanding of a God that is relevant and that requires their agency and cooperation in responding to the communal concerns around them.

The term *public theology* (or *public theologian*) is not without issues or problems; in some arenas it is highly contested. It's difficult to succinctly define public theology. However, my discussion of public theology draws upon two working definitions. Ethicist Robert M. Franklin introduced me to the concept of public moralists and public theology. In a sermon for incoming students at Emory University, he admonished them to offer a new type of leadership for the church and world:

Since the time of Reinhold Niebuhr, we have called them public theologians. [Public theologians] are women and men who take their faith out of the comfort of the sanctuary into the public square of the nation and the globe. In times of stress and uncertainty, they "go public" not to impose their faith upon other people, but to give voice and to give body, yes to embody, a radical idea – the idea that love is the greatest force available to humanity for solving its ills. Not the weak and superficial sentimentality that passes for love in our time, but love as a force of the soul. Love as a movement of the Spirit... *Public theologians show before they tell the world the meanings of faith, hope, love, justice, and reconciliation.*[17]

Additionally, Duncan Forrester offers the following definition of public theology:

> Public theology, as I understand it, is not primarily and directly evangelical theology which addresses the gospel to the world in the hope of repentance and conversion. Rather, it is theology which seeks the welfare of the city before protecting the interests of the Church, or its proper liberty to preach the gospel and celebrate the sacraments. Accordingly, public theology often takes "the world's agenda," or parts of it, as its own agenda, and seeks to offer distinctive and constructive insights from the treasury of faith to help in the building of a decent society, the restraint of evil, the curbing of violence, nation-building, and the reconciliation in the public arena, and so forth. It strives to offer something that is distinctive.[18]

From these definitions, it's possible to see five constitutive elements of public theology.

1. Public theology is not about conversion or explicitly sharing religious traditions, practices, or views in the public square.

Both Forrester and Franklin argue against public theology as an attempt to convert persons to particular religious views or faith traditions. Over time, uneasiness has developed surrounding religion in the public square, particularly in government.[19] As a scholar of religion and a practitioner of Christianity, I am not always comfortable with religion in public life, because I am afraid that it will either tend toward proselytizing or else completely disregard the views or beliefs of others. However, despite my unease, there is both a tradition of bringing religion into the public square and a real need for us to draw upon the resources of religious traditions and communities.

2. Public theology seeks the good of the community ahead of church needs or religious agendas.

Even though public theology is grounded in particular religious convictions and institutions, the work of public theology is not to protect the rights and privileges of the institution at the cost of a larger goal or common cause.[20] These are issues of great concern, but they are more aptly discussed as issues of jurisprudence or the separation of church and state. Instead, Forrester notes that often the agenda of the public theologian looks like the agenda (or an agenda) of the community or world. It puts the needs of the community above the needs of the church.

3. Public theology is not simply Christian theology.

Clive Pearson, Associate Director of the Public and Contextual Theology Strategic Research Centre, writes that "public theology assumes that it is relevant for all humanity, not just Christians. It should be conceived from a perspective that recognizes both the marginal location of the Christian faith in a post-Christendom world, and the value of other disciplines."[21] Christianity cannot corner the public theology market. Public theology includes being in dialogue with persons of other religious traditions and faiths, learning and working with them as they draw upon the resources of their traditions to address issues and concerns in the public arena.

4. Public theology draws on the resources of religious traditions to offer distinctive and constructive response to crises of the community and world.

Public theology is more than a simple concern for society to become better. It is people working to create a society that goes beyond what policymakers can envision under their current structures; it is people lifting up an eschatological or hopeful view of what can be. Public theology undergirds the fight and struggles to create a more just society, pushing members of particular religions to work for a common cause. It draws on religious convictions and ideals to work for a common good. Reflecting on James Gustafson's understanding of public theology, Mark Toulouse writes that "the church's task is to convey publicly the best that Christian tradition has to offer. Theology joins the conversation without apology… [and] must offer an interpretation of people and communities that take seriously their activities as moral agents."[22]

5. *Public theology is embodied theology.*

Public theologians must embody their theological ideals. Academic theological reflection is often criticized as disengaged reflections from the ivory tower. But public theology (both by definition and in the nature of those called to be public theologians) engages in rigorous research and thoughtful reflection and lives out theological principles in the public arena. Public theology corresponds with particular and specific action in and on behalf of the wider public. Public theology calls us to *do something*, not to simply believe something.

Public theology, at its best, is theology that is relevant to the lives and lived experiences of all humanity, and one that challenges, critiques, and helps us make sense of the complexities of our lives. It calls us to goals and interests other than our own. Public theology is the antithesis to much of the privatized and individualistic spirituality that has emerged in society. It asks and encourages young people to think about and reflect on how they can work for a common good and respond to crises and issues in the world around them. Public theology calls into question the public/private divide, challenging whether it is possible or feasible for us to separate our private beliefs from our public duties and participation. Public theology draws upon particular traditions and world views to ask what it is that God wants us to do and how we can work so that all humanity can thrive.

Public theology is theological reflection for the benefit of both the church and the world. It means demanding that our faith, our religious and ethical beliefs, and our practices and traditions connect with public life (and become an integral part of our public life). But more importantly, it means that we take our experiences of public life and push back and demand something of our faith convictions

The purpose of public theological reflection is not to impose particular political, religious, or social views upon youth. However, public theology should invite youth to explore questions and concerns that arise for them, and it should equip them with resources to reflect on those concerns in light of a larger concern for the common good. Part of this process involves engaging with youth about what the common or public good is and why youth should work for it.

This kind of dialogue is difficult, and often youth resist engaging in it. On occasion, parents and teachers also resist, saying things like, "What are you trying to do to my child?" Parents may ask how youth can fit into the goals and dreams which they have for them, such as a great education, a great job, a piece of the American dream. This is a dream that often does not have space for radical public voices, for questioning the status quo, or for working for systemic change.

Empowering Youth to Be Public Theologians

Despite the difficulty of the dialogue and the resistance of youth and parents, there is still a need to empower youth to become public theologians. As public theologians, young people encounter a faith that is relevant both to their own lives and to public life. As public theologians, youth can find something beyond the world as it is (be it a transcendent God or a vision of a "beloved community") that calls them to work for change and to honour the human strivings for freedom and justice around them. Public theology calls youth to pay attention to their world, to the particular places they inhabit, and, further, to give up the comfort of apathy to work for a cause beyond simple self-interest.

For many, adolescence is a time of great questioning and upheaval. It is a time when the myths and narratives that sustained youth as children no longer work. As caregivers begin to entrust youth with more responsibilities, youth also begin to explore larger spheres of influence and develop the capacity to carefully attend to the perspective of others. By extension, adolescents become aware of a much larger world, and while many early adolescents may still be very self-centred, the developmental period lends itself to interactions in which empathy and passions often emerge.[23]

Because of the newfound capacity for empathy and a yearning to answer the questions of "Who am I?" and "What should I do with my life?", adolescence becomes an ideal time to engage young people in theological reflections about their lived experiences and the experiences of people around the globe. Engaging youth in theological reflection on social issues is of benefit to the communities in which they live and will work, but it is also of benefit to their own lives. It empowers them to make a difference in the world, and in many cases it helps them answer questions surrounding their purpose(s) beyond being "just a kid" with few rights and privileges.

Therefore, it is necessary to help youth reflect on the concerns in their lives and to see how they, as youth – right now and not later in the future – have something to offer their communities and the world. The reflections of 17-year-old Danielle from Georgia reiterates the need to invite youth into theological reflection and action now, when they are youth:

> When I look around my community and my school, I feel like we're too laid back. And I see it in myself, because I presently feel like I want to change the world but I feel like I don't have all the tools yet. I'm furthering my education, like when I'm finished with my education then I'll have all the tools that I need. So I still feel like I'm in the wings based on the process of getting all the tools. But I still don't feel right just waiting and I feel like the environment I'm in is kind of like this waiting stage. They are all waiting for something.
>
> My community…it's…not really a community where you can gung ho go out and do community service and…change something… It's more like we're going to stay in our home and if we each individually…make our little homes better then it will work out better.
>
> But I don't feel like that. I don't feel like that's how it's going to work. I feel like we all have to come together… [But] we're all trying to make ourselves better. We're not really worried about too many other people… That's hard for me.
>
> Do you feel like God is calling you to work for change? Yeah… like that's why I do law. I want to represent rape victims.

Danielle is a prime example of how a young person may have a vision for how her community should come together, and a desire to work to change things, but at the same time feel constrained by the expectation that she has to wait until she gets all the tools of her education, and by her communal environment that focuses on individual achievement and development. Not only does Danielle demonstrate that she is frustrated with how things are going and the lack of support available in her community to help her affect the kind of change and response to social concerns she envisions, but she also feels "called" by God to do something, and she has a plan for later, after she gets her education. But she does not see what she can do now as a young person, as a young religious person.

Danielle's narrative reminds us that a first step toward empowering youth to reconnect the disparate areas of their lives, to see beyond an individualistic and personal Jesus, and to become public theologians, requires that we say to her and all other youth, "God is calling you now. You have something now. You have what you need to change the world now."

Chapter 14

Inheriting the Earth

Ben Lowe

What does environmental stewardship have to do with raising up young generations of disciples? For many people, the answer to this question may be, "Not much." In fact, when I told people that I was writing this chapter for a book about ministry and formation with youth and children, most people were surprised. For many, environmental stewardship isn't on the radar for children's and youth ministry.

I grew up within the nurture of Christianity in the United States and have served in various youth and children's ministries for over a decade. In my experience, creation care is all too often viewed as an add-on instead of part of the core curriculum. But caring for creation is an integral part of Christian discipleship and belongs on the priority list and within the core curriculum of our work to form young disciples. After all, we can't form faithful disciples of today's young people without also teaching them to care for God's creation.

So what does it look like to faithfully engage youth and children in caring for creation? This is a big question that would take far more than one chapter to fully unpack. But while I can't cover everything in these pages, I'll offer the beginnings of a biblical foundation along with three postures and three practices that can help us get started in forming young disciples who care for creation.

Ben Lowe is on staff with the Evangelical Environmental Network and serves as the national organizer for Young Evangelicals for Climate Action. A dedicated activist and organizer, Ben was born and raised as a missionary kid in Southeast Asia, where he experienced first-hand the impacts of poverty and pollution. He is author of *Green Revolution* and a regular contributor to RelevantMagazine.com.

Creation Care is Essential to Biblical Discipleship

According to scripture, caring for creation is integral to what it means to be human. Human beings are made in the image of God, distinct from the rest of creation, so that we have both the unique capacity and the divine authority to co-rule the world on God's behalf, according to God's will.[1]

Discussions on the first two chapters of Genesis that focus solely on the creation-versus-evolution debate which can often happen in youth groups and Sunday school classes – risk missing the main point of the text, which is less about *how* God created the world and more about *that* God created the world. God brought order out of chaos, established functions and installed functionaries, and then commissioned us as God's image-bearers to continue cultivating the world. As the saying goes, when we see God face-to-face, God probably isn't going to ask us to explain how God made everything, but rather what we did (or didn't do) to take care of it.

Moving to the New Testament, we read that when Jesus was asked to identify the most important commandment in the Law, he pointed to the *Shema* in his reply:

> "The most important one," answered Jesus, "is this: 'Hear, O Israel: The Lord our God, the Lord is one. Love the Lord your God with all your heart and with all your soul and with all your mind and with all your strength.' The second is this: 'Love your neighbor as yourself.' There is no commandment greater than these."[2]

Simply put, we cannot follow these great commandments without caring for creation. We cannot love God fully unless we take care of the world that God created, sustains, and loves. And we cannot love our neighbours as ourselves unless we protect the environment that we all depend on for our survival and well-being. As a good friend often reminds me, when the land isn't healthy, the people aren't healthy.

All of this is especially relevant to younger generations, like the Millennials (my generation), who are inheriting an increasingly beleaguered planet. Inheritances are supposed to be blessings. This one, however, is becoming more of a curse.

It is easy to look at the interconnected environmental and social crises of today – water, food, energy, climate, global pollution and toxification, disease, natural disasters, wars, and violence – and fall into despair. But these crises, while very real, are better understood as symptoms of deeper problems. In the words of environmental leader James "Gus" Speth,

> I used to think that if we threw enough good science at the environmental problems, we could solve them. I was wrong. The main threats to the environment are not biodiversity loss, pollution, and climate change as I once thought. They are selfishness and greed and pride. And for that we need a spiritual and cultural transformation, something we scientists don't know much about.[3]

At its heart, the environmental crisis is not just a technical crisis with political or technological solutions. It is a moral and spiritual crisis. To put it more precisely, the root of our environmental and social problems is sin. Therefore, what we ultimately need is a solution to sin.

The Bible speaks directly to this. The first three chapters of Genesis show that God created the world in a state of peace and wholeness, where right relationships flourished between God, humanity, and the rest of creation. But as sin infected the world, all our relationships, including our relationship with God, were broken. In Romans 8, 2,000 years ago, Paul described what science today is quantifying: that all of creation is groaning from the effects of our sin. This is the bad news.

The good news is that God has not given up on creation. The rest of the Bible is the story of God saving the world from sin, first by working through the law and a chosen people known as the Israelites, and then ultimately by redeeming the whole world through Jesus Christ: "For God was pleased to have all his fullness dwell in him, and through him to reconcile to himself all things, whether things on earth or things in heaven, by making peace through his blood, shed on the cross."[4] Through Jesus' life, death, and resurrection, the door was opened for *all things* to be reconciled back into a right relationship with God and, consequently, with one another. Everything that is broken as a result of sin is to be healed.

Thus, through the undying love of God, there is a solution to sin: Jesus Christ. And because sin is the root cause of our interconnected environmental and social crises, there is ultimately no answer to these problems apart from Christ, his death, and his resurrection. Jesus is the true hope of the planet and he invites us to be both the recipients and the agents of his reconciliation, living into God's kingdom here on earth as it is in heaven. This is summarized beautifully in *The Cape Town Commitment*, the official statement published by the most recent Lausanne Congress on World Evangelization, hosted in South Africa in 2010:

> Integral mission means discerning, proclaiming, and living out the biblical truth that the gospel is God's good news, through the cross and resurrection of Jesus Christ, for individual persons, and for society, and for creation. All three are broken and suffering because of sin; all three are included in the redeeming love and mission of God; all three must be part of the comprehensive mission of God's people.[5]

With this foundation in place, I'll share three postures and three broad practices that I believe are essential for integrating creation care into ministry with youth and children.

Three Postures

Incarnation

We who live in developed countries increasingly tend to live insulated lives. We're largely disconnected from how we impact the earth and our neighbours near and far. Do we know where our water comes from? Or our energy? Or our food? And what happens to the pollution and waste that we generate? Many of us do not know the answers to these questions.

My generation may be the first one without first-hand experience in raising, killing, and cleaning our own chickens. For us, chickens don't come from the coop; they come in plastic-wrapped Styrofoam packages at the supermarket. When my grandmother was growing up, however, her family would get together every Sunday and kill one of their chickens for dinner. First they would chop its head off and watch its body run down the driveway until it collapsed. Then they would pluck its feathers, pull out its guts, and throw it into the oven. This is what it meant for them to eat meat. They knew exactly where it came from and they did the dirty work to prepare it. Previous generations were much more in touch with the world around them, and with where their food, water, and resources came from.

We need to recover this sort of awareness and understanding among younger generations. Jesus modelled a thoroughly incarnational way of life. And we are created to be intimately connected to the land, people, and creatures around us. But today we're often more connected to our smart phones, televisions, and other gadgets than anything else. We've become isolated within an increasingly digital and virtual reality, and because of this, we often don't know how to live well as part of God's creation.

Moving to a posture of incarnation involves the hard work of getting back in touch with the world around us and uncovering how our lifestyles impact the rest of creation. It involves researching our energy options, starting a vegetable garden, learning the names of the trees and birds in our neighbourhood, and much more. As the saying goes, we will not care for what we do not love – and we cannot love what we do not know.

Responsibility
The second posture is one of responsibility. Our society models entitlement and selfish consumption; we need to teach young generations to see themselves as responsible agents of renewal and reconciliation. We all need to take responsibility – in ways we often haven't – for the impacts of our lifestyles and societies and for the well-being of the world that God entrusts to our care.

I live as part of an intentional Christian community called Parkside. We're based in a predominantly refugee and immigrant neighbourhood in a traditionally white, wealthy, and conservative suburb of Chicago. Some of us have nicknamed our neighbourhood "Burfrico" because our apartment complex is made up mainly of families from Burma (Myanmar), Mexico, and the continent of Africa (hence Bur-fri-co).

Burfrico is a diverse and beautiful community in which to live and grow up. But we also deal with significant problems. Littering may not be one of the darker struggles in our neighbourhood, but it is one of the most systemic and visible. There's trash everywhere! On one hand, this is understandable, since many of the people living here came from refugee camps where litter and trash often just pile up. On the other hand, this contributes to a growing strain on our relationship with our surrounding suburban community, which expects us to conform to their standards of living and cleanliness.

To help address this ongoing conflict, some of us launched an aware-ness campaign that included teaching our Burfrico kids not to litter and involving them in efforts to clean up our neighbourhood. They made signs (in multiple languages) that discouraged littering, and many even excitedly picked up trash on several occasions.

We also have a community garden. When we launched it, many peo-ple warned that we would have trouble keeping the kids from trampling all the plants. Instead, however, the children are the biggest champions for the garden. They are the ones who help out the most and they com-plain loudly if we exclude them from any aspect, especially when it in-volves power tools.

By getting involved in the community garden, the young people in our neighbourhood started loving the garden and taking responsibility for it. Instead of becoming the greatest threats to the garden (as some assumed they'd be), they became its greatest protectors. That's the kind of responsibility that we need to teach our kids – care for the earth that God so loves.

Meekness

The third posture is one of meekness. "Blessed are the meek," Jesus teaches in the Beatitudes, "for they will inherit the earth."[6] Frequently misunderstood as weakness, meekness is best perceived as power under control. It's a posture of humility and restraint that's often sorely lack-ing in our interactions with the world around us. As a result of a lack of meekness, we're now trying to undo damage caused by our past hubris.

Once upon a time we thought it was a good idea to build dams and straighten river channels – but now we're spending millions of dollars undoing many of these changes and restoring surrounding habitats and fish populations. Once upon a time we thought it was a good idea to drain wetlands so that we could build and farm on them (most notably in the Everglades of South Florida) – but now we're trying to control the resulting floods and conserve the biodiversity that remains. Once upon a time we thought it was okay to carelessly pump all manner of pollutants into the atmosphere in order to increase production and profits – but now we're struggling with the resulting health impacts (such as asthma and mercury poisoning) and the climate crisis, which is one of our greatest global challenges today.

If young generations and those yet to be born are going to avoid repeating some of these mistakes, they will need meekness. And the church can play a role in fostering a meek generation. A good place to start would be to have youth measure their environmental footprint (many straightforward footprint calculators are available online) and find ways to reduce it by conserving energy, water, and other resources.

Great power without great wisdom is a recipe for disaster, and just because we have the capacity to destroy the planet doesn't mean that we have the right to do so. Being good and godly caretakers of this world includes having a healthy respect for God's creation, along with a healthy reverence for the Creator of it all.

Three Practices

Postures lead to practices. So I share three broad steps toward forming youth and children into faithful stewards of God's creation.

Teach It

As a missionary kid and a pastor's kid, I practically grew up in church. But it wasn't until I was 19 years old that I finally heard a sermon on caring for creation. I had listened to countless sermons by this time. But not one of them had ever addressed environmental stewardship as part of what it means to follow Jesus.

Creation care needs to be taught regularly in our churches in order to integrate it into our faith. And we need to start early with our children and youth. While the message should come from the pulpit, it should also be taught at Sunday school, mission conferences, youth camps, music festivals, and vacation Bible schools.

Many churches around the country are doing better in their efforts to teach environmental stewardship, and more and more pastors are speaking out on environmental issues and the climate crisis. Seminaries also include creation care in their curricula so that future pastors will enter the ministry better prepared in this area. And para-church organizations such as the Evangelical Environmental Network are doing their part to help as well. So the church as a whole seems to be making progress in this respect.

But will there be another generation of Christians who don't hear churches address caring for creation until they reach adulthood? Or will we integrate environmental stewardship into our ministry with young people, teaching them that disciples of Jesus care for God's creation?

Experience It

But youth and children don't just need to hear about creation care. They need to experience it and to experience the majesty of God's good creation. We need to take kids out to our many parks and nature preserves, to bring them hiking, exploring, and camping.

I serve in the youth group in my local church and our youth pastor isn't a big fan of camping. But every summer he dutifully organizes a camping trip for the youth group. We go to the kind of campground where you drive up to a big open field, open the trunk of your car, pop out the tent, and everything is ready to go. This is not my kind of camping – my ideal would be canoeing deep into a wilderness area with a few friends for a week – but it's a step in the right direction and I want to support this initiative.

Ironically, the theme of our recent camping trip was "surviving the wilderness," and the messages were based on the Israelites' wanderings through the desert after they escaped from Egypt. Meanwhile, our youth group's "wilderness" experience involved lounging for a couple days under shady trees in a grassy field, where we enjoyed cool drinking water, all-you-can-eat hot dogs, and a playground. To top things off, we even had hot showers within a short walking distance!

While this may not have been my ideal camping trip (I made it a little more authentic by skipping the showers and pooping in some nearby woods), that's okay! It's important to start somewhere. So go camping, go canoeing, go hiking. Get kids outdoors and experience God's creation together.

Do It

At the end of the day, creation care isn't just something to talk about; it's something to live out. And when it comes to youth and children, there are many successful models to follow and myriad opportunities to live out our mandate to serve and protect creation.

Churches can commission an energy audit and then work with youth to implement the resulting recommendations. They can start a vegetable garden on church property that children can take some responsibility for. And groups can organize service projects to clean up streams or nature trails in the surrounding communities.

Many times, I've found that young people have their own good ideas to offer, such as replacing Styrofoam coffee cups in the church with mugs that can be washed and reused indefinitely, or offering practical workshops featuring local experts – such as "How to Compost" or "Basics of Bike Repair" – that are open to the surrounding community. And, in my experience, getting the youth or children involved in creation care projects is usually one of the quickest ways to bring the whole church on board.

For youth who want to get further involved in activism and advocacy, there are many good ministries working to make a difference at local, state/provincial, national, and global levels. For example, the Evangelical Environmental Network (where I work) sponsors a national (USA) initiative called Young Evangelicals for Climate Action, where young Christians are building a movement to help overcome the climate crisis. Another Christian organization called A Rocha USA runs community-based conservation projects in numerous locations across the United States and also helps set up internships at field sites on five continents. A quick Google search will return many other potentially promising opportunities.

Faithful, Hopeful, Green

This is hopeful work. And there is plenty to be done, for the God we serve is not only determined to save the world but also includes us in the process. At the end of the day, however, we remember that all of this is about more than fixing the planet; it's ultimately about worship. As Fred Van Dyke, one of the great environmental teachers and leaders of our time, once said to me, "Even though the stewardship we offer is intended to benefit God's creation, the offering itself is one that we direct to Almighty God, maker of heaven and earth, and Jesus Christ, his only Son our Lord."[7]

May God find us faithful as we nurture new generations to inherit God's good but groaning world.

Chapter 15

Bringing Sexy Back:
Forging a Theological Framework

Dave McNeely

I recently led a seminar for college students about the intersection of spirituality and sexuality. In a moment of clairvoyant clarity, I took a page from Justin Timberlake and launched our advertising campaign with the slogan, "We're Bringing Sexy Back to Church."

Not everyone was as smitten by this clever phrase as I was. Within weeks of posting the new flyers around our church, we hosted a youth choir festival with scores of teens from the southeastern United States attending. While at our church, the teenage boys huddled around the flyers as though the greatest mysteries of their world might finally be revealed. One adult chaperone accosted our music minister with this telling accusation: "This is completely inappropriate for teenagers to see!"

This woman is not alone in her sentiments.[1] As a minister to youth and college students, I've noticed that many churches hope that the deep and perplexing questions posed by contemporary expressions of sexuality might simply go away if we just ignore them. But, far from going away, questions around sexuality exert tremendous influence over youth. The freedoms won in the sexual revolution of the 1960s to the 1980s corrected many problems, oppressions, and the repression of earlier sexual norms and practices. But they also led to new norms and practices

Dave McNeely is a member of First Baptist Church of Jefferson City, Tennessee, where he currently serves as Minister to Youth and College Students. In addition, he serves as an adjunct professor of religion at Carson-Newman University. Dave is married and has two children.

that may be liberating in some ways but also cause pain and struggle for young people both inside and outside the church.

As a minister, I've seen the more problematic aspects of sexual liberation as high school and college students sit in my office expressing frustration, suffering, and sorrow over what they came to name in hindsight as mistakes. And I'm not the only one who sees these more problematic aspects of contemporary sexual liberation. Through his research with teens and emerging adults, Christian Smith has found that this "shadow side" of sexual liberation plagues young people across the United States, regardless of religious affiliation. He and his colleagues raise questions and doubts about young people's views and practices not because they are prudes, but, in their words, "because we have heard too much directly from the mouths of emerging adults themselves about the major pain and damage that their free pursuit of sexual pleasure has often caused in their lives."[2]

So while the sexual revolution made many gains, it opened the door to new struggles and problems that remain ignored or under-addressed and do damage to young people. Whether we believe "anything goes," "true love waits," or "sex-talk isn't for church," young people (this goes for Christians, too) are being hurt and damaged by more common responses to contemporary sexual views and practices. Thus, I've come to believe that, regardless of where Christians stand on issues of sexuality, we can agree problems exist that need to be addressed.

Such pain and problems go hand in hand with the lack of a theological sexual ethic faithful to both our tradition and our time. And this void includes a flawed approach, shared throughout various streams of the Christian tradition but most recently and publicly modelled by the "culture warriors" of some streams of evangelical Christianity in North America. This approach, drinking deeply from Augustinian wells, views sexuality fearfully, with a careful eye to restriction and reproach rather than embrace and expression. Examples of this primarily negative posture include the anti-abortion movement, the plethora of initiatives opposing premarital sex (for example, "True Love Waits" and purity balls), and congregational bylaws restricting the ministerial service of divorced members. Recent research indicates that a sexual ethic centred on such prohibitions has a minimal, if not disastrous, effect.[3] In addition, such an antagonistic atmosphere has served to undermine faith in the plausibility of a healthy and positive Christian sexual ethic.[4]

In another approach, other Christians seeking to affirm the goodness of sexuality have found difficulty moving beyond using a simple ethic of freedom and pleasure to guide their sexual expression. Fleeing abusive restrictions that hindered sexual maturity, such Christians often err on the side of permissiveness, to equally questionable and problematic results.

At their core, both of these approaches wrestle with the question of sin, those distortions and abuses within our lives that are destructive and dehumanizing. The restrictive approach places greater emphasis upon the vertical/transcendental aspects of sin, that is, our actions and thoughts that represent an affront to God. The permissive approach, in contrast, focuses on the horizontal/interpersonal aspects of sin, our actions and thoughts that damage others. While both approaches ultimately make difficult but necessary presumptions about the nature of sin, each runs the risk of discounting one dimension in favour of the other. Furthermore, we often fall into a dangerous trap of presuming that we can determine what actions harm others or ourselves or offend God.

Fortunately, the Christian tradition allows for a robust and encouraging appraisal of sexuality, even if such a strain has far too often been dismissed and/or buried under a pile of regulations. Lutheran theologian Laurie Jungling, for one, views the creation accounts of Genesis as pregnant with possibilities for constructing a sexual ethic that balances the tensions of freedom and faithfulness. She writes, "Erotic freedom requires erotic faithfulness for embodied relationality to reach its full potential in creating, sustaining, and empowering the abundant life of all creation."[5] Taking our cue from the creator God in whose image we are made, Jungling proposes a sexual ethic that is modelled in God's very creative act, "the divine call [that] emerges not from a capricious freedom but from fidelity and promise."[6] Furthermore, this freedom is incomplete and prone to abuse without the boundaries instituted by faithfulness.[7] Such an approach, then, avoids the mistake of dismissing either the vertical or horizontal dimensions of sin, but rather properly places them in relationship with each other.

While Jungling and others have provided valuable contributions to our reappraisal of Christian sexual ethics, there is still a need for a holistic and constructive framework that embraces and addresses the gamut of sexuality. Such a framework can offer helpful guidance for those of us who want to "bring sexy back to church," that is, who want to engage young people in conversation and reflection about what it means to live into the sexuality of our lives in ways that remain faithful to the gospel.

Forging a Framework

In the late 1970s, Stanley Hauerwas wrote, "I suspect that the 'crisis' concerning sexual behavior in our society is not what people are actually doing or not doing, but that we have no way to explain to ourselves or to others why it is that we are doing one thing rather than another."[8] These words ring as true today as they did when Hauerwas penned them 35 years ago.

Without some framework for understanding and discussing sexuality, problems surrounding young people's sexual views and practices (and those of adults as well) are not likely to subside anytime soon. Thus, in an attempt to forge a "third-way" approach for responding to contemporary sexual practices, I will sketch out a framework for a new kind of sexual ethic that I find helpful when addressing matters of sexuality with the youth and young adults with whom I minister.

Creative

At the heart of this framework is a creational ethic imagined in light of the narratives of creation preserved in the first chapters of Genesis. Before the presumed "marital mandate" of Genesis 2, God issues a call to all of humanity: "Be fruitful and multiply." While this directive is often taken solely to refer to the procreative act of childbearing, the full scope of this commandment is much wider and has broader implications. As the childless Jesus makes abundantly clear in John 15, "bearing fruit" is the work of all God's children and extends far beyond mere procreation. To be human is to be wonderfully creative in any number of ways.

The call to creativity extends to sexuality. To be faithful in our sexuality requires, at a minimum, that we create, bear fruit, produce, and multiply – and not solely in the more literal manner (making babies) to which we are accustomed. Any sexual norms, practices, and views that fail to meet this mark fall short of sexuality's true fruit-bearing intention.

Rather than reducing sexuality to procreative sex, a creative sexual ethic moves toward the broad force that gives direction to our sexuality: erotic desire.[9] Catalyzed by the generativity of such desire, our relationships of all types become locations of creative and redemptive work, often in ways that parallel their more literal procreative counterparts. For instance, rather than limiting our creative impulse to the biological bearing of children, we find ways to "bear" children through adoption, sponsorship, godparenting, and caregiving, thus creating a "faith family" born of mutual creative desire.

Furthermore, such a broadened transformation of "pro-creation" mitigates against the overly consumptive posture that characterizes many modern relationships. In these sorts of relationships, dating centres upon consuming food and entertainment, the "high holy day" belonging to Valentine is sponsored by Hallmark and Nestle, sex reduces partners to products, and even marriage devolves from a covenant into a contract protecting its signatories not from abuse and injustice but the consumptive heresy of dissatisfaction. In contrast, a relational ethic based upon mutual fruit-bearing seeks creative collaborative outlets such as cooking, art, and play; outlets through which the work of creativity becomes a greater measure of our relational and erotic health than consumption.

Incarnational

One of the reasons that sexuality can evoke difficulty, disagreement, and controversy in the church is the reality that it is an intensely physical phenomenon. As many religious traditions have shown, those with a keen interest in the spiritual dimension of life can have a troubled relationship with the physical dimension (as if the spiritual and physical dimensions can be separated from one another). From asceticism to hedonism, the spiritual/physical pendulum can swing far and wide and balance is often both difficult and rare.

Nonetheless, Christianity has retained a unique if often neglected emphasis upon the importance of the body. Few Christian sources have summarized this better than the Catechism of the Catholic Church, which states, "'The flesh is the hinge of salvation.' We believe in God who is creator of the flesh; we believe in the Word made flesh in order to redeem the flesh; we believe in the resurrection of the flesh, the fulfillment of both the creation and the redemption of the flesh."[10] In short, where there is no flesh, there is no Christianity. Without flesh, there can be no faith. We are bound to and by matter – and this is bound to matter.

Despite this rich tradition of embodiment, Christians can exhibit a deep ambivalence toward things "of the flesh," a term which has often been a second-hand way of naming something as sinful. Matters pertaining to sexuality have suffered from a notoriously questioned reputation. But we can work to change this reputation. It is important that we restore the notion of embodiment to a place of virtue within our Christian ethical systems. Thus, a new kind of sexuality must be unapologetically *incarnational*.

Incarnational sexuality is an embodied sexuality that understands and celebrates the body as part of God's good creation, a wonderfully-made site of sacredness. At the same time, it must come to terms with the reality that, although the body is not inherently sinful, sin (broadly defined) often manifests itself through bodily experience. Thus, incarnational sexuality recognizes the body as the site not only of the goodness of creation, but also of its distortion and brokenness. Yet sin does not have the last word on matters of the flesh. Incarnational sexuality embraces a belief that the flesh is also the site of redemption, one of the many dimensions of creation that will ultimately be restored to wholeness.

Covenantal

The "third-way" framework that I am sketching neither advocates strict codes of conduct nor unexamined gratification. It calls for boundaries and channels that give our sexuality and our relationships order and direction. In the context of the body of Christ, we have a rich word for the appreciation of limits: *covenant*.

Christianity characterizes God as a serial covenant-maker and a covenant-keeper *par excellence*. Beyond the biblical witness, churches have often linked membership with the idea and practice of covenant. And, of course, marriages are viewed through the lens of covenant.

Simply stated, a covenant is an agreement between two or more parties that is intended to express and preserve the nature of their relationship, implying expectations, responsibilities, goals, and consequences for failure. Much like a greenhouse environment, covenants create settings by which we faithfully grow into the fullness of our relationships by ordering and shaping our desires. In the words of Jenell Williams Paris, "Desire warrants discipline and care, not fulfillment and affirmation."[11]

It is important to note that our covenant-making and covenant-keeping take place within communities that make sense of these covenants. This is clearly illustrated in wedding services where the congregation serves not as an "audience," but as "witnesses" to the cutting of a covenant. Hauerwas points to the intimate connection between community and covenant when he writes, "From the church's perspective the question is not whether you know what you are promising; rather, the question is whether you are the kind of person who can be held to a promise you made when you did not know what you were promising."[12] The community of faith holds us accountable in our covenants.

Communal

Theologian Linda Woodhead stated, "It is the body of Christ which forms the basis of a new society – not the body of the individual."[13] This statement brings us to another dimension of the framework being forged in this chapter: sexuality as *communal*.

Few statements will make those of us raised on a steady diet of individualism cringe more than saying that sexuality is inherently public. But, as it turns out, when we consider the problems and struggles disclosed by post-sexual revolution statistics, our private parts are no better off now as "our personal business" than they were as "our little secret" (prior to the sexual revolution). While marriage has understandably been held up as a prime example of a covenant relationship, we need to remember that Christians live by a communal covenant that is more primary. That covenant is baptism. As Jana Marguerite Bennett has beautifully rendered the Christian order of allegiance, "water is thicker than blood."[14]

In this light, our experience and expressions of sexuality become a community endeavour – faithfully discerned, accountably explored, and graciously promoted. It is for this reason that, clichéd as it may be, I believe 1 Corinthians 13 ought to retain its place as a beloved staple of wedding ceremonies. While this famous "love chapter" is not directly a treatise on marriage, few passages are more appropriate for marital union, not because its poetic musings make great needlepoint, but rather because it situates marital (and other) relationships within the context of the Body of Christ. Such communal love is awkward, risky, and uncomfortable, but it calls us to faithfully live out our God-given sexuality within God's family.

Covenant-making and community go hand-in-glove. Covenants are not contracts; they are entered into as acts of trust rather than distrust, and instead of being adjudicated by disinterested third parties, covenants are adjudicated by the communities that bear witness to them. When sexual covenant-makers struggle with the commitments they've made, they should be able to come to their communities in trust for encouragement, guidance, counsel, and support. As Paul suggests in Galatians 5 and 6, not only should covenant-makers be able to look to their covenantal communities to help "bear each other's burdens," but within God's family they have the right to expect to be nourished by the sweetness of the spirit in which that help comes.[15]

Compassionate

While the four aspects already mentioned would no doubt support a formidable and robust Christian sexual ethic, one final dimension needs to be spelled out. Just as Jesus subsumed all of the commandments into a simple twofold call to love both God and neighbour, a new kind of sexuality could similarly be wholly embodied in the call to be *compassionate*.

While the communal nature of the sexual ethic I am proposing certainly mitigates against self-centredness, the fact remains that the other four dimensions could be reasonably accomplished while simultaneously failing to demonstrate the fullness of love. The work of creativity has often been a solo project, exemplified by great artists and writers; the work of incarnation ultimately begins with an inward focus on one's own inhabited flesh; the call to communal sexuality may put one in relationships of reciprocity, but these relationships may be used to satisfy one's own needs and desires; and even the work of covenanting can be manipulated to fulfill only oneself.[16] But it is impossible to be compassionate and only serve oneself. To borrow from Paul,[17] without compassion, we would still have nothing.

Compassion goes by many names – *agape, hesed,* love – and takes many forms. It is characterized by sacrifice, care, and respect. It is an inward disposition and an outward practice of putting others before oneself. And it is only through such service that our sexuality becomes whole. As Quaker author Robert Grimm puts it, "Sexuality becomes...the dynamic force which enables the personality to attain its goal – to exist for others, to love."[18]

From Framework to Fruition

If Christian Smith[19] and Mary Eberstadt[20] are correct, the "shadow side" of sexual liberation has fallen particularly hard on young people. Adolescents and young adults are stumbling into significant pain and stress as a result of sexual practices and views that are promoted by the wider culture in which they live. As Christians, we are called to be Christ's presence in the world, offering healing where there is pain and hope where there is sorrow. The framework I propose in this chapter can help the church to offer an alternative vision of sexuality, a vision that is creative, incarnational, communal, covenantal, and compassionate. But if we are to provide nurturing and fruitful environments for the sexuality of our children and youth to flourish in, we must not only hold to frameworks; we must allow our frameworks to shape our lives and our ministry.

A new kind of sexuality must be fluid enough to faithfully take on many forms in contexts as diverse as the communities and individuals living out such principles in their lives together. But just as every ripple in a pond begins with one small disruption, so I offer here a few considerations to contemplate on the journey toward a more faithful sexuality, especially for those entrusted with the nurture of the children and youth among us.

Developmental Considerations

Beyond adopting a theological framework, any first steps, fledgling though they may be, must take human development into account. Rather than reducing sexual education to "the talk" – a one-time event at puberty – churches can work toward a plan for addressing and nurturing sexuality throughout the lifespan. Although further work needs to be done in examining the compatibility of our theology and various lifespan development theories, some conclusions and first steps are already available to us.

First, we can seek to help young children receive their bodies as gifts, an attitude that is quite compatible with infancy and young childhood, but is all-too-easily forgotten as we grow up. Children, after all, are gifts.

Additionally, it's no coincidence that significant religious rites of passage such as bar/bat mitzvahs and confirmation have traditionally occurred virtually concurrent with puberty, both ritually and physically welcoming the child into adulthood.[21] Regardless of our particular tradition's blend of biology and ritual, we can embrace the pubescent transition as the most fertile time for integrating the spirituality and sexuality of teenagers. The time to bear fruit (both literally and figuratively) is awakened in an intense and confusing vortex of change, and adolescents often long for positive directions toward which to direct this newfound energy.

Finally,[22] emerging adulthood (or post-adolescence) as a stage of life is a reality that has complicated Christian sexuality even further. As more young adults postpone marriage and childbearing, greater stress for a longer period of time is placed on these young adults to find outlets for their sexual impulses. Far too often, the church has failed to notice these demographic changes and respond with anything more substantive than a reiteration of rules designed for 16-year-olds, or the subtle aversion of attention and implicit condoning of "do whatever you need to do – just be safe." Any attempt to forge a new kind of sexuality will wrestle with a more substantive and beneficial response to the unique needs of young adults, perhaps beginning with Lauren Winner's timely cry for a renewed embrace of chastity – which is more holistic than mere abstinence – as a spiritual discipline.[23]

From Segregation to Integration

Along similar lines, if we wish to promote a more robust and faithful Christian sexuality among our children and youth, we can seek ways to eliminate many of the boundaries that deter, rather than enhance, sexual maturity. In particular, we ought to do a better job at reducing the age and gender segregation common within ministry with children, youth, and adults. Many Christian scholars and commentators of various and divergent traditions have lamented the loss of intergenerational relationships in our faith communities, particularly for the negative effect such a loss has on children and youth. In the area of sexuality, an increased focus on intergenerational relationships would provide opportunities for healthy models of mature sexuality to more intentionally shape the lives of those in the midst of an emerging sexuality.[24]

In a similar fashion, I wonder if the proclivity of many churches for separating males from females (during childhood, adolescence, and even adulthood – think of men's breakfasts and women's luncheons or denominational women's and men's organizations) has unwittingly fostered unhealthy sexual attitudes that in turn cultivate unhealthy sexual behaviours. For example, when teenage boys and girls are segregated largely due to a perceived "sexual tension" (whether or not it's complemented by a theology of gender separation), they are taught to view each other primarily in sexual terms, a view that reduces Christian relationships to biology and rejects authentic brotherhood and sisterhood.[25] Practices of gender segregation can also pose significant problems for young people who self-identify as gender-variant, transgender, and intersex. A healthier and more faithful approach to sexuality, and one that acknowledges that sexual tension exists and gender matters, will seek ways to cultivate Christian inter-gender friendships among children and youth.[26]

Embracing the Body
In addition to establishing a lifelong commitment to developing a healthy sexuality in various ways and reducing age and gender divisions within faith communities, Christians wishing to move forward in living out a framework for a new kind of sexuality would do well to look backward. Fortunately, although deep ambivalence and mistrust of the body and sexuality run through Christian history, our tradition has providentially maintained many practices and disciplines that greatly enhance our reception and development of our embodied nature. Even in the most non-liturgical of traditions, it is almost impossible to escape the bodily dimensions of the Eucharist (a meal) and baptism (a cleansing, a rebirth, a resurrection).

A new approach to sexuality need not necessarily invent new practices. It can appropriate the rich abundance of bodily expressions available in the storehouses of Christianity. In addition to Eucharist and baptism, practices such as foot washing, laying hands, fasting, singing, dancing, and the often-forgotten "corporal works of mercy" – feeding the hungry, giving drink to the thirsty, clothing the naked, sheltering the homeless, visiting the sick and imprisoned, burying the dead – provide a cornucopia of physical graces that show young people that their bodies are part of God's good creation even though they can be used short of God's hopes, dreams, and desires.[27] Perhaps the easiest, but also most opportune, avenue for new forms of sexual faithfulness to be passed on to young disciples is to embrace these traditional disciplines and maximize their potential for the celebration and nurture of our bodies as God's gifts.[28]

Much more could be said regarding how to live out a new kind of sexuality and pass it on to children and youth. More likely than not, however, such considerations will be most faithfully discovered and expressed through local communities of faith committed to exploring this theological framework for sexuality within their specific contexts. Bound to offer hope to some and anxiety to others, a faithful Christian sexual ethic grounded in a shared theological framework might take on different expressions in different situations – and the real work to be done is not in books, but on the ground in the dynamics of everyday relationships.

Toward "Dangerous Futures"

In Mark 12, Jesus drives a stake through any romantic notions of love we might harbour, revealing that the transformation of our sexuality in the eschaton will create sexual realities unrestricted by time-bound customs and conventions. Dismissing post-resurrection marital puzzles as blind to both God's power and scripture's wisdom, Jesus reimagines incarnate sexuality beyond the scope of legal obligations and constitutes an embodied ethic grounded in creation and covenant.

Reflecting on these perplexing and challenging words of Jesus regarding eschatological sexuality, Elizabeth Stuart writes, "Christianity is as much about dangerous futures as it is about dangerous memories."[29] Indeed, while we carry with us memories of a rule-driven and repressive form of Christian sexuality, there is something more dangerous, more risky, and more subversive in the communion of the resurrected Christ which bids us beyond the romantic entanglements in which we find ourselves.

The true measure of any framework for sexuality will be its ability to create and inform communities and individuals whose lives grow more faithfully into the likeness of Christ – people who are maturing in the redemptive work of creation, incarnation, communion, covenant, and compassion. I harbour no illusions that such a framework will provide a simple or complete answer to some of the most pressing questions related to sexuality that we face today. Yet I believe that it is a step in the right direction. May we boldly venture together with young people into these "dangerous futures."

Chapter 16

A Letter to My Granddaughter, Growing Up as a Christian

Tony Campolo

Dear Miranda,

I grew up believing the things that an evangelical Christian is supposed to believe: the Apostles' Creed, the infallibility of scripture, and that salvation is a gift of God through the work that Jesus did for us on the cross.

The importance of being a Christian didn't dawn on me until I began to ask two ultimately important questions about my life. First of all, I wanted to know how I could become a fully actualized human being. I began to ask that question when I was in graduate school dealing with students steeped in a secular mindset. While they affirmed nothing of religion, they did, as humanists, want to know how to become self-actualized human beings in the sense that Abraham Maslow had suggested.

Secondly, I wanted to know what to do with my life. I was desirous of figuring out how I could best invest my time and energies for the work of Christ and his kingdom.

The first time it dawned on me that there was a difference between existing and living was when I was 12 years old. With my school class, I went to New York City and we all travelled to the top of the Empire State

Tony Campolo is Professor Emeritus of Sociology at Eastern University, a former faculty member at the University of Pennyslvania, and the founder and president of the Evangelical Association for the Promotion of Education. Author of more than 35 books, Dr. Campolo lives with his wife, Peggy, near Philadelphia, and has two children and four grandchildren.

Building. As I looked over the city and took in the magnificence of Manhattan that lay before me, I experienced what some would call a deep moment. As I stared through the fog onto the scene that lay before me, I was thrust into a state of awe and reverence. In that moment, I was fully alive.

From that moment on, I wondered how I could have more times like that. Beyond that, I sensed that my life to that point had been the meaningless passage of time between all too few moments of *real aliveness*.

It wasn't until my college years that I came to understand what hindered me from being fully alive in what would have to be called "the now." Gradually I came to grasp the relevancy of the gospel to this existential longing. I came to see that to be fully alive required intense spiritual energy and also that two things dissipated that energy and kept me from full awareness of the moment. Those two things were guilt and anxiety.

Guilt siphoned off my energy because things in my past haunted me; things that I had done and should not have, and, perhaps more importantly, things that I hadn't done and should have.

Anxiety drained away much spiritual energy because I worried about the future. Would I make the right choices? Would I be at the right place at the right time in order to seize life's opportunities in an optimum fashion? Did I have the intelligence and skills to measure up to the challenges that life would bring my way?

As I struggled with these concerns, I found exceptional help in scripture. Fortunately, I had been socialized in an environment wherein scripture had become part of my DNA through my experiences in Sunday school (I never missed a Sunday for 15 years) and vacation Bible school; being dragged to hear endless numbers of what my mother called "Bible-believing preachers"; attending summer Bible conferences; and most of all – *Bible Buzzards*.

Bible Buzzards was a weekly Saturday night gathering of young people to study scripture. We were together for two or three hours and the teacher, who was a layperson with the vocation of accountant, was steeped in the Bible and made it come alive for us. I regret that my own children and grandchildren never had the opportunity to be raised in that kind of biblically saturated environment. I fear that as they ask the same questions that I asked myself as I was coming of age, they will not be able to reach into a biblical treasure chest and take out "some things old and some things new."

About the past: I recall from scripture that God who is the ground of all being forgives and forgets. The dark things of my past, the Bible taught me, were forgiven and forgotten. They were buried in the deepest sea and remembered no more. The scriptures taught me that though my sins be as scarlet, on Judgment Day I would be presented to God as one who is "white as snow." Through faith in Christ, I was able to lay aside the dark burdens of the past that "so easily beset me." As recorded in Philippians 3, I forgot those things which were behind and would press on to the goal of becoming fully alive, even as Jesus Christ was fully alive.

Scripture also enabled me to handle my anxieties about the future. I learned from the Bible not to fret about the future, and that God would not judge me on what I might accomplish in the days that lie ahead. I learned the word *grace* from the Bible, meaning that I would not earn my salvation through any "good works" that I had done but that God's grace – God's unmerited favour toward me – would make me acceptable to God on that final day before the Judgment Seat.

Now, in my waning years, even the ultimate cause of anxiety – the fear of death – is a sting that has been removed by the One who assures me that he is the Resurrection and the Life and that believing in him, though I die, yet shall I live. I may not know what the future holds, but I know who holds my future.

Growing in freedom from the fears of the past and anxieties about the future, I am more and more gaining energy to focus on what lies before me in the here and now. *Carpe diem* is now my raison d'être. More and more, I am aware of the sacredness of what was once ordinary, and the preciousness that I experience in the existential now. There are times when I feel a mystical sense not only of the sacredness of other people, but of all of nature. As Jesus commands, the lilies of the field and the birds of the air become increasingly sacramental as I am freed from guilt and anxiety to focus on what confronts me in the present. In short, I am free to experience God's creation in ways that feed my soul.

My emotions about nature nurture within me commitments to rescue the environment from the groanings of nature that have been caused by humanity ignoring its sacredness. Harming the environment has a quality that is close to blasphemy; the awareness of the sacredness of nature makes me cognizant of how sinful it is to hurt it in any way.

Most important is this: With the freedom I have in Christ, I am able to *connect* with others in an awesome mystical manner. This is hard to express. It has been called by some the *mysterium tremendum*. I am talking about encounters in which I no longer look *at* the other person – as though through a glass darkly – but increasingly, through the power of the indwelling of God's Holy Spirit, I see *into* the eyes of the other and reach the inner recesses of that person's being. I know the other as "also I am known." Then it happens! I feel Jesus coming at me through that other person. In this spiritually charged encounter I sense a meeting with the living Lord, and the other becomes sacramental.

Encountering Jesus in the other, regardless of whether that person is white, a person of colour, heterosexual, homosexual, bisexual, transgender, Christian, Jew, Muslim, or secular humanist, is what has made me into a social activist. I am coming to realize that Jesus waits to be discovered in every person, and that whatever is happening to that other person is happening to the Jesus I love. If the other person is hungry or naked or sick or an undocumented immigrant or in prison, increasingly I can sense the presence of Jesus in that person, and that person's oppression becomes intolerable. I must address it. If I see the other as a victim of racism or sexism or homophobia or poverty, I experience a compulsion to respond and cry out for justice. If the violence expressed toward the "sacred other" via capital punishment or war is something that I experience, I feel a need to cry out, "Stop! In the name of Jesus! Stop!"

Sin has gradually come to be redefined for me. It is no longer simply the violation of some transcendentally ordained rule or regulation. Sin, for me, is whatever diminishes the humanity – or the sacredness – of the other person.

Living with this kind of hyperawareness of the world around me, and the people in that world, and the pain of other people, is exhausting. I cannot do that all the time. It would deplete my spiritual dynamism. That is why I have to stop and set aside time for renewal and regeneration. This is what drives me to embrace spiritual disciplines. I won't begin to describe them here and now, but I feel I must explain one of them. It is *centring prayer*.

Each morning I try to awake and spend time lying flat on my back in bed before I have to get up. During this time, I try to empty myself of everything except for Jesus. I try to drive out "the animals" (the animals being the 101 things that come into my consciousness the minute I wake up), the worries about the things I have to do that day, and the concerns about the things left undone from the day before. I have to go to what the ancient Celtic Christians called "the thin place."

I wish I could say I discover this thin place every morning. I wish I could say that every time I try to open myself and surrender in stillness to the infilling of the Spirit that it happens, but it doesn't. But it does happen. It does happen.

In Isaiah 40, we read that those who wait upon the Lord will be renewed. The emphasis on *waiting* is my emphasis. If I wait in quietude for the Spirit of God to flow into me, I sense myself being empowered. It's not long before I can, in the words of Isaiah 41:31, mount up like an eagle and fly. Afterwards, I can still run with my commitment to live life fully, but eventually I become exhausted and as I walk (or better described, I stagger), I know it's time to go once again "into the closet" where I can meet God in secret, so that God can reward me with spiritual energy in a way that will be visible to all of those who come to know me. As I have already said, in giving myself to others in the deep sense that Christ calls me to encounter, I become spiritually exhausted; but then joy cometh in the morning, when in stillness and quietude I go to that "thin place" and wait patiently for the Lord and for the renewal that God gives me.

You have probably figured out by now that in my strivings to become fully human I have discovered my mission for life. Ironically, it was not in trying to "find myself" as a self-actualized human being, but rather in losing myself in the sacredness of others that I began to find myself – myself being my mission. The growing awareness of the sacred waiting to be met in "the other" is what humanizes me and calls me to change the world. I struggle every day against the principalities and powers and the rulers of this age that have diminished the possibilities for humanness in others. This is a calling that challenges me to work to change the structures of society in order that God's will might be done on earth as it is in heaven.

I long for the day when all people are fully alive and the kingdoms of this world have become the kingdom of God. I long for the day when God reigns in love and justice forever and ever.

I hope this hasn't left you too confused as to who I am and what I am about. But I am old and getting older and I don't know if I will get to write much more in the future, so I did the best I could in the time I had.

Love,
Your Poppop

Chapter 17

Jesus on the Autism Spectrum

Dixon Kinser

One in 88.

That is the frequency at which children are being diagnosed with autism spectrum disorders. This is up by 28% from 2009 and 78% from 2007,[1] which means that now the rate could be even higher. We who are in ministry with youth and children will probably encounter autism spectrum disorders (or ASD) soon if we have not already, as there is a wave of ASD diagnoses headed our way. But it is not something we need to fear. We already have what we need in our faith communities to welcome young people with ASD and to invite them into authentic spiritual formation. That is the point and purpose of this chapter: to provide a crash course on autism spectrum disorders, to help readers recognize how it manifests itself, and to empower leaders to welcome youth with ASD into ministries and disciple them in the way of Jesus.

My first experience of ASD was not clinical, but personal. In 2005, my son was having what were then deemed to be "behaviour troubles" at his pre-school. He was not reading social cues from other children and his response to certain stimuli (like loud noises) was extreme. After a period of observation, my wife and I were called into a meeting with the director of the school who told us two things: first, my son's needs were beyond what this pre-school could offer him; and second, while they were not suggesting a diagnosis, we should explore getting him evaluated for autism.

Dixon Kinser is a husband, father, writer, speaker, musician, amateur filmmaker, and Episcopal priest. He is the author of *Exploring Blue Like Jazz* (with Donald Miller), works in youth and young adult ministry, and lives with his family in Nashville, Tennessee.

"Autism?!" I thought. "Wait, what is that?" Questions flooded my mind. Is that what Dustin Hoffman had in the movie *Rain Man*? Are you saying my son is like Rain Man? Am I saying my son is like Rain Man? That seems a little extreme, right? Right?! But what if it's true… and would I be okay with it even if…and…well… I figured I should stop panicking and go look this thing up.

So I took the vague notions I had from a Tom Cruise movie I'd seen in high school and did what any anxiety-ridden parent might do when their child isn't well – I went on the Internet. A month and two separate diagnostic procedures later, my son was diagnosed with something called PDD-NOS which stands for Pervasive Developmental Disorder Not Otherwise Specified. My wife likened the time before and after the diagnosis to something like watching *The Sixth Sense* (or any movie with a great plot twist) a second time through. Now that we knew the ending, we could see how the evidence for the twist in the plot had been there all along. We just hadn't known to look for it.

Autism Spectrum Disorders: Instant Expert

ASD is a term used for a range of neurological disorders that affect brain development, which is why the *Diagnostic and Statistical Manual of Mental Disorders vol. IV* (DSM IV)[2] classifies it as a Pervasive Developmental Disorder (PDD). Yet what can make ASD so hard to grasp is that it exists on a continuum.

ASD has a spectrum, sort of like an umbrella, that includes a wide variety of conditions ranging from mild to severe. On the severe end, we might find individuals who are completely non-verbal in their communication and demonstrate little or no social interaction even with close family members. (Think again of Dustin Hoffman's character, Raymond, in the 1988 film *Rain Man*.) On the mild end, however, we might find someone who is a brilliant intellectual with profound mastery of a given subject, yet who remains unable to pick up on even the most basic of social cues. Imagine Sheldon Cooper from the ABC comedy *The Big Bang Theory* on this end of the spectrum.

Under this umbrella called the autism spectrum there are a few named diagnoses that each represent a particular collection of symptoms. Some more familiar diagnoses are autism, atypical autism, and Asperger syndrome. However, if someone shows all but one of the symptoms for a particular diagnosis, this person ends up with a diagnosis like my son's, PDD-NOS, which references the type of disorder it is according to the DSM IV (a pervasive developmental disorder), but recognizes that, unlike autism and Asperger syndrome, it is not otherwise specified.

What this means is that no two persons with ASD are exactly alike. Yes, they will have similarities and their therapeutic strategies will be analogous. But because ASD is a spectrum of disorders, the old maxim from the ASD community holds true: "If you've met one person with autism, then you've met one person with autism."

Which brings me back to Sheldon Cooper from *The Big Bang Theory*. I'm sure most people can recall meeting someone like him, someone who is brilliant but who lacks social awareness or tact. And that's the point. This ASD thing is not as uncommon as we might believe. In fact, when I first began to attend support group meetings for parents with kids on the spectrum, the meeting leader asked us to raise our hand if we had a relative in our family that always seemed "a little quirky." More than half of us raised our hands. She then made the point that if they were children today, chances are they might receive an ASD diagnosis.

ASD is more common than we may realize. Statistically, the vast majority of people are probably already familiar with it. It is not the looming monster that some fear it to be, rolling in to overtake us unless we act fast. It is a present reality that is easier to accommodate than we might think, especially if we have a plan.

Trendy ASD: Five Helpful Facts

While it is true that every person with ASD is unique, there some definite trends that tie people together on the spectrum. Understanding a few of these trends can be helpful in getting a handle on how ASD manifests itself in the lives of people, and how people on the spectrum can be integral parts of the common life of the church.

A Specialist Mind

Persons with ASD have what we might call the mind of an expert. Their brains tend to be naturally good at some things and not-too-good at others. Sometimes what makes an ASD mind unique is the marked contrast between skill and deficit. All people are good at some things and bad at others. But a person with ASD tends to be *very* good at some things and *very* bad at others. What's more is that some deficiencies in the mind of a person on the spectrum can be in things that develop "naturally" in other children, like muscle tone and nerve development. So while an eight-year-old child on the spectrum may be able to multiply, divide, and factor in their head any number thrown at them (no matter how large), that child may lack the strength and dexterity to tie their own shoes. The child's mind is that of a specialist.

Preferring the Trees to the Forest

Persons with ASD tend to focus on details rather than large patterns. While this is not always the case, trends show that more and more people with ASD gravitate toward details instead of larger connections and purpose. This manifests itself in my son's life quite regularly.

One day I was running late to pick up my daughter from school. As I grabbed for my keys I misspoke and said to my son, "Come on buddy, we need to get in the car now so we can pick up your sister at dance." Instead of recognizing that the overwhelming social push of this moment was to get out the door and into the car because we were running late, my son wanted to put everything on hold and fixate on the one detail of my sentence that mattered (to me) the least: the fact that I said we would pick her up at "dance" and not at "school." The whole process of getting into the car to pick up my daughter was derailed so that my son could correct and comment on my mistake. He did not respond in this way to be petty or annoying. For him, this detail mattered most, because in the mind of a person with ASD, it's easy to miss the forest in order to carefully examine the trees.

Missing Social Cues

It has become fairly well-known that persons on the spectrum tend to miss or misread even basic social cues. This trait even spawned a fantastic *Seinfeld* episode about a "close talker," played masterfully by Judge Reinhold. Missing and misreading social cues can range from avoiding eye contact, violating personal space, or even laughing in response to anger. It can be especially problematic in youth work, in which relational ministry is the order of the day, and it can create overt friction in the public lives of persons with ASD. After all, relational youth ministry often requires youth to have the ability to build and sustain relationships according to conventional social cues.

Sensory Issue

Many persons with ASD experience something called sensory integration dysfunction (SID). [3] In lay terms, SID means that a person's sensory input either has the volume turned way up or way down. Persons with ASD may experience a sound that others would consider loud, to be painful and deafening. Likewise, they may believe the hug they are giving a friend is gentle, when it is actually being experienced as threatening and aggressive. The details will differ but the trend is the same: on the spectrum, senses may be experienced differently.

No Cause. No Cure?

Questions about ASD are some of the most researched of our day and yet at this time no one knows what causes ASD. Its origins are most likely a combination of environmental and genetic factors, but until we can determine what these factors are, the causes of ASD remain a mystery. What this also means is that there is no cure. What we do know, however, is that ASD is on the rise (especially in boys[4]) and that there is a wave of children and youth on the spectrum moving toward children's and youth ministries. We would do well to be prepared for it.

Youth Ministry and ASD: All in the Family

When my son was diagnosed with ASD our family life changed...again.

When our children were born and came into our home, they ignited a revolution in the family rhythm that had existed for my wife and me. They changed the way we slept, the way we ate, and the way we worked. Our kids even demanded changes in our architecture (we couldn't walk through the house without climbing over baby gates) and our social life. So when our oldest was diagnosed with ASD, I was not sure what would happen next. Should we expect another revolution in the Kinser family? What would acknowledging, parenting, and raising a child on the spectrum require of us?

As time passed and I understood more about ASD, I realized that in our case, raising a child with ASD was actually going to be a matter of incremental adjustment rather than drastic change.[5] As I watched my son's teachers work with him, I observed that they did not radically alter the curriculum for him, but instead made strategic amendments to their instruction to accommodate the way his brain worked. In education lingo, these adjustments are called *modifications* and though they vary in form from student to student, their goal is the same: to facilitate the learning and inclusion of persons with ASD in the classroom.

We hadn't been calling it *modification*, but that was precisely what we were doing in our family. The more we understood about who my son is and how his brain works, the more incremental adjustments we made so that all members of our family could succeed. Our little community was not blown up by ASD. We were shaped by it to accommodate the developmental needs of one of our own – but we did not explode.

In several instances in the gospels, Jesus portrays what he is doing as creating a new family. He describes those who do the will of God as his brothers and sisters,[6] expects a devotion from his disciples that transcends birth families,[7] and while on the cross commends the care of his own mother to one of his disciples.[8] Whenever we invite youth and children to follow in Jesus' way with us, we are inviting them to be part of God's new, big family.

Perhaps a helpful metaphor for bringing students with ASD into our ministries is that of a family raising a child on the spectrum. Of course, this metaphor has limitations. But it could be a useful place to begin. Thinking about ministry from the perspective of family life frees us to imagine how we might make modifications to help students with ASD not just be *with* our community but to actually be *in* our community too. It releases us from temptations to send youth with ASD somewhere where there are "better equipped leaders" and it challenges us to create scenarios where all our young people can be full participants in our common life – no matter how their brains work. Our youth groups, as they exist today, can be exactly the right kinds of places for students on the spectrum because when it comes to youth ministry on the autism spectrum, we may already have what we need!

Best Practices

I've been involved in youth ministry for two decades and, like my family life, my work with youth has changed as a result of learning about ASD. I'd like to offer some of the "best practices" that have helped me move youth on the spectrum in my church from being *with* our community to actually being *in* our community. While I speak out of my experience as a youth minister, many of the practices and strategies I share can be helpful for ministry with children as well.

Make a Spiritual Formation Individualized Education Plan
When a young person on the spectrum is in a school setting, educators often make use of what is called an Individualized Education Plan (IEP). An IEP is a strategic document that is developed collaboratively by education professionals who interact with the student with ASD and his or her parents. The IEP takes the specific educational and developmental goals for the student and outlines modifications and programs that will help the student to accomplish them.

As a youth pastor, creating an IEP is where I begin with the youth in my ministry who are on the spectrum. I meet with the young person's family and try to develop what I call a Spiritual Formation IEP (SF-IEP). This SF-IEP serves the same purpose as an educational IEP, except the objective is the soul care and nurture of the teen.

I tend to follow four steps as I build a SF-IEP. First, I initiate a meeting with the parents of the youth. In so doing, I maintain a relaxed and friendly posture to make it clear from the outset that I'm on their side.[9]

My second step in creating a SF-IEP is to ask the parents to tell me about their teen. I invite them to share any diagnosis (if a diagnosis has been given), and then ask how their teen's struggle manifests itself in her or his life and personality.

Third, I follow up by exploring what strategies, vocabulary, and modifications the family uses with their child and think together about how to implement them in our youth ministry.

Lastly, I ask the parents what goals and dreams they have for their teen that year and how the teen's involvement in the community can work toward achieving these goals. This process has allowed us to move beyond triage mode and just trying to "make the programs work," toward exploring how the church can play a part in the larger life goals of the youth.

It is important to note that the church ought to be the one to take the initiative. When a child is diagnosed with ASD, the family members – parents and guardians – act to find resources for their child. And so it should be with the family of God. The church family first needs to reach out to teens with ASD and their families so we can make a plan together. If we wait for families to reach out to us, it may never happen. Our responsibility toward modification begins here, not as an act of law, but as an expression of love. Getting strategic and intentional about teens with ASD is a key way we embody the love of God. For this reason, I have found that meetings with parents and other family members[10] communicate an incredible level of pastoral care and support to the families involved. They are a manifestation of love. And I think this is one reason why all my SF-IEP experiences so far have been win-win.

Schedules Can Simplify Things

A common trait among youth on the autism spectrum is anxiety around unknown or unexpected circumstances and sudden changes. Being flexible and shifting gears at a moment's notice are learned skills that do not always come easily to persons with ASD.

One way I have found to minimize the stress and anxiety that a new place like youth group can cause teens with ASD is to give everyone a basic schedule of events at the outset of the year, program, or event. This schedule can be as simple as a list of activities or it can be an entire agenda complete with how long each program component will last.[11] Either way, a schedule can give youth with ASD peace of mind and allow them space to be present during worship without worrying about what is coming next.

Remember the Buddy System

I remember going to summer camp as a child and being introduced to the buddy system. Any time that we were going swimming in the lake, we had to have a partner with us. My "buddy" kept an eye on me and I kept an eye on my buddy to make sure that our swim time was safe and fun. Sometimes wisdom from summer camp can be adapted in all sorts of unexpected ways, and a "buddy" or "peer mentor" system for youth with ASD is one adaptation.

I've found it incredibly helpful to pair teens on the spectrum with a peer mentor, a pre-screened and trained peer in the group who volunteers as a social surrogate for a teen with ASD. This means that they do everything from meeting the young person at the door to the youth gathering and walking in with him or her, to helping the teen have conversations with other youth group members and reminding her or him when it's time to stop taking cookies off the snack tray.

Peer mentors can also advocate for teens with ASD by giving youth leaders and parents real-time data about the challenges and needs their partner is facing, as well as her or his successes in youth group. Selecting peer mentors requires intentionality, wisdom, and energy on the part of the youth leader but, when done well, the benefits to all greatly outweigh the costs.

Make ASD Talk-about-able

On whatever level I engage ASD in youth ministry, I try to make the diagnosis talk-about-able. I allow ASD to be something my faith community can discuss and learn about in the open, rather than ignoring it or fearing it. If the church is a family, I don't want my family to become a dysfunctional family that dissuades its members from listening to one another or discourages truth telling. The Body of Christ is not that kind of family – or at least we're not supposed to be that kind of family. Bringing ASD into the open and exploring its implications are crucial ways to practice relational health in the family of God.

Furthermore, because of youth ministry's relational nature, the social deficits of a teen on the spectrum will not go unnoticed. This, again, is not a boogeyman to fear, but it *is* an opportunity for honesty and truth telling. ASD is a reality, and its increasing visibility in entertainment media and news coverage makes talking about it far easier than even a decade ago.

How, when, where, why, and with whom to disclose a diagnosis within a church must be decided on a case-by-case basis. It requires consultation between the youth pastor, the teen, and the family. However, keeping an open posture toward the situation and taking concrete steps to make

ASD talk-about-able will make a significant difference in demonstrating what it looks like to love God and love our neighbour – especially if that neighbour is on the spectrum.

The Gift of ASD: A New Normal?

The increase in the number of autism spectrum disorder diagnoses shows no sign of slowing down. In fact, as we develop better diagnostic tools and learn how to screen for ASD in younger children, chances are that the rate of diagnosis will actually increase. Couple this with the fact that there is no cure for ASD and it begs the question about the point at which an epidemic becomes the new normal.

To put it another way, consider why the word *disability* is used to describe an ASD diagnosis. It's used because the autistic mind is not built to succeed in our current social and educational systems (or perhaps it's more accurate to say that our current social and educational systems aren't built to help the autistic mind succeed). Within existing systems, individuals on the spectrum find themselves *dis*-abled when it comes to what they are expected to do and how they are expected to do it. But we need to remember that these systems – including how we gather for worship and formation in community – are not sacrosanct or handed down on stone tablets. We made them up, which means we can also change them! At what point are so many of our children, friends, and family members diagnosed with ASD that the present systems bend to meet them, instead of asking them to accommodate the status quo?

I ask this question with the utmost sincerity. Is there a tipping point ahead where we will need to change how we gather and scatter as the family of God? And if there is, what are the implications for the way we do church? At what point does the way we arrange our ecclesiastical and liturgical life need to be transformed in order to welcome the least of these? What would that mean for us and for our churches? What does that mean for our ministry with children and youth?

There are parts of my son's personality now that are inexorably linked to his ASD. So many of the little quirks and idiosyncrasies that make up his personality flow from the way his brain works – and I love that! Is it possible that in the new heaven and new earth, my son's ASD will be reflected in his resurrected body? If the holes in Jesus' hands and feet are any indication, I wouldn't be surprised at all if it were. And if that's the case, and if we as children of God are to join God as God brings heaven to earth, then might we not be called to embrace ASD as a gift in the here and now? I am not saying it is easy or simple. However, ASD could be the gift that opens our hearts to new ways to love and challenges us to pursue a new kind of Christianity, one that has the imagination to hear Jesus say, "I was on the spectrum, and you welcomed me."

Chapter 18

Let's Say Grace

Joy Carroll Wallis

When Jim and I had been married for just four months, we strolled hand-in-hand along a beach in Florida. It was January 1998 and we were enjoying a break during a Sojourners board retreat. We were at the beginning of a new adventure together and feeling very grateful that God had brought us together. But we wondered if there would be children in the picture. We both married later in life – I had just turned 38 and Jim was 49 – and we weren't sure that having children would be easy or possible for us. But that afternoon, we decided that we would both love to be parents and that we would try.

I have always loved children. I babysat as soon as I was old enough, and later I taught Sunday school and led youth camps. Before I became a priest in the Church of England, I was an elementary school teacher. My brother had children while he was young and so I was the devoted aunt to three nephews, and also godmother to a legion of godchildren!

Jim is the oldest of five siblings, all of whom have children. He spoiled them, prayed for them, and loved them all, along with a bunch of godchildren that he too had gained along the way. We had both reached a point in our lives at which we were sadly resigned to the fact that we

Joy Carroll Wallis is a preacher and communicator who regularly contributes to church press, public radio, and television. Joy was one of the first women ordained as a priest in the Church of England and still speaks on behalf of women and others marginalized by church and society. She was the inspiration and role model for Richard Curtis' hit sitcom series *The Vicar of Dibley* and her book, *The Woman Behind the Collar,* details her life and work as a priest in the Church of England.

might never have our own children. Little did we know as we walked and talked on that balmy January day in Florida that I was already pregnant. Luke was born in September and we celebrated our first anniversary in October with our son.

We immediately learned the truth of the saying, "to love someone is to see the face of God." The gift of a child opened for us a completely new awareness of our capacity to love unconditionally and sacrificially, and it seemed quite extraordinary. And yet at the same time, we realized that of course this is a "common grace" experienced by the vast majority of parents. In a Sojourners column that Jim wrote a few days after Luke was born, he shared, "Holding him in the delivery room, I did pray, as many parents do, that Luke would be everything that God desires of him and created him to be. Offering your child to God is a way of offering yourself to God again, and it felt that way to me. For the religious and not, there is a powerful spirituality in the birth of a child. Already, we're learning a little about the unconditional love of God for us in the way we feel about our own child. Through one of the most universal human experiences, parent after parent is taught the lessons of love and life. And all is grace."[1]

After the disappointment of two miscarriages, Jackson was born almost five years later, another amazing gift for us at the ages of 43 and 54. Jack was born just a few days before the start of the war with Iraq, which Jim had been working very hard to stop. Sojourners had just launched the six-point plan, an initiative offered by United States church leaders as an alternative to war with Iraq, and in less than two weeks it had spread around the country and the world. Suddenly, right there in the delivery room of Washington Hospital Center, Jim's cellphone began to ring. On the other end were British cabinet ministers and members of Parliament who had seen the plan and were facing a parliamentary debate the next morning. "Jim, is this a good time to talk about the six-point plan?" they asked. While the nurses looked horrified, I told Jim that he should take the call and take his best shot at stopping the war. After all, what else could he do? I wasn't even pushing yet.

As we drove Jackson home from the hospital two days later, the war began. We were filled with a mixture of deep sadness that the war hadn't been stopped and sheer happiness over this new little life that had joined our family. It was a poignant reminder of how precious life is at a time when so many were about to lose their lives amid the madness of war.

Today our boys are 15 and 10 years old and grace has been the continuing theme of our family life. We often feel that it is by the grace of God that our kids are doing well. We have worked hard and put in an enormous amount of effort to make them our priority and raise them as best we know how. But it often feels like we are making it up as we go along. We point them in what we think is the right direction and hope for the best. Perhaps that's what trusting God with our children is all about.

In this chapter, I share some of the things that we have learned as a family, and some of the mistakes we have made. At the 2012 Children, Youth, and a New Kind of Christianity conference, our family shared about what it means for us to be a Christian family. I offer some of those musings of joy and struggle in humility. Every child and every family is different and we are all cracked or broken in some way. As I have often preached about Jeremiah's jars of clay moulded by God . . . the cracks are how the light gets in.

Grace at Home

Jim and I grew up in Christian families, which brought with it both advantages and disadvantages. My father was a clergyman in the Church of England in the inner city of South London. Jim's parents were the founders and leaders of a Plymouth Brethren congregation in Detroit. We both rebelled and returned, and our stories are well documented in the books we have written.[2]

One of the best gifts that we experienced as the children of Christian leaders was that of an open home. Exposure to family, and friends from many different cultures and walks of life helped shape us. But, more importantly, it allowed us to grow up participating in the ministry of hospitality – and that has stuck. The Wallis home is known to be an "open house." Our guest room belongs to many people: from a professor teaching a course in town, to a church leader participating in a fellowship program or conference; from a patient recovering from major surgery or illness, to a summer intern visiting from a far-flung part of the world. To add to this, the basement and boys' rooms are often filled with teenagers or most of a baseball team, and our dining table is full to capacity on a regular basis.

One day when just the members of our family were sitting down to eat dinner, Jim asked who would like to say grace. Jack, who was about four at the time, looked around and said, "But we don't have enough people!"

We don't have to have a quorum to give thanks to God for our food, and indeed these prayers before we eat have been a good introduction to praying together with our children. Luke and Jack are now comfortable in offering to God what is on their hearts together as a family and with any guests that may be with us. I remember one evening when one of Luke's friends was with us for dinner. As we joined hands to give thanks, this friend said, "Wow! This is just like in the movies." Of course, there are those occasions, such as when someone is in a bad mood or in the middle of a squabble, where the call to prayer is more difficult and the prayers are short and grumpy. But these times of sharing prayers and meals as a family have been highlights in our common faith life.

Praying with our children has been a priority for Jim and he has been most faithful in praying with each of the boys at bedtime. These occasions have been a way for the boys to work through questions they have about God, about the purpose of prayer, and about what to expect in the way of answers. Although we could share all sorts of examples, one evening prayer sticks out the most. After an evening conversation with friends about poverty and the outrageous number of preventable child deaths around the world, Luke, who was quite young at the time, was clearly moved by what he had learned. At bedtime, as his dad tucked him in and prayed with him, Luke said, "Lord, I pray for the 30,000 children who will die tomorrow... Please don't let them die... Well, I know that's not possible, so please let them have their best day ever... But of course it won't be their best day ever... so... Lord, please help us to stop this from happening."

Sometimes their prayers leave us awestruck. But at other times, their ability to integrate their whole lives into their prayers makes us smile. Jack is used to the "responsive classroom" at school and he once prayed, "I want to pray for all the poor people in the world, but that's a lot... God, there really are a *lot* of poor people in the world... Any questions or comments?"

To balance the open house, we've found it important that we all have the space and full permission to be ourselves, even if the result is not always very attractive. We think that living in a family is the most serious commitment to community that anyone will ever make. Unconditional love, forgiveness, and fresh starts are foundational in our family community, each of which is made real through God's grace. Many of our friends' families are rooted in varying traditions or values. Our family is firmly rooted in the Christian tradition and we all attempt to be followers of Jesus. And we hope that our daily actions and decisions reflect this.

Forming and Living a Christian Identity

It seems to me that aside from our prayers and external Christian practices, which certainly have their place, the most important way to identify as a Christian family is to actually follow the teachings of Jesus – together. Putting love, forgiveness, justice, peace, and reconciliation into practice is what forms Christian identity. Every day, Luke and Jack see and hear Jim helping to shape policies that make a difference in the lives of the poor and vulnerable, and they learn the importance of speaking up for those with no voice. To balance the usual brotherly arguments and bickering, I am often encouraged by conversations I overhear which show that what they hear in our family conversations is taking root. For example, after the tragic suicide of a young man who had been bullied and tormented for being gay, we had many conversations about gay bullying (and bullying of any kind) and how important it is to take a stand against it. One day when Jim was driving the boys to school, Jack told him about a problem with a child who was being a bully in his playground. Luke immediately offered Jack strong advice. "Jack, it's your job to stop that. You are an athlete, a smart kid, and the other kids like you. It's your job to stand up to the bullies and make them stop."

As we prepared to speak as a family at the 2012 CYNKC conference, we sat down and discussed together what it means to be Christian. Luke said his Christian faith expressed itself in service and the way he treats other people. Luke has always been very thoughtful and sensitive to others' feelings and needs, so it didn't surprise us last year when he told us that once a week after school he was going to help his mentor/coach with an after-school baseball program for underprivileged kids. Every Tuesday throughout the school year, he travelled on the metro to the school, taught baseball skills, and built relationships with these kids. He became a mentor to them.

Now Luke is in a public high school, which he chose to attend after being accepted at a fantastic private school because he wanted to be in a school that reflects the real world. We totally support this decision and feel certain that, with God's grace, Luke will find his way in life, being salt and light wherever he goes. His friends come from families of all faiths (and no faiths) and, for him, it is quite normal to be part of a crowd made up of people with all sorts of identities and who respect one another for who they are. I hope our children have learned the language of openness, acceptance, and appreciation of the strengths of the faith traditions of others, rather than judgment.

We often say that Jack lives in the security of his older brother. Jack is a carefree soul. He is a risk taker, he is funny, and he has a strong sense of self and will not ignore an injustice… including one against him. He is kind, he talks a lot, he's a star on his school's "Geoplunge" team, and he plays baseball, basketball, and soccer – all good Christian virtues! He walks a neighbour's dog twice a week for $4 a walk and is getting ready to ask for a raise. He is well-liked by his peers and will always say what he thinks. He doesn't doubt that he is a Christian, partly because that's what we are as a family (which is what I love about the theology of infant baptism, about which I could write enough to fill another chapter). I have no doubt that he will have lots of questions as he grows older and begins to figure out what his own faith looks like.

As Jack got ready to take the microphone in our family presentation at the CYNKC conference, he had a twinkle in his eye and proceeded to bring the house down several times. "First of all, I want to say… in the beginning, God created baseball!" Although he opened with a joke, he moved on to more serious observations about what it means to him to be part of a Christian family. "Being in a Christian family is a big commitment…sometimes you have to make difficult choices. Like sometimes you have to choose between church and baseball. Me…I usually choose baseball!" Some of the youth leaders in the audience were very kind to him afterwards and told him, "I'd choose baseball too!" Of course, Jack has had to make more difficult decisions than how to spend his Sunday mornings. But as he grows up, we hope and pray that when he is faced with tough decisions, he will remember that being Christian is a commitment that involves discerning the best path for following Jesus.

The Stories that Inform Our Lives

As a family, we try to find times to read and talk about the Bible. This usually takes the form of some prepared readings or devotional books that follow the church calendar. For example, in Advent, we have a giant Advent book that we pull out every year. Each page has a section of the Christmas story behind a door and Jack reads the story as each door is opened. We are not always successful in doing this on a regular basis, but we do what we can together.

We have found that one of the best ways to discuss theology or Christian faith is by talking about films and books. Jack proudly read *The Hunger Games* before he saw the movie and had some wonderful insights as we discussed the differences between the book and the movie. One of our favourite movies was *The Perfect Game*, which told the true story of a Mexican Little League team that won the Little League World Series in 1957. The resilience, determination, and faith of the players helped them overcome bigotry, great hardships, and the odds that were stacked against them. We really enjoy times when we see good movies together, or discuss books we've read, or talk together about world events and politics. These are all opportunities for our kids to see how our Christian faith informs and undergirds our views, perspectives, and actions in the world.

Recently our family went to see the movie *Lincoln*. We were especially interested in the presidency of Lincoln because Jim's newest book has a quote from Lincoln on the cover and is a rallying call for us all to embrace the "common good."[3] Although Jack is still young, he takes in and contributes much to our discussions about films like *Lincoln*, *The Hobbit*, *The Lord of the Rings*, and *The Chronicles of Narnia*. Only last week we all saw *Les Misérables*, which sparked all sorts of ideas and gave us lots to talk about as a family. It highlighted the importance of forgiveness and redemption. As a family, we talked about how both adversaries – the main characters – claimed God as their guide. Jean Valjean experienced a God of compassion and mercy, while the inspector's God was vengeful and legalistic. The power of the story enabled us to point to Jesus and the gospel stories of forgiveness, hope, and redemption.

The Village Priest

As for the mom in this family, I am privileged to be able to focus my energy in the communities in which our boys grow and thrive. I am the president of Jack's elementary school Parent-Teacher Association and the commissioner of Northwest Washington Little League baseball. I am sometimes referred to as the "village priest" in a world where it does indeed take a village to raise a child. At present we worship and minister at First Baptist Church in Washington, D.C., which I've found to be a little surprising for an Anglican priest.

When I was elected to serve as a Baptist deacon, I was reminded that we are what God calls us to be wherever that happens to be. I have discovered that priesthood is unconfined and spills over into all areas of my life – including raising a family. Whether or not the priest has a church, the vocation lives and finds expression. The priestly part of my being goes with me into Jack's elementary school, it goes with me onto the Little League baseball diamond, and it goes with me as we build a community of moms and dads who playfully call ourselves "the village" in our efforts to support one another as we raise our kids. I listen, I support, I pray, I encourage, I explain, I take initiatives. I am there in the middle of life in Washington, D.C., as a person, as a mom, and as a Christian; and from time to time God uses all this.

When I was a parish priest in England, I remember a bishop explaining that priests are paid a stipend as opposed to a salary. The stipend was a sum of money that enabled us *not to work;* it enabled us to be present to a community as a priest. This was quite liberating for me – I was not being paid for my performance as a priest but was financially enabled by the diocese to *be* a priest where I was.

These days I remain thankful for the grace of being able *not to work* and the great thing is that although I have chosen to be an "at-home" mom, the priest has not disappeared. I have discovered a wonderful integration of priesthood and family that is immensely satisfying. There is a richness about my life right now that makes me thankful that I have so much, if not all at once, of what priesthood and family life have to offer. And by God's grace, our family will continue to honour the "big commitment" of being Christian together.

Chapter 19

Yours, Mine, and Ours

David M. Csinos

When someone has a surname like mine, people often ask about it. For as long as I can remember, people have been wondering about how to pronounce my name and what culture it's from. I'm quick to reply that it's a Hungarian name. Sometimes I explain how to pronounce it in Hungarian. Once in a while I even mention what it means. (For those wondering, it means "sharp" or "good-looking.")

Because I have been asked by others to identify my cultural background for my whole life, it was easy to build this heritage into my identity. I've always known that I am Hungarian, and so did my classmates, coworkers, and friends. Growing up in northern Ontario, I was involved in the local Hungarian club, a community that instilled in me a sense of pride about my culture. I learned to play Hungarian folk music, dance traditional Hungarian dances, and even picked up some Hungarian words. In my family's house, we didn't wash dishes with a dishcloth, we used a *mosogatórongy*. And I have boxes filled with school projects and assignments that cover all sorts of aspects of Hungarian culture, from music and food to history and geography. Clearly, my Hungarian heritage and identity were (and continue to

David M. Csinos is the founder and President of Faith Forward, the organization born from the 2012 Children, Youth, and a New Kind of Christianity conference. He speaks regularly about faith formation and is author of several resources about ministry with young people, including *Children's Ministry that Fits* and *Children's Ministry in the Way of Jesus* (with Ivy Beckwith). Dave is a Teaching for Ministry Fellow and a doctoral candidate in practical theology at Emmanuel College of Victoria University in the University of Toronto.

DAVID M. CSINOS

be) sources of great pride for me. They helped me to know where I came from and gave me value as a member of a community. I have fond memories of my involvement with the local Hungarian society, through which I formed friendships, learned about my heritage, and came to understand why my surname tends to stand out.

But despite the joy, value, and pride that came with knowing I was Hungarian, the cultural identity I developed as a child was problematic. After all, my background is not only Hungarian. My paternal ancestors may have been from Hungary (actually, they were ethnic Hungarians who, because of post-World War II border changes, emigrated from land that had recently become part of Romania, but let's not complicate things further), but my maternal roots run in different directions. My maternal grandfather's family was British and had lived in Canada for many generations. But my mother's mother's genealogy goes back to a man named Barnabé Gagnon, who made the arduous journey from France to North America in 1620 when the European population of Nouveau France was only a few hundred.

So why didn't I know about this part of my background when I was a child? Why did I grow up defining myself as Hungarian and not also as one of the other cultures woven into me? How did my family lose the ability to speak Hungarian in only one generation, and why don't I speak English with the francophone accent that's shared by so many members of my mother's family? These are political questions with political answers. And how we answer these questions affects how we do ministry with children and youth in our world of cultural diversity. We need a perspective of diversity encased within mutuality, respect, and appreciation for one another's differences: for the sake of our children and youth, for the sake of the church, and for the sake of the world.

Triangulating Me

I grew up in a city in northern Ontario that, from my perspective, was defined by three major people groups. The first group consisted of white Canadians who spoke English as a first language. They were the ones who, at least to their own ears, "didn't speak English with an accent." This was the group that held power and privilege and didn't need to push or pull to exercise their rights and have their voices heard.

The second group consisted of French Canadians (or *Canadiens*). They bore privilege because of their white skin, but their privilege was undercut by their French names and accents. Like many French Canadians in other parts of Canada, this group tended to operate out of a collective memory of the conquest of the French at the hands of the British in the 1760s and the ongoing persecution that resulted from this defeat.

The third major group consisted of people of colour and immigrants, whose skin colour or language excluded them from one of the other groups. In a city marked by English-French tensions, members of this group held the least privilege, faced the most oppression, and experienced the most hostility.

Although I defined myself as Hungarian (rather than as one of the other ethnicities woven into my identity), my accent and my skin colour placed me squarely within the first group, the one that held the most privilege. And my perceived membership within this group coloured the way I grew up seeing the world and the way others saw (and continue to see) me. I took it as my prerogative to educate those who would define me as simply "Canadian" (read: white, English Canadian) about my true cultural background. I felt I had to work at being seen as Hungarian because this part of my identity remained hidden behind my visage.

But at other times, my hidden identity and sense of self protected me. Although I didn't name it as such, life in northern Ontario was marked by racism and ethnocentrism. And one way that these attitudes surfaced was through jokes told in the schoolyard. Sometimes the jokes were directed toward someone fitting within the immigrants and people of colour category, like the young son of a local couple whose schoolmates taunted him because of his Hungarian accent and his broken English. As I got to know their son, I learned that his schoolmates taunted him because of his Hungarian accent and his broken English. At other times, the jokes were at the expense of French Canadians. But while my identity included some of these "otherized" groups, personally I never became a punch line for these racist and xenophobic jokes. Regardless of the self-identity I held to, my accent (or lack of accent to some ears) and skin colour inducted me into the dominant Canadian culture. I was able to blend in and avoid having these insulting jokes directed my way in ways that my ancestors weren't so lucky.

I share these recollections as a way of locating myself within the complex context through which I write this chapter. I remain aware of the fact that I am a child of privilege, a child who is integrated into the dominant culture of my homeland, and despite my best efforts to avoid problematic ideas and phrases that assume cultural dominance and privilege I imagine I have not been able to shed them altogether. The effects of colonialism are woven deeply into my bones and despite my best efforts to overcome them I am left knowing that I often fall short.

The Politics of Multiculturalism

In the 1970s the government of Canada adopted an official policy of multiculturalism that was shared and strengthened across political parties throughout the latter decades of the 20th century. When I was growing up, federal dollars and policies supported countless initiatives to help people learn about the cultures that make up Canada. And I probably wouldn't have been involved in my local Hungarian society and I probably wouldn't be such a proud Hungarian if it weren't for those programs. Thanks to multiculturalism I learned about my heritage, was involved in multicultural events where I performed Hungarian music and dance, and – perhaps most importantly – developed a rich appreciation for the wonder that is Hungarian food. Multicultural policies and initiatives contributed to the development of my strong Hungarian identity. In a sense, then, I am a poster-boy for Canadian multiculturalism.

But after I moved away from Canada and returned a few years later, I began to see cracks in the multicultural veneer, cracks that had remained invisible to me until I temporarily removed myself from the culture and context in which I'd been raised. I began to realize that multiculturalism falls short of the ideals of mutuality, respect, and appreciation that I believe we need in our world of growing diversity. I began to see another side to multiculturalism, one that often remains hidden from those who have the privilege of being part of the dominant culture.

For one thing, multiculturalism can simplify and "essentialize" culture, a claim that Neil Bissoondath makes in his bestselling book, *Selling Illusions*.[1] It can cause people to see cultures as static, monolithic entities when in reality they are fluid, dynamic, and contain much internal variation. Furthermore, multiculturalism can force people to choose one aspect of their identity over several others. In my life, this meant waving the red, white, and green horizontal stripes of the Hungarian flag while ignoring the Union Jack, the Fleurdelisé (the flag of the province of Québec), and even, to a degree, the Maple Leaf. It's only been in the past few years that I've come to intentionally learn about my diverse family history and to embrace the multitude of cultures that work together to construct my sense of self. But as I do so, I see that my identity cannot be reduced to one culture or another. I now agree with author Lawrence Hill, who wrote, "I have many different sides. They all fit together into the configuration of who I am."[2]

Multiculturalism can also turn culture into a commodity and put it on display for others to "taste" without experiencing its full flavour. In this case, multiculturalism can rob culture of its life and make it stagnate as stereotype. In Bissoondath's words, "Culture becomes an object for display rather than the heart and soul of the individuals formed by it."[3] Multiculturalism assigns people (particularly people of colour, and immigrants) various roles as cultural "others" who must preserve and display a stereotyped heritage rather than evolve and adapt to new times and places, as cultures have always done. Rather than asking people to simply homogenize into the dominant culture, multiculturalism pushes the pendulum to the opposite, equally problematic end of the spectrum by encouraging people to maintain their cultural distinctiveness in ways that can rob cultures of their inherent evolutionary impulses.

Another problematic aspect of multiculturalism is that it can be used by dominant cultures to manage "otherness." It keeps the dominant dominating and keeps the marginalized at the margins. Multiculturalism proclaims that it's okay for people to live out their Indian, Trinidadian, Russian, or Congolese cultures – but they must do it according to the guidelines that the dominants set in place. "Feel free to live according to your own cultural traditions," multiculturalism might say, "but do it by our rules." An attitude like this often underlies toleration: "We'll tolerate you and your otherness, but we're not really going to accept you as one of us."

Sociologist Himani Bannerji argues that this dynamic creates a category of "insider-outsider" for people who at once do and do not belong to a society.[4] These "nominal citizens" are subject to the laws of the land but, because of their race or culture, aren't really seen as true members of

DAVID M. CSINOS

a society, a community, or even a congregation. This also applies to other forms of otherness, like gender, religion, sexual orientation, and ability.

In Canada, the term "visible minority" is often used to refer to non-European cultural groups. But this implies that there's also an "invisible majority" who maintains control and power. After all, it's through the eyes of the majority that minorities are deemed visibly so.[5] These majority groups, who are white, are seen as the cultural norm and in some cases their cultures are overlooked while the cultures of people of colour are accentuated.

I saw this normalization of the majority culture in a paper that a student wrote for a seminary class I was teaching. This student wrote about differences between "Hispanic churches" and "Christian churches," using these terms in a way that implied that non-Hispanic or white churches are the norm for Christianity while Hispanic churches are the cultural other. This way of ignoring the culture of the dominant majority helps to maintain their dominance, since the way they do things is seen as just the way things ought to be done.

Bissoondath believes that the idea of hyphenated cultural identity feeds out of and into this marginalizing process.[6] It encourages people who aren't part of the dominant culture to self-identify as a hyphenated citizen. European-Canadian folks who speak English as a first language are seen as "just Canadian," while those who don't share their skin colour or language are identified as Italian-Canadian, French-Canadian, or Chinese-Canadian. And south of the border, it may be common to hear adjectives like African-American, Asian-American, and Native American, but it's still rare to hear the term European-American. The hyphen becomes "a sign of an acceptable marginalization."[7]

I'm not trying to imply that cultural diversity is inherently negative or riddled with problems. In fact, I believe that cultural diversity is a blessing, a sacrament through which we can glimpse God and God's reign here on earth. But sin leads people, communities, congregations, and societies to hijack cultural diversity and use it in ways that maintain the status quo and even solidify the power already held by dominant groups. And when this happens, we need humility and courage to name and struggle against problems in our societies, our churches, and even our own lives as we encounter diversity in the world around us.

Learning and Unlearning Attitudes towards Culture

Often we pass on problematic ideas and attitudes about cultural diversity to younger generations without intending to do so. The harmful assumptions that lie behind multiculturalism are learned, but this means that they can be unlearned. We can change what we impart to young people, whether explicitly or implicitly, about what it means to be black or white, Francophone or Anglophone, Israeli or Palestinian, Tutsi or Hutu, and everything in between.

The dynamics at work within and behind multiculturalism also operate in many other contexts, including in churches. They can exist in the way we worship. The songs that churches sing, the silent attentiveness expected during homilies and sermons, the seats we sit on, the types of bread we break, and even how we meet together as churches; these practices evolved out of certain cultures and cultural norms. And because they are so deeply interwoven within Christian tradition, these cultural behaviours and the attitudes behind them can seem like they are given or endorsed by God.[8]

Culture also has a hand in how we understand the Bible, theology, and belief.[9] For much of church history, the plumb line for measuring orthodoxy and orthopraxy was largely based on dominant Western understandings of what it meant to think and act as a Christian person. And it's important to remember that this westernized version of Christianity is the one that justified "manifest destiny" and the colonial expansion, invasions, genocide, slavery, and wars that followed. While there are countless ways to read and interpret the Bible and the classics of Christian theology, so-called "correct" understandings are often dictated according to the dominant culture within a given context. Thankfully, some are now moving beyond culturally dominant theologies and biblical interpretations. But the road ahead is long.

The dynamics of multiculturalism also play out in how we educate Christians and how we pass on the faith to younger generations. Sunday school, educational programs, and practices used in the spiritual formation of young people are culturally based. For example, do we teach adolescents to memorize prayers or to pray spontaneously? Do we separate children and youth at church into age-segregated classes or do we expect them to join the rest of the congregation for corporate worship? Do we want children to silently pay attention to the teacher or do we want them to ask questions throughout a lesson? And if we want them to ask questions, do we expect them to raise their hands or just blurt them out? Everything we do to pass on the faith is related to culture.

For those of us who are part of the dominant and majority cultures in society and church, it can be easy to assume that the way we do things is the way things ought to be done. We might try to be welcoming of children and teenagers from cultures other than our own, but are we really just inviting them to come and do things the way we do them? This is a crucial question for churches. And it's a question that invites a different response to diversity than the shallow tolerance and oppressive hegemony of multiculturalism. It invites a response of interculturalism.

While some people use *multiculturalism* and *interculturalism* as synonyms, many in Canada are starting to use the word intercultural to subvert the racist and oppressive tendencies that underlie multiculturalism. For example, the United Church of Canada is intentionally moving toward being intercultural by asking how it can become a more justice-seeking and inclusive church that affirms and celebrates "diverse ways of being church together."[10]

United Church of Canada ethicist Roger Hutchinson calls for a view of interculturalism that "shifts the emphasis to encounters among persons and groups with cultural differences."[11] At its best, interculturalism moves the focus from issues of tolerance, assimilation, and integration to issues of mutuality, respect, and relationship. It proposes that one single ethno-cultural group no longer dominates a space, speaking instead about how, to use Hutchinson's words, "the public realm is, and should be, both *shared* and *contested*."[12]

Interculturalism changes our response to diversity from one of coexistence to the sharing of power; from inviting people into *our* churches to being willing to shape what it means to be church *together*; from worshipping in one way to worshipping in several ways. Faith communities no longer become something that is either *yours* or *mine*. They become *ours* as we live into our calling to be Christ's church together.

Interculturalism challenges the assumption that the way we've always done things is the way things ought to be done. And this challenge has been a driving force within new expressions of Christian faith that have sprung up not just in recent decades, but throughout the history of the church. Daring to make the church a place of interculturalism is one way of being faithful to the gospel in our contemporary, globalized world.

Clearly, interculturalism is disruptive and disturbing, at least for those who have heretofore been privileged. (For others, it can be quite liberating!) It disrupts socially conditioned and culturally constructed ways of being church and empowers us to work together to discover anew what it means to follow Jesus and be the church. It disturbs the way we do Sunday school, catechesis, confirmation classes, and youth groups as we learn from one another how people from different cultures do faith formation. It liberates us to explore new ways of nurturing faith in young people, a faith that is radically inclusive of the many cultures that exist in the world that God so loves.

Jesus and his early followers acted in intercultural ways and disrupted the orders of their day. Whether Joseph, Mary, and Jesus were becoming refugees in a foreign land, or Jesus was being opened to change through an encounter with a Syrophoenician woman; whether Philip was baptizing an Ethiopian, or the church in Galatia was reading that we are all one in Christ Jesus; it's clear that our God is a "boundary-breaking God."[13]

Following this God isn't easy.

And intercultural ministry isn't easy either. It takes courage and commitment to help children and youth think and act interculturally. That's why so many people opt for multiculturalism and its shallow approach to tolerance. It's fairly easy to welcome a family from Somalia, Syria, or another part of our own country to the way *we* do Sunday school or youth group. It is more difficult to open ourselves to being changed by the involvement of these families. When we think and act interculturally, we open ourselves to admitting that how we've always done it doesn't cut it anymore. We start recognizing that there are different *we's* who do things in different ways.

Toward Intercultural Ministry with Children and Youth

So how do we become leaders who foster intercultural communities? How do we integrate a spirit of interculturalism into ministry with youth and children?

An important step is to recognize the cultural nature of children's and youth ministry. When we acknowledge that the ways we minister with young people and the kinds of faith into which we form them come out of particular cultural assumptions and norms, we can become open to changing them in light of other cultures. This is a crucial first step in moving from monocultural or multicultural ministry to ministry that is truly intercultural; ministry that encourages relationships of mutuality, respect, and appreciation across differences.

Secondly, pastors, teachers, and parents can surround young people with diversity. We can expose them to cultures that are not our own or their own through books we read together, food we share with them, music we enjoy with one another, and so much more. Diversity can start simply. Instead of ordering pizza at youth events, why not serve kebabs, bannock, or couscous and vegetables? When we help youth and children encounter elements of diversity through our ministry with them, we help open their hearts and minds to tasting, touching, hearing, and seeing how people live their lives and their faith in all sorts of contexts and cultures.

A third idea is to invite and be invited. The Korean church down the road, the Mosque a few blocks over, the predominantly white church on the other side of town, even the Nigerian congregation that meets in your church building on Sunday afternoons: why not invite these folks to come and share with young people about how their cultures and faiths intersect? And perhaps a visit to their congregations will help the young disciples at your church get to know what it means to be part of faith communities that worship God and follow Jesus in ways that are different from their own.

We can also be open to the traditions of others. Or better yet, we can work across cultures to create new traditions with the young people in our midst. While some people rail against what they deem to be "cultural syncretism," a buzzword for a watering down of the gospel, when we accept that all aspects of Christian faith and tradition are culturally conditioned we can be open to working with young people across cultures in order to form new ways of practicing our common-if-varied faith. But as we explore different traditions and create new ones together, we need to guide young people as to how to question and affirm what faithfulness to God looks like in other cultures and in our own cultures.

Of course, being open to other traditions requires respect and appreciation for others and that we hold the view that culture and cultural traditions are gifts given by others. Like so much in scripture, interculturalism moves toward practices of one-anotherness. We must go out, forge new friendships, and wait for the gifts to be given, rather than pick and choose the parts of other's cultures that we find exotic, innocuous, or intriguing. Without this commitment, this practice can all too easily resemble the colonial tendency to co-opt other cultures, which is deeply disrespectful.

The way we read the Bible can help foster intercultural community and appreciation for diversity. What would happen if we read the Bible as a book that celebrates diversity as part of God's magnificent intention for the world? In *God's Big Table*, Elizabeth Caldwell writes that "the Bible offers us a way of seeing and understanding, a lens through which we can look and see the world in all its difference."[14] When helping young people enter God's story in the Bible, let's do so in ways that promote respect, appreciation, and mutuality among cross-cultural differences. True, the Bible has some stories of what seems like God-ordained cultural genocide, but it is also rich with narratives of people who crossed literal and metaphorical borders in their quest to be faithful to God.

Often when persons of majority cultures talk about diversity, they use their own culture as an assumed norm or reference point. I remember some teachers in middle school would talk to us about the way "we" do things and then teach us how "they" (Aboriginal, Pakistani, Peruvian, French-Canadian...) do things. Implicit in this language is an assumption that what *we* (members of the dominant culture) do is the norm and anyone who does things differently is, in a sense, abnormal. This is a tendency that we need to intentionally avoid in the spiritual formation of young people.[15]

Gradually and in age appropriate ways, as we live interculturally we can help children and youth notice and analyze racism and prejudice. This isn't easy. It involves dealing with tough questions and complex issues that even adults may struggle to understand and accept. And it involves not only uncovering prejudice out there in other people's homes, churches, and communities, but also finding it in our own places and lives. It may be difficult work, but it's part of what it means to live into God's kingdom here on earth.

And why should we stop at cultural diversity? We can help young disciples develop appreciation and respect for differences that exist in our abilities, our sexual orientations, our families, our gender identities, our faith traditions, and other manifestations of God's plan for a world of glorious differences.

The Challenge Before Us

Clearly, this is challenging work. And those of us who take up the task of nurturing an intercultural spirit with children and youth have our work cut out for us. We're going to make mistakes. We're going to say and do the wrong things sometimes. So we ought to remain open to being corrected and even rebuked by one another. We need to acknowledge the challenges that come with living interculturally within new kinds of Christianity. But welcoming diversity brings blessings with it as well. What would happen if we took time in every Sunday school class or youth group meeting for each person to list one way that they were challenged and one way that they were blessed by diversity during the past week?

In her brilliant children's book *Cain and Abel: Finding the Fruits of Peace*, Rabbi Sandy Sasso paints a mesmerizing picture of the Garden of Eden.[16] Through the Jewish art of Midrash, she describes the radical diversity that God kneaded into the dough of creation and set within the garden, a place where different kinds of fruit – orgapples, limeberries, pinangos, and banangerines – grow on the very same tree. It is an image of God's kingdom on earth, a place where there is room for all to live, grow, and thrive through mutual interconnectedness and appreciation.

Sadly, however, Martin Luther King, Jr. was right when he said that eleven o'clock on Sunday morning is the most segregated hour of the week.[17] We in the church have often dropped the ball of our mandate to be a church united across differences. But hope comes in the morning. We find ourselves at the dawn of a new day for the church. Let's seize this day and raise a generation of young disciples who live into God's plan for marvellous diversity.

Chapter 20

Drawing Future Maps in Pencil

Melvin Bray

While participating in the inaugural Children, Youth, and a New Kind of Christianity gathering, I put the finishing touches on a recording of a dramatic re-imagining of the Noah saga that I had been working on for some time. It was quite an emotional moment for me. Perhaps that was because before that point my story work had largely been my little secret, shared primarily with folks without professional interest in how we pass on faith to children and youth.

I've been involved in a writing project called *The Stories in which We Find Ourselves* for the past several years. It was inspired by my struggle (what was it Frederick Douglass said about struggle?[1]) with the frustration and annoyance I felt over having constantly to deconstruct the colonialism so deeply woven into the fabric of so many Bible story series. I couldn't help but wonder what foolishness and, worse yet, violence my children were absorbing from these stories in my absence (can a child "take fire in his bosom and... not be burned?"[2]). How would these colonial messages shape them? The possibilities disturbed me. So I started writing with an eye toward the future.

Melvin Bray is an Emmy® award-winning storyteller, writer, educator, and social entrepreneur embedded with his wife, three kids, and innumerable worms in the West End neighbourhood of southwest Atlanta, Georgia. He is an active member of several vanguard networks working to cultivate more sustainable approaches to life. On his favourite work days, Melvin gardens with kids (and occasionally with adults) and helps them discover what nature has to teach about life well lived. www.kidcultivators.org

However, the Noah saga represented a daunting test of my ability to see past the scripts of my own childhood. It's amazing how intractable those scripts can be, even though I had long ago deconstructed the basis for their power in my life. For example, as much as I realize that Christians seldom recount the Genesis telling of Eve and Adam but rather John Milton's telling of *Paradise Lost*, and I have myself gone back to re-imagine that script in technophonic detail, I still find myself wrestling with latent notions of depravity and fall and condemnation that weren't even explicitly embraced as doctrine in the denominational tradition in which I was raised.

So when it came to the story of Noah, all I could see was a story of God as Big PUN[3] (as in PUNISHER) who had gotten fed up with humanity and gone about the business of wiping the slate clean and starting over. I saw a cautionary tale of what happens when one gets on the wrong side of the Almighty. As the *brothas* in the *a cappella* quartets used to sing (and often still do), "It's gonna rain / It's gonna rain / Better get ready and bear this in mind / God showed Noah the rainbow sign / It won't be water but fire next time."

It strikes me as despairing if I really think about it. What hope is there in the eyes of that God? And then to discover that God would be so capricious as to save only Noah (and his family), one who would later do metaphorically the same to his own offspring by cursing them for seeing his nakedness as he stumbled about drunk (with power?), destroying his family's camp as he went. It's not only despairing; it's disgusting to think that this is a God to whom some allegiance is owed.

And it is this realization that Almeda Wright alludes to in her chapter when she speaks of "a time when the myths and narratives that sustained youth as children no longer work." This realization comes at different stages in life for different people. It happened for me in my early twenties. But Wright's statement inspires an interesting question. What if the process of deconstructing one's myths were to happen younger and younger?

Most of us first accept myths[4] at face value, the way they are handed down to us. But somewhere along the line, life happens. The stories around which we've organized our lives stop adding up to be consistent with the circumstances in which we and those around us find ourselves. In our stories, we see battle and victory in the name of our Lord. In life, we find the death and devastation that lie in the battle's wake. In our stories, we hear of a thing some have called "redemptive suffering." In life we see certain commonalities between those so often "called to suffer" and that becomes the source of indignation. In our stories, we tell of God creating Adam and Eve. In life, we encounter Adam and Steve, and recognize the spark of the divine in the love they share for each other and together for their own and other people's children. In our stories, we may catch the faint aroma of a call for religious purity. In life, we taste the global crises caused by a lack of respect for religious plurality. "What then shall we say to these things?"[5]

The natural tendency of any community bound together by certain ideological commitments is to doubt what contradicts its stories, which is not always a bad thing if one is holding out hope for the beauty of what can be. However, anyone involved in a thriving love relationship can tell you that neither faith, hope, nor love make one blind to the shortcomings and deficiencies of their circumstances. Quite the opposite. So why would we ever insist that those raised in the Christian tradition – let alone those adopted into it – must embrace not only the stories of our faith but also specific interpretive tellings of those stories, when we ourselves see their shortcomings and deficiencies? We shouldn't. We mustn't. And we do so at our own peril.

The perils I see come in at least two forms. One is the peril of those for whom the psychic dissonance in their uncritical belief systems becomes so great that for sanity's sake they have to leave those systems of belief behind. Sadly, the baby often goes out with the bathwater: God is abandoned as a result of the need to jettison certain untenable notions about God. In such a situation, how is someone supposed to keep one without the other? How can someone even tell the baby from the bathwater if no one has ever given her the resources to do so, or allowed her to cultivate her own? What criteria are we to use in determining what's inherent and what's construct to our understanding of God when we've never been allowed to raise the question?

The other peril is that of those who double down on their uncritical belief systems despite the evidence to the contrary. I'm convinced something insidious happens to the mind taught to deny the light of day. I fear that mind loses its ability to perceive truth. When we teach our children to embrace our prejudices and certitude and to argue for a thing that does not exist, long after the rationality of our argument has broken down, it has to impact their ability to function rationally in a broader perspective. Do we actually lose our reason, as Anton Chekhov's protagonist in *The Bet* suggests? Do we begin to take "lies for truth, and hideousness for beauty"? Do we "exchange heaven for earth"? If the ideas of abiding poverty in homage to the one who explicitly says "I never knew you" if we do; or maintaining our right to bear arms in the name of the Prince of Peace are any indications, we have good reason to think so.

Thus, we are left with one sensible option. We must tell better – more beautiful, more just, and more virtuous – stories.

I could elaborate, but it really is that simple. If we don't tell better stories, our children have no reason to continue on this journey with us. Without better stories, we don't have a credible answer for where we're headed, let alone how best to travel on the journey. What we do know is where we've been, and it's incredibly hard for a thoughtful person not to be pissed off by that, particularly if one has been on the oppressed end of the colonial experiment or the embattled side of the culture wars. While I believe it is true that the path that has brought us to this point has been far from what can be honestly called "the way of Jesus," my intuition is that the way of Jesus has been the only means by which we've escaped devastation heretofore. And my faith that the Jesus way, like true north, is discernible is the only reason I hold out hope that we can move in a positive direction together. However, I'd have no basis upon which to make these claims without some hint of a better story – this myth of the kingdom of God – than the ones I've known.

Mythologist Joseph Campbell provides explanation (a lot of it) for why our myths are so utterly important. Even though he's written volumes on the subject, his explanation is one of the most concise yet comprehensive. Campbell says myths serve four vital social functions:[6]

1. Myths awaken a sense of wonder before the mystery of being.
2. Myths explain the shape of the universe.
3. Myths affirm the existing social order.

4. Myths guide the individual through the stages of life.

Add to Campbell's list a fifth function espoused by historian William McNeill:[7]

5. Myths give humans the means by which to act in concert with one another (like instinct functions in other animals).

Without a whole lot of explanation, we can see how critically important each of these functions is in general. But we should also not miss the pertinence of each to our particular desire to sojourn in faith and community together. Without a sense of respect for the mystery of life, how can we appreciate one another's presence in it? How many battles have been fought over whose understanding of the shape of things is correct or true? Is it possible to hold a vision of the universe that acknowledges the abundant diversity of it as beautiful and the way it is meant to be? Without an understanding of our chosen social order (or options that run counter to it), how do our children find their places within it? What are our duties to ourselves, our families, our communities, our God-beloved world at each stage of our journeys through life? How do we move together in embracing our fleeting glimpses of God's hopes, dreams, and desires in the earth, particularly when those glimpses are taken from a variety of different vantage points?

These are some key questions (there are so many others), and our myths (our faith stories) help us to answer them. So we can continue to tell the story of Noah as the story of a pouty and petulant child-in-the-sky[8] who throws a tantrum because he doesn't like how others are playing. Or we can tell it anew as the story of a Creator bent on saving creation from drowning in the flood of its own hubris, and of a family the Creator challenges to exemplify the quiet grace of a neighbourliness powerful enough to forestall the flood, or at least ride it out.

Either way, perhaps the hardest lesson of all is learning to make room for more than one telling of the story. The band The Cobalt Season sings a song "Careful Not to Draw Your Maps in Pen and Ink," which opens and closes with the startling line, "You are going to change your mind someday." There are, of course, tellings of our faith stories that don't allow for this possibility. However, the journey on which we find ourselves in this volume not only allows for this possibility, it encourages it. It depends on it for its very life. We change our minds, and we should. How can anything live and grow yet stay the same? Take it from a gardener: it can't.

Scripture may tell us that God is the same yesterday, today, and tomorrow, but that cannot mean our understandings of God should be. So as we journey together, whether our traditions are the same or not, we look to hear the differences in how fellow travellers taste the divine or smell the divine at work in their stories. In so doing, our hearts are touched and our minds, our lives... changed.

The challenge is to preserve the space for this to happen; for ourselves as keepers of faith, and for the children and youth to whom we hope to pass faith along. One way to accomplish this is to pay attention to how we tell our stories. A few years back a friend of mine, Russell Rathbun,[9] did some work with me around how we read and process scripture. Though our backgrounds are littered with varying kinds of literary theory, textual criticism, and a whole mess of academic holdovers from theological training, we realized that our process is far more straightforward nowadays. Our work in homiletics and theatre led both of us to become storytellers: he as a Lutheran priest who dons a new character each week he preaches at his church; and me as some random friend of far too many pastors who thinks it more important to tell better stories within emergence Christianity than it is to just talk about them.[10]

Based on the notions that no telling of the biblical narrative is neutral (not even the biblical tellings), and that scripture can't be broken (so it doesn't need to be treated as "precious" in a *The Lord of the Rings* sort of way), Russell and I invited people to step inside the text as the Rabbis of old would:

> They bring themselves to it and step across the edge of the scroll onto its body, bouncing a little, believing it will hold their weight. And then on hands and knees crawl through the furrows of words, examining, brushing away dirt, not unlike a botanist examining growth patterns and evidence of the soil's mineral content, water content and whether there is deep clay below the cracks in the

soil from which the words emerged. The cracks and the gaps allow them a way in. [Rabbinical] Midrash is the exploration of the gaps. Stories and parables, proverbs and legal case studies come from mining these gaps. The text is changed by [the rabbis] having been there. There are footprints left behind, indentations, great hollowed out places and covered over, smoothed out portions. The tents of opposing camps are set in the text side by side. Conclusions leaned up against refutations, some decaying, some flourishing. Having once been an oral wisdom that required a speaker – and what is an individual speaker if not a unique interpreter – the text was not allowed to pass into stone, to become hardened, but was kept alive and fertile, even malleable. But with deep and unknown roots.[11]

And we asserted that it is the birthright of every person of faith to interrogate her or his stories in this way.

Russell and I took people through a reading of a common scripture narrative, giving them these directions:

1. Read the passage for what it says and doesn't say.
2. Think about how you have traditionally heard this story told.
3. List three things you love about the passage as you are now reading it.
4. List three things that have bothered you in the past about the story itself or the way the story is typically recounted.
5. Articulate three questions that come to mind when you think of this story.
6. Select one thing from each of the three preceding categories and use them to re-imagine the story.[12]

The responses to every facilitation of this simple process have been amazing. Once youth sink their teeth into the text in this way and find out that this is how a living tradition is supposed to function, they seldom want to let go. Russell and I call this kind of re-imagining of the biblical narrative "stories that compost."[13] Our hope is to pass along tellings of the stories of our faith that our children can use for as long as the stories nourish them. But when the stories cease to be of value, they can "psycho-degrade" if you will, and be reconstituted into something more relevant and useful for the specific times in which our children (or grandchildren) live. That starts, however, with current keepers of the faith – parents, teachers, children's ministers, youth workers, all of us – opening up that possibility by the way we handle our stories and articulate our expectations.

This is not to suggest that all paths lead forward, that every journey will bring life. To the contrary, some tellings of our stories lead back to from whence we came, which is not necessarily where we want to go. So how do we find true north and avoid making it up as we go along? If nothing else, every so often we happen upon a signpost left behind by those who have gone before us. I remember one that read, "Finally, friends, whatsoever things are true, whatsoever things are honest, whatsoever things are just, whatsoever things are pure, whatsoever things are lovely, whatsoever things are of good report; if there be any virtue, and if there be any praise, think on these things."[14] As long as we continue to hold these virtues dear as we re-imagine our myths, they will do their good work.

It is fairly certain that we find ourselves in uncharted – not completely unfamiliar, but uncharted – territory this side of the new millennium. We need to remain mindful of who we are and where we come from. We need to remember the allure of the better place we seek. We need better stories; we need new maps. Remembering The Cobalt Season's advice, might I suggest going forward we map our journeys in #2 pencil (with a good eraser close at hand) as a way of signifying to our children that our confessions of faith are simply the best we've apprehended to this point. Better yet, let's draw our new maps in a Google doc[15] so it can track changes for us and allow for real-time, collaborative updating.

Remembering our stories is important. Far from trying to undermine the sanctity of our faith stories, I want to see them alive and vital for time to come. Otherwise I wouldn't put the energy I do into reminding people of them. When I think back over my own cultural story, I can't help but be in awe of the ancestral wisdom found there. I often speak of post-this and new-kind-of-that, but not for one nanosecond is it lost on me that the seeds of all I am lie in the stories of those who came before me. It's amazing to me how effective our forebears were at distilling great truths into a few words. For example, they would sing, "Walk together children / don't you get weary / there's a great camp meeting in the Promised Land," and in those simple words imply just about everything salient said herein.

Our journeying is not just for us. It is for our children. In fact, we may not get to the Promised Land with them, but we have to keep alive for them the memory and hope of the promise given. The way has been and will likely continue to be wearying, but the important thing is that we walk it together. And we have this song, which in itself is a story that binds us together as pilgrims of a common hope. The story tells of a great camp meeting – a gathering of the Creator's good creation – just over the horizon, where all are welcome. And if we just keep walking, finding new ways to tell our stories so that all can hear them and all can be heard, we will get there together.

Mapping a Lifelong Journey

We are disciples in training,
we're learning from the master,
we're on the road with Jesus,
wherever he may lead.

We are disciples in training,
we're part of the adventure,
we're on this road together,
let's see where it will lead!

–Bryan Moyer Suderman[1]

Chapter 21

So the Gift Can Be Given:
The Journey of Faith Formation
John H. Westerhoff, III

I was amazed by the eclecticism of the group of people who gathered in Washington, D.C., for the 2012 Children, Youth, and a New Kind of Christianity conference. Perhaps the group was so eclectic because we do not represent any ideology, only that we are people on a search. But while we come from all kinds of places and all sorts of traditions, we have a question in common. And that common question is what brought us together.

That question is, how do we nurture faith in children and youth? And not just any faith, but a faith that is living, imaginative, curious, provocative, beautiful, seeking, peace-loving, and healing.

For the past 55 years, I've been striving to answer different versions of this common question. And I would like to share my search. To help us ask some new questions and search for new answers, I'll create the rhetorical equivalent of a Jackson Pollock painting. Pollock was a contemporary artist who would place a canvas on the floor and splash and dribble colours all over it. And something would be created. That's what I'm going to do in this chapter; splash some words, spread around some questions, dribble a few ideas, and hopefully create something that you might want to look at and reflect on.

John H. Westerhoff, III was professor of theology and Christian nurture at Duke University Divinity School for 20 years. An Episcopal priest, he has published over 500 articles and 34 books, including the classic *Will Our Children Have Faith?* He serves as Priest Associate and Resident Theologian at Saint Anne's Episcopal Church in Atlanta, Georgia.

Making Sense of the Present

In order to make sense of the present or to envision a possible future, we need to try to remember the past, at least as we experienced it. As William Faulkner wrote, "The past is never dead. It's not even past."[1]

We are our stories. And so we need to continually ask what we remember, and why we remember what we remember. There are some things we remember, some things we never remember or refuse to remember, and some things that we remember that never really happened. But what's stored in those memories is important because we are our stories. Each of us has a story and those stories are always in relationship with God's story. And out of this conversation involving our personal stories, our common stories, and God's story, we are able to discern new answers.

Memory is a matter of writing history. And history is very complex. It is a work in progress. It's something we are always revising. No single account of the past can ever completely describe it. And so I'm going to look at the past with very broad strokes. And I admit that the past that I'm going to discuss is primarily in the tradition of the Western world, because that is my context. But I am aware that it doesn't represent a total or even accurate understanding of the past.

I've found it helpful to reflect on history in terms of ages and transition periods. Transition periods run about 100 years and ages run for a few centuries. In the first century we entered into the Apostolic Age; the fourth century saw the birth of the Age of Christendom; the 10th and 11th centuries birthed the Age of Faith; and then came the Age of Reason (or the Age of Modernity) in the 16th century. It is this age that many people today continue to call their own even though, as evidenced all around us, we are transitioning out of modernity and into a new period.

In transitioning from the Age of Faith to the Age of Reason, the Western world depreciated the importance of intuitive thinking and knowing, which is nurtured primarily through the arts. The intellectual way of thinking and knowing, nurtured primarily through the sciences, replaced intuition. One must remember that this is not a question of either-or, but one of both-and. We need to keep intuition and intellect together. But in the Age of Reason, humanity basically denied intuition, and everything began to change, including how we define ideas and terms. There were huge shifts in understanding. For example, faith came to mean propositional truths or beliefs rather than perception; and ethics focused on particular moral behaviour rather than character. It is this Age of Reason that we were born into. For many of us, it's the only world we've ever known.

Some who were living during the transition between the Age of Faith and the Age of Reason rejected the new age. Within the church, those who rejected reason went underground, so to speak, and began to create anti-intellectual movements. For them, the church became a place where thought and reason weren't used because these would only cause difficulty. Some also became literalistic. They took everything literally and forgot that the gospel is a story. And if we take any story literally, we destroy the story because we miss out on what it's really about.

After about 500 years of prioritizing reason over all other ways of knowing, many have recognized the limits of over-reliance on the rational mind. Particularly since World War II, astute individuals have been wondering what it may mean to bring intuition back into the world. It's not going to be easy: that much is clear. After all, the first people fired and the last people hired in schools teach the arts. And if art is taught at all, it's often the history or philosophy of a particular art and rarely the practice of the arts themselves (they have special schools for the arts).

The church has depreciated the arts in its educational programs. Most of what we do in the church that we call art isn't art at all. So the church has often rejected the arts, accepted the arts but failed to use them, or misused them. Sunday schools may put an art activity at the end of a lesson, but rarely is dance, the visual arts, music, drama, or any other art form the primary means for teaching and learning. We are more apt to teach what the Bible says than to interpret the Bible through the arts.

Our Transition Period

I'm convinced that the key to understanding any historical age is to understand its transition period. We have been in transition from the Age of Reason (the Age of Modernity), since the 1950s, which is when I was beginning the study of theology. I have experienced the end of the Modern Age and the birth of postmodern times. Although the word *postmodern* is used in many different ways, I use it to speak of this period of transition that seemed to begin in the 1950s and is only now starting to come to a close as a new age is birthed.

And so if this transition, like others, lasts about a century, then we're in the middle of it. Living in a transition period is much more difficult than living in an age in which there's some stability.

The challenge of living in a transition period necessitates that we engage our imaginations to discern what is needed in a new age. Something was lost in the Age of Reason (and something was gained – we shouldn't only judge it negatively). But there are limits to modernity's way of thinking and being present in the world. During this transition time, we need to experiment with alternatives.

Technology is one aspect of this transition period that we need to examine imaginatively. I believe that, while it connects us in new ways, digital technology can also reinforce loneliness. I don't think that technology is inherently negative, but as MIT professor Sherry Turkle points out, the way that we often use it adds to the sense of loneliness and isolation when we don't counter it with intimacy and community, both of which we need and search for. And fostering community and intimacy is one role for the church in this transition period, because the church is called to be counter cultural, offering the opposite of what the culture is offering.

Digital technology and globalization have also led to the "shrinking" of the world. All of a sudden we live in a smaller world and we have to interact with people from different cultures, religions, and social realities. Suddenly humanity is brought together across different religions, different cultures, different memories of history, and we find that not everyone wants to follow in the ways of the Western world.

An earlier product of modernity predating digital technology and globalization is specialization. Everything became specialized. From physicians to clergy, people were educated in highly specialized fields. In the church and seminary, this meant dividing theology into three parts: foundational (or dogmatic) theology, which established the basic foundations of Christian faith; systematic (or constructive) theology that explored how to make these foundations appertain to particular people; and practical (or applied) theology, which applied ideas developed in the other two fields to those practicing the faith. Each of these fields in turn developed a number of specialized sub-fields. In my own discipline of practical theology, areas such as homiletics, ethics, pastoral care, spirituality, ecumenism, and catechesis (teaching and learning) all emerged.

Another product of modernity is functionalism, which objectified the world. Functionalism is about what we do as human beings. Doing replaced being. We became defined by what we do and our worth was bound up with our function in the world. In the church, we got busy trying to perform our functions of care and service in the world, sometimes forgetting that being cared for and being served is also necessary and can give a person worth. We were always trying to *do* something and that's how we messed up the world. We thought that we were building God's reign, forgetting that God builds it, God has already built it, and we are to abide in it, to live as if it's here in its fullness until it can come in its fullness. We are meant to *be* in God's reign, which is a very different thing than building God's reign (but that's not to say that our actions in the world don't matter!). The church is to be a mission, not have one.

Modernity made it easy to forget that life is not all doing. And our consequent one-sided view led us to hold problematic conceptions of children and adults. Modernity defined a child as being dependent, non-rational (intuitive), and non-productive (playful). Adults came to be defined as people who are independent, rational, and productive – qualities held up as desirable during this age. This led to a split in how we understand children and adults. We turned human beings – children, adolescents, and adults alike – into objects for study so that we could understand and control them. For example, ever since G. Stanley Hall wrote a book called *Adolescence*[2] in 1904, we have believed that adolescence exists. We rarely ponder if the phenomenon really exists. Perhaps it's a social construction of reality.

This, by the way, is also what we have done with scripture. Modernity has turned the scriptures into pieces of literature for us to analyze. Instead of a book that questions us, we turn scripture into a book that we question. This is a result of seeing the world as an object and seeing ourselves as doers, a product of the Age of Reason.

Another product of modernity is institutionalization. The church became seen as an institution, a highly structured organization with a specialized purpose (for example, religion). Some people today, as a reaction to this, want to express their Christian faith without being part of the church. And when church is perceived solely as an institution, this seems possible. But while the church has some of the characteristics of an institution, it must be much more. Church is people on a way, people learning together to follow Jesus. So it is impossible to be Christian and not be part of the church, at least when the church is seen as the Body of Christ rather than as one institution among many.

We need to distinguish between the church as an *institution* and as a *community of faith*. We can have faith without an institution, but we can't have faith in relation to God without a community. We are communal beings by definition. No one can be human alone. One person is no person. One Christian is no Christian.

But even our discussions about communities of faith can become functional (and this is what leads to institutionalization). Christians often talk about building a community – a functional idea. But we can't *build* a community. Community is a gift from God. Nevertheless, there are certain criteria we can meet and follow so the gift can be given.

People on the Way

A community has a common story that holds people together. We are our stories, and our stories encompass our interpretations of our existence and our memories. We who are Christian share a common story – God's story – that helps us to understand our personal stories.

Communities may also have a common authority, such as scripture, tradition, reason (reflection on experience), and this authority is a resource for our thinking and decision making. When a community has a common authority, it can make room for a vast number of differences. But if all members do not have the same authority, they will just argue and fight and pass each other like two ships in the night. A common authority holds the community together.

Communities of faith share a common ritual or liturgy (liturgy means "the work of people"). Common rituals shape our faith, character, and consciousness. Our daily life and our cultic (or ritualistic) life are directly related to each other. Our daily life influences our worship, and our worship and prayer influence our daily life.

This brings us to a common life, the final aspect of communities of faith that I'll mention. At their best, faith communities are more like families than institutions. In a family, life is encompassed and lived together. In institutions, we specialize. In families, it's the total person that is important. In institutions, we become task-oriented and people are known by what they do. Emotions in a family (at least in a healthy family) can be expressed. But in institutions, emotions need to be kept at bay. Families keep customs and covenants out of love. Institutions keep laws and regulations through contracts. In a family, it's your being that is valued. In institutions, performance, or behaviour, is valued.

Three Perspectives on Human Nature

Christian educators have conceived of human nature in different, distinctive ways. And the way we understand human nature greatly influences how we understand and do ministry with children and youth.[3]

One way to conceive of human nature is in terms of chronological age. From this perspective, we speak of childhood, adolescence, emerging adulthood, adulthood, old age, and so on.[4] Life is seen as a cycle, a process of aging. The metaphor for the curriculum or the course to be run within this understanding of human nature is to see the learner as a valuable piece of raw material. The teacher or adult is understood as a skilled technician. And the process is one of moulding each piece of raw material into the adult's predetermined design. We do things *to* young people. And so we set up our programs (and I use this word intentionally) to mould children and adolescents into our notions of what it means to be adult, to be faithful, to be Christian.

A second way of understanding human nature is as a series of developmental stages, as a process of maturation. As people grow, they mature from one stage to the next, from a lower (and less-desirable) stage to a higher (and more valuable) stage. In this understanding, the metaphor is now that of a greenhouse. The child is a seed. The teacher or parent is a gardener. And the process is one of caring for each individual seed until it grows in the way that it is inherently supposed to do so. But of course, the gardener always has a book on plants and their growth, a manual for how much water to give, how much fertilizer to add, and how much sun or shade is needed, all so the seed can develop into a whole plant. In this understanding, we don't do things *to* young people, but *for* young people.

But there is a third possibility, one that envisions human beings in terms of characteristics of life, characteristics of being human. This means thinking less about events or stages of life and more about relationships. Rather than bringing people together by age or developmental stages, community centres on interests. For example, a drama group can include young children, teenagers, and older people because they are all interested in acting. If we organize by interest, we may end up with a group consisting solely of fifth-grade girls, but this is not intentional segregation based on age or gender. Perhaps they are the only ones interested in some particular subject. They come together not because they are fifth-grade girls, but because they share a common interest, a common need, a common characteristic of life.

This perspective naturally fosters intergenerational communities. And as these communities are received as gifts, members can help one another learn and grow together. And so the metaphor is not one in which adults do things *to* or *for* young people, but *with* young people. The metaphor for being with each other is that of pilgrimage. The child is a pilgrim. The adolescent is a pilgrim. The adult is a pilgrim. And the community consists of co-pilgrims who do things *with* each other. The child and adolescent have as much to offer the adult as the adult has to offer the child and adolescent. They need one another. They can all share their stories.

While we are all pilgrims on a common journey, the pathways we take are different. There are multiple pathways possible on the Christian journey. And our abilities, interests, and preferences are some of the qualities that determine which pathways we choose and which are more appropriate for us. It is like climbing a mountain: some people want to follow a well-worn trail and others want to bushwhack. Take a compass bearing and head up over the cliffs. There are different ways of making pilgrimage.

A (Not-So-) New Understanding of Faith

This third perspective calls for a new understanding of faith (or perhaps it is really an ancient definition). During the Age of Reason, faith became synonymous with belief. Faith meant believing *that* something is true.

Faith became a set of propositional truths to be accepted intellectually.

While this is how faith has been understood during modernity, it is not the only way that the church has understood it. I believe that faith is best understood as perception – how we see, imagine, and envision reality. The way we perceive reality is what is real to us. In fact, perception is not just perception; perception *is* reality. There is no reality apart from perception. How we see things is the way they are for us. After all, we are the images we create.

So faith is not a set of cognitive beliefs that we have to accept as true. It is a way of seeing the world. This is why the creed begins in Latin with the word *credo*. This word translates as "I believe in," not "I believe that." This is a very important distinction, for to say "I believe that," is to say that I believe something is true. But to say "I believe in," has another meaning entirely. A less literal translation would be "I give my love to," "I give my loyalty to," "I give my heart to a particular image of God." It's less about literal truth and more about fidelity, love, and relationship.

In this second understanding, doubt is not a lack of faith. In fact, without doubt, you cannot have faith; but with faith, you will always have doubt. Certainty, then, is a lack of faith. This idea makes sense when we perceive truth as opposites in a healthy tension. In this view, heresy is seen as a truth-gone-mad. A heresy may possess truth, but it's a truth that has denied its opposite. A simple example is that Jesus is both fully human and fully divine – an absolute impossibility. If we go too far one way or the other, human or divine, we have a heresy. Somehow we have to maintain these opposites in a healthy tension. Similarly, faith and doubt are not mutually exclusive. Faith and doubt are opposites that must be held in a healthy tension.

Faith is foundational to our perceptions of life and to our imaginations. Through the imagination, in spite of all evidence to the contrary, we see God present and active in our lives. There are two ways to think and know: the intellectual and the intuitive, through use of reason and imagination. The intellectual is shaped by scientific method and the intuitive by the arts: music, drama, dance, visual art. Faith is also foundational to our character, our dispositions to behave in particular ways. And faith is foundational to our consciousness, our awareness that makes particular experiences, like the grace of God, possible.

We who care about the faith of young people need to recapture this understanding of faith if we are ever going to bring up our children in the Christian life of faith.

Made, Not Born

Tertullian, one of the early church fathers, had a lapidary phrase that "Christians are made, not born." This was a radical idea. In the ancient world, a person was a Jew because her mother was a Jew. A person was a Muslim because his father was a Muslim. But within Christianity, having Christian parents was not going to make you a Christian. Christians are made, not born. Parenthetically, Christians cannot "be made," as in they cannot be shaped or manipulated into being. There are many influences within and around, but each person is free to accept or reject these institutions.

But what does it mean to make Christians? How do we "grow up young Christians" as Shane Claiborne says in the foreword to this book? The answer, I believe, is "catechesis," a Greek word that literally means "to echo."

When the early church used the word *catechesis*, it referred to echoing the Word, which is a person, Jesus. So catechesis is to echo Jesus, to reproduce Jesus, to become Christ-like. It is a lifelong journey of becoming Christ's presence in the world.

Thus, catechesis is related to our learning to teach as Jesus taught. Jesus didn't teach through the schooling-instructional model that was common in his day as well as today. He didn't teach through lectures, memorization, and the regurgitation of information. He taught a way of life that was based on a particular faith, on a way of seeing life, understanding life, and imagining life. Jesus taught a way of living based on our identity as believers in Jesus Christ and members of his church. Catechesis is the uniting of knowing and doing, of orthodoxy and orthopraxis.

So we are called to teach as Jesus taught. Jesus said, "Identify with me, observe how I live, and imitate me." That's what it means to be Christian and that is what we are called to do as the Body of Christ, as the church. We're called to live out this call to radical ongoing discipleship. And we're called to make new disciples of Jesus.

Over the years people have asked me what I think a Christian looks like. I find this question misguided because there is a difference between a noun and an adjective. To be *a* Christian is to use the word *Christian* as a noun, as an object. So if somebody asks, "Are you a Christian?" it can be very easy to answer in the affirmative. But if someone asks, "Are you Christian?" responding becomes more difficult. To be Christian is to be Christ-like. So a person may be forced to respond to this question by saying, "Am I Christian? At noon, somewhat. By 4:00 p.m., iffy. By 8:00 p.m., not at all." It is easier to be *a* Christian than it is to be Christian, and it is easier to teach people how to be a Christian than it is to teach them how to be Christian, to be like Christ. It is easier to create programs that help young people learn all about Christianity than it is to help them learn how to be Christ-like.

Catechesis has three distinctive elements: instruction/training, education, and formation.

Instruction and training are how a person acquires the knowledge and skills necessary for living in a Christ-like manner. But all too often we focus only on knowledge (such as learning what the Bible says) and we ignore the skill of learning to interpret it. It isn't enough for us to know about the Bible; we need to acquire the skill of interpreting the Bible. It isn't enough for us to know what is right and wrong; we need to know how to make moral decisions and to discern God's will. In other words, it's not enough for us just to know about theology, about what Christians believe; we must learn to think theologically.

Education is a natural process of reflecting on experience. Experiences only become spiritual when we reflect on them. Education assumes a process of reflecting critically on our lives, day by day, in order that we might become more faithful and more like Christ.

The problem is that instruction and education are better suited for adults than for children. What young people need more than instruction/training and education is formation.[5]

Formation is a process of enculturating a person into the Christian life of faith. It is similar to an apprenticeship. Churches need to provide environments where children along with adults can participate in and practice the Christian life of faith.

Christian formation involves a number of interrelated, intentional lifelong processes, such as the organizing of our life together, the use of our time and talents, how we ask others to use their gifts, how we live day by day, who our role models are, how we practice discipline, how we speak, how we critically reflect on the world around us. Our responses to these concerns are central to the spiritual formation of our young people.

I would like to reflect on just two of those concerns as examples. First, we need to show young people what it means to resist. And by this I mean that we need to demonstrate how to identify and resist the influences of evil and injustice that are present in our contemporary experience.

Second, how we interact with each other is important to learn. If we treat each other with kindness, if we honour each other, respect each other, show one another compassion and love, then we model the dignity of every human being and the image of God that is in them. Instead of splitting off into new communities of faith because we can't get along with one another, we can show children what it means to love and respect one another, even though we may disagree with each other. And we can go outside of our own faith communities and demonstrate how to honour and treat with dignity those who are members of other churches, religions, cultures, sexual orientations, gender identities, abilities, and so on.

A Painting Completed

And so I come to the final drops of paint on this canvas. I have not said all I have to say on this important topic of nurturing new kinds of faith in children and youth. But hopefully the painting I have created is one that you want to look at and reflect upon on your journey to be Christian with another generation in our common quest to be like Christ and to echo Christ in a community of faith.

Almost 40 years ago, I asked if our children will have faith. Now more than ever, I am convinced that faith is formed in communities of faith. As we live together as disciples of the risen Christ in our contemporary, postmodern world, we can walk together in ways that make the gift of God our own.

Notes

Introduction

[1] "New World Coming" words by Bryan Moyer Suderman on CD *Detectives of Divinity.*

Signpost: Unloading Our Ideological Guns

[1] I Can Hear Your Message" by Bryan Moyer Suderman, from the CD *A New Heart.*

Chapter 1: After the Maps Change: Children, Youth, and a Church Yet to Be – Brian D. McLaren

[1] David Kinnaman, *You Lost Me: Why Young Christians Are Leaving Church… and Rethinking Faith* (Grand Rapids: Baker, 2011), 21.

[2] Kinnaman, *You Lost Me.*

[3] This is the topic of my book *Why Did Jesus, Moses, the Buddha, and Mohammed Cross the Road? Christian Identity in a Multi-Faith World* (New York: Jericho, 2012).

Chapter 2: Confessions of a Sunday School Superstar – Janell Anema

[1] Ralph Waldo Emerson, "Resources," in *The Works of Ralph Waldo Emerson, vol. 8: Letters and Social Aims* (Boston: Fireside, 1909).

Chapter 3: In Search of a Raceless Gospel – Starlette McNeill

[1] "Jesus Loves the Little Children" words by C. Herbert Woolston (1856–1927).

[2] For example, the Hamitic curse is associated with Genesis 9:18–27. But "nothing is said in Genesis about the descendants of either Ham or Canaan being Negroes. This idea is not found until the oral traditions of the Jews were collected in the Babylonian Talmud from the second century to the sixth century A.D. In this source, the descendants of Ham are said to be cursed by being black." Thomas F. Gossett, *Race: The History of an Idea in America* (New York: Oxford University Press, 1997), 5.

[3] Winthrop D. Jordan, *The White Man's Burden: Historical Origins of Racism in the United States* (New York: Oxford University Press, 1974), 51.

[4] Ibid.

[5] 2 Corinthians 5:14–18 (NRSV).

[6] A term coined by sociologist John McKnight, *redlining* is a practice wherein African-Americans or those socially coloured black were denied mortgages in an effort to ensure that particular neighbourhoods were not integrated. A red line was drawn on a map to indicate where banks would not invest.

[7] Isaiah 11:6.

[8] Michael Omi and Howard Winant, *Racial Formation in the United States: From the 1960s to the 1990s* (New York: Routledge, 1994), 55.

[9] Ibid. 55–56.

[10] John Calvin, *The Institutes of the Christian Religion*, 1536 ed., trans., Fred Lewis Battles (Grand Rapids: Eerdmans, 1995), 15.

[11] Matthew 5:3 (NRSV).

[12] Romans 8:37 (NRSV).

[13] Romans 12:2.

[14] 2 Samuel 16:7.

[15] This phrase is commonly employed by African-American preachers to describe the powerful nature of the cross and Christ's resurrection (see Revelation 1:18).

[16] William H. Willimon, *Peculiar Speech: Preaching to the Baptized* (Grand Rapids: Eerdmans, 1992), 7.

[17] Ibid., 12–13.

[18] Helmut Thielicke, *The Freedom of the Christian Man* (New York: Harper & Row, 1963), 10.

[19] Quoted in Thielicke, *The Freedom of the Christian Man*, 15.

[20] Romans 2:11.

[21] "God is not a racial, national or denominational deity... [so] there is no racial discrimination in God's family." T. B. Maston, *The Bible and Race: A Careful Examination of Biblical Teachings on Human Relations* (Nashville: Broadman, 1959), 24–25. What I am arguing for is a post-racial theology, a theology that does subject God to the stereotypes and prejudices of race. This theology can also be defined as pre-racial in that race did not exist before God. Thus, the goal is for the Christian faith to be purged of this social construct.

[22] John 17:22 (NRSV).

Chapter 4: Welcoming Rainbow Kids – Melinda Melone

[1] David Kinnaman and Gabe Lyons, *unChristian: What a New Generation Really Thinks about Christianity . . . and Why it Matters* (Grand Rapids: Baker, 2007).

[2] Brian McLaren, *A New Kind of Christianity: Ten Questions That Are Transforming the Faith* (New York: HarperOne, 2010).

[3] The "It Gets Better" project is a series of videos on YouTube initiated as a response to several suicides by LGBTQ youth. Each video encourages young people to hang on and gives examples of how life gets better for LGBTQ folks as we get older.

[4] "Clobber Passages" are those few Bible verses that are used to condemn homosexuality and, too often, homosexual people. It's important to be aware of them and avoid arguing about them, for when scripture is used as a weapon, nobody wins. Clobber passages include Genesis 19:1–11 (Sodom), Leviticus 18:2 and 20:13 (abomination, death penalty), Romans 1:21–27 (unnatural), 1 Corinthians 6:9–10 and 1 Timothy 1:9–11 (sin lists), and sometimes Genesis 1 and 2 (Adam and Eve, not Adam and Steve).

[5] However, the term "queer" has negative associations for some people, especially older gay men.

[6] Videos available on YouTube.

[7] Another cute take on this issue is the "Genderbread Person" infographic by Sam Kellerman on the website, "It's Pronounced Metrosexual," http://itspronounced metrosexual.com/2012/03/the-genderbread-person-v2-0/, accessed May 26, 2013.

[8] Sometimes these people encourage those with "same sex attraction(s)" to act, and even marry, in opposition to their feelings, not acknowledging that by attempting to do so, LGBTQ people may do themselves (or their spouses and families) possible harm.

[9] For more information, see http://www.gaychristian.net/greatdebate.php? and http://www.gaychristian.net/eric_buildingrelationships.php?$FBB_SESS.

[10] "Side B" adherents may support marriage equality politically, but do not support same-sex sexual relationships as an option for Christians.

[11] "Side X" members are rare in GCN and are usually moving toward more accepting positions.

[12] GCN has hosted Tony and Peggy Campolo as speakers at their annual conference to model unity despite different opinions and views. Tony holds to "Side B" and Peggy affirms "Side A."

[13] Young people who don't have a mother or a father, or have two or more of each, can feel excluded, confused, and hurt by the emphasis on these exclusive holidays if they are celebrated in more traditional ways. I've known some organizations to move toward a "Loved Ones Day" celebration in late May as an alternative to both Mother's Day and Father's Day. Another option may be to celebrate Mother's Day

and Father's Day, but in ways that are explicitly inclusive by including "spiritual mothers" and "spiritual fathers," grandparents, godparents, and other people who children hold close to their hearts. Inclusiveness may also mean encouraging children to make more than one card or to recognize more than one person or people who don't fit traditional parent categories.

[14] There are thousands of local and national organizations serving rainbow kids, including many faith-based ones. Some of my favourites include Believe Out Loud, CO-LAGE, GLAAD, GLSEN, HRC, National GLBT Youth Hotline, NGLTF, PFLAG, SoulForce, The Trevor Project, and Welcoming Resources.

Chapter 5: Rescripting Youth Education – Carl Stauffer

[1] Donna Hicks, Dignity: The Essential Role It Plays in Resolving Conflict (New Haven/London: Yale University Press, 2011).

[2] Paul Richards, Fighting for the Rain Forest: War, Youth and Resources in Sierra Leone (Oxford : James Curry, 1996).

[3] Names have been changed in order to protect identities.

[4] Paulo Freire, Pedagogy of the Oppressed (New York/London: Continuum, 1970).

[5] Augusto Boal, Theater of the Oppressed (London: Pluto, 1979).

[6] Advocates for Youth, "Youth and the State of the World," http://www.advocatesfor youth.org/publications/455?task=view, accessed May 26, 2013.

[7] Firoze Manji and Sokari Ekine, eds., African Awakening: The Emerging Revolutions (Cape Town Dakar Nairobi Oxford: Pambazuka, 2012).

[8] Jane Vella, Training through Dialogue: Promoting Effective Learning and Change with Adults (San Francisco: Jossey-Bass, 1995).

[9] Richards, Fighting for the Rain Forest.

[10] Malcolm Gladwell, The Tipping Point (London: Abacus, 2000).

[11] David Kolb and Ron Fry, "Toward an Applied Theory of Experiential Learning," in Theories of Group Process, edited by Cary L. Cooper, 33–57 (London: John Wiley, 1975).

[12] Ervin Goffman, The Presentation of Self in Everyday Life (New York: Doubleday, 1956).

[13] Belinda Bozzoli, Theatres of Struggle and the End of Apartheid (Johannesburg: Wits University Press, 2004). See also Carl Stauffer, Acting Out the Myth: The Politics of Narrative Violence in Zimbabwe (Saarbrucken, Germany: Lambert Academic, 2011).

[14] Mark Juergensmeyer, Terror in the Mind of God (Berkley/Los Angleles: University of California Press, 2000).

[15] Lisa Schirch, Ritual and Symbol in Peacebuilding (West Hartford, CT: Kumarian, 2004).

[16] William Cavanaugh, *Torture and Eucharist: Theology, Politics and the Body of Christ* (Malden, MA: Blackwell, 1998).

[17] Jill Freedman and Gene Combs, *Narrative Therapy: The Social Construction of Preferred Realities* (New York: W.W. Norton and Company, 1996).

[18] John Winslade and Gerald Monk, *Narrative Mediation: A New Approach to Conflict Resolution* (San Francisco: Jossey-Bass, 2001).

[19] Stanley Hauerwas and L. Gregory Jones, eds., *Why Narrative? Readings in Narrative Theology* (Eugene, OR: Wipf and Stock, 1997).

[20] John Paul Lederach, *Preparing for Peace: Conflict Transformation across Cultures* (New York: Syracuse University Press, 1995).

[21] Michelle Alexander, *The New Jim Crow: Mass Incarceration in the Age of Colorblindness* (New York: The New Press, 2010).

[22] Howard Zehr, *Changing Lenses: A New Paradigm for Crime and Justice* (Scottdale, PA: Herald, 1990).

[23] Sandra Bloom, *Creating Sanctuary: Toward the Evolution of Sane Societies* (New York/London: Routledge, 1997).

[24] Amartya Sen, *Development as Freedom* (New York: Knopf, 1999).

[25] Charles Taylor, *Multiculturalism*, edited by Amy Gutmann (Princeton: Princeton University Press, 1994).

Chapter 6: God Moves Sideways – Samir Selmanović

[1] Hannah Arendt, *Men in Dark Times* (San Diego: Harvest, 1955), 7.

[2] Brian D. McLaren, *Why Did Jesus, Moses, the Buddha, and Mohammed Cross the Road? Christian Identity in a Multi-Faith World* (New York: Jericho, 2012).

Signpost: Cultivating a New Imagination

[1] Tell Me What You Wish For" words by Bryan Moyer Suderman from the CD *Can't Keep Quiet*.

Chapter 7: Reason for Hope - Ivy Beckwith

[1] Barna Group, "Six Reasons Young Christians Leave the Church," http://www.barna.org/teens-next-gen-articles/528-six-reasons-young-christians-leave-church, accessed May 26, 2013.

[2] "The Pew Forum on Religion and Public Life, "Religion Among the Millennials," http://www.pewforum.org/Age/Religion-Among-the-Millennials.aspx, accessed May 26, 2013.

[3] Christian Smith with Melinda Lundquist Denton, *Soul Searching: The Religious and Spiritual Lives of American Teenagers* (Oxford: Oxford University Press, 2005).

[4] Barna Group, "Six Reasons."

[5] Pew Forum on Religion and Public Life, "Religion Among the Millennials."

[6] Smith with Snell, *Souls in Transition,* 223.

[7] Ibid., 145.

[8] N. T. Wright, "Imagining the Kingdom: Mission and Theology in Early Christianity," (Lecture, University of St. Andrews, October 26, 2011).

[9] Walter Brueggemann, *The Prophetic Imagination,* 2nd ed. (Minneapolis: Fortress, 2001).

[10] 1 John 2:17 (TNIV).

[11] Mark 1:15 (TNIV).

[12] Brueggemann, *The Prophetic Imagination,* xxi.

[13] Ibid., 35.

[14] Ibid., 25.

[15] Ibid., 40.

[16] Ibid., 39.

[17] Ibid., 64.

[18] Ibid., 65.

[19] Psalm 30.

Chapter 8: Expanding Children's Imaginations for Peace – Amy Gingerich and Rebecca Seiling

[1] This curriculum, called *Shine,* will be published for use starting in fall of 2014 by MennoMedia and Brethren Press.

[2] Violence and peace are outlined in Article 4 in *The Schleitheim Confession,* translated and edited by John Howard Yoder (Scottdale, PA: Herald, 1973), 12–13.

[3] See Jeremiah 31:17.

[4] Bruce C. Birch et al., *A Theological Introduction to the Old Testament* (Nashville: Abingdon, 1999), 376.

[5] Genesis 1:27.

[6] Genesis 2:20b–25.

[7] Matthew 18:1–9.

[8] Adapted from Rebecca Seiling, *Plant a Seed of Peace* (Scottdale, PA: Herald, 2007) and Elizabeth H. Bauman, *Coals of Fire* (Scottdale, PA: Herald, 1954).

[9] Peter Dyck and Elfrieda Dyck, "Foreword," in *Growing Toward Peace,* edited by Kathryn Aschliman (Scottdale, PA: Herald, 1993), 12.

[10] Ibid.

[11] Romans 12:2, 18 (NRSV).

[12] Seiling, *Plant a Seed of Peace*.

[13] Mary Clemens Meyer, *Walking with Jesus: Stories about Real People Who Return Good for Evil* (Scottdale, PA: Herald, 1992).

[14] Seiling, *Plant a Seed of Peace*, 9.

Chapter 9: Nurturing an Imaginative, Inquiring Spirit – Susan Burt

[1] Michael Morwood, *Praying a New Story* (Melbourne: Spectrum, 2003), 6.

[2] From a 2011 TED talk, available at http://www.ted.com/talks/louie_schwartzberg_nature_beauty_gratitude.html.

[3] Seasons of the Spirit, "Theological and Education Foundation: The Vision of *Seasons of the Spirit*," http://www.seasonsonline.ca/files/TEF-paper.pdf, accessed May 26, 2013.

[4] Avi Weiss, "Shabbat Forshpeis: A Taste of Torah in Honor of Shabbat," http://www.hir.org/a_weekly_gallery/8.16.02-weekly.html, accessed May 26, 2013.

[5] Lindsay McLaughlin, "Moving Spirit," in *Creating Change: The Arts as Catalyst for Spiritual Transformation*, edited by Keri K. Wehlander (Kelowna, BC: CopperHouse, 2008), 82.

[6] Henry J. M. Nouwen, *The Return of the Prodigal Son: A Story of Homecoming* (New York: Image, 1992).

[7] "Interview with Mem Fox about *Hunwick's Egg*," http://www.memfox.com/hunwicks-egg.html, accessed May 26, 2013.

Chapter 10: Girls and God When Everything's Changing – Joyce Ann Mercer and Dori Grinenko Baker

[1] Joyce Ann Mercer, *Girl Talk, God Talk: Why Faith Matters to Adolescent Girls – and their Parents* (San Francisco: Jossey-Bass, 2008), 135–136.

[2] Dori Grinenko Baker. *Doing Girlfriend Theology: God-Talk with Young Women* (Cleveland: Pilgrim, 2005).

[3] Names of girls with whom we have spoken have been changed.

[4] See Joyce Ann Mercer, "Vampires, Desire, Girls and God: *Twilight* and the Spiritualities of Adolescent Girls" *Pastoral Psychology* 60, no. 2 (2011): 263–278.

[5] Dori Grinenko Baker, *The Barefoot Way: A Faith Guide for Youth, Young Adults and the People Who Accompany Them* (Louisville: Westminster John Knox, 2012), 55–57.

[6] Judith Siqueira, "Editorial" *In God's Image* 13, no. 4 (1994): 2–4.

[7] Pierre Bourdieu, *Practical Reason: On the Theory of Action* (Stanford University Press, Stanford, CA 1998), 9.

Chapter 11: Missional Youth Ministry – Todd Hobart

[1] Where appropriate, I have used pseudonyms for persons and churches referenced in this chapter.

[2] The websites used were: Youth Specialties, Fuller Theological Seminary, Luther Seminary, Churchstaffing.com, Youthpastor.com, The Southern Baptist Convention, and The United Methodist Church.

[3] Darrell Guder, ed., *Missional Church: A Vision for the Sending of the Church in North America* (Grand Rapids: Eerdmans, 1998).

[4] Dwight Zscheile and Craig Van Gelder recently documented the various streams of the missional church conversation, as well as advancing the conversation significantly through their own contribution: Craig Van Gelder and Dwight J. Zscheile, *The Missional Church in Perspective: Mapping Trends and Shaping the Conversation* (Grand Rapids: Baker Academic, 2011).

[5] For example: Mark H. Senter III et al., *Four Views of Youth Ministry and the Church* (Grand Rapids: Zondervan/Youth Specialties, 2001); Brian Kirk and Jacob Thorne, *Missional Youth Ministry: Moving from Gathering Teenagers to Scattering Disciples* (Grand Rapids: Zondervan/Youth Specialties, 2011).

[6] Pamela D. Couture, *Seeing Children, Seeing God: A Practical Theology of Children and Poverty* (Nashville: Abingdon, 2000).

Chapter 12: Beauty in Brokenness: One Family's Story of Serving Children and Youth through United Compassionate Action – Steve Park and Mary Park

[1] Matthew 25:30; see also Ched Myers and Eric DeBode's exegesis of Matthew 25 in the article "Towering Trees and 'Talented' Slaves," *The Other Side* 35, no. 3 (1999).

[2] M. Scott Peck, *The Road Less Traveled: A New Psychology of Love, Traditional Values and Spiritual Growth* (New York: Touchstone: 1978).

[3] Huston Smith, *The World's Religions: Our Great Wisdom Traditions* (New York: HarperCollins, 1958/1991).

[4] For churches and leaders interested in partnering with existing organizations, a good resource for finding such organizations is the Christian Community Development Association (www.ccda.org).

[5] Gareth G. Davis and David B. Muhlhausen, *Young African-American Males: Continuing Victims of High Homicide Rates in Urban Communities,* Center for Data Analysis Report #00–05, *May 2, 2000,* pp. 2, 4.

Signpost: Infiltrating the World

[1] "Infiltrating the World" words by Bryan Moyer Suderman from the CD *A New Heart.*

Chapter 13: Personal Jesus, Public Faith: Cultivating a Generation of Young Public Theologians – Almeda M. Wright

[1] Tonéx, *Personal Jesus,* Verity Records, CD recorded 2000

[2] The cellphone application is available at www.personaljesus.com. The product is described by the following blurb:

It's time to wake up to a new App! JESUS IS CALLING YOU! ... a SPEAKING ANIMATED JESUS who delivers more than 200 quotes from the Bible directly into your iPhone or iPad. Personal Jesus allows you to share His word in social networks. ...Since Jesus is all around, you can watch him walking on water, having his last supper, being crucified, resurrected or in heaven. And since he is also universal and personally done for you... pick his color! White, Black, Asian or Celtic! Your own Personal Jesus.

[3] The Youth Theological Initiative is an ecumenical Christian summer academy, where rising high school seniors from around the country live together in a diverse intentional community to explore questions of theology, ethics, and social justice, participate in service learning, and experience a variety of religious practices and communities in the Atlanta area. Each year surveyed, the academy accepted 48–60 students. The interviews and surveys were collected in 2006, 2007, and 2008.

[4] Brian Campbell, paper presentation for *Imagining America Conference*, Conference Theme: Layers of Place, Movements of People: Public Engagement in a Diverse America, University of Southern California, Los Angeles, CA, October 2008.

[5] This also parallels the findings of national studies on youth and religion, such as that of Christian Smith, et al. in the National Survey of Youth Religion, where his team found that youth across traditions were remarkably inarticulate about their faith and beliefs.

[6] This young man, though affiliated with Methodist and Lutheran churches, described himself as agnostic. Therefore his uncertainty about the presence of God was consistent with his self-identification.

[7] Another young woman said this:

I feel like God is allowing things to happen in politics... I feel like things, all things are being set in order. I feel like God allowed that – you know, because... divine prophecies are going to have to be fulfilled... He's setting things in order to prepare for his son to come again. I feel like...because of sin there will always be tragedy. But I feel like, yes, he is working and he's just setting the table. In the whole world, I think he is just setting the table up, and he's doing something big.

[8] Christian Smith with Melinda Lundquist Denton, *Soul Searching: The Religion and Spiritual Lives of American Teenagers* (Oxford: Oxford University Press, 2005), 162-164. See their work for a more complete discussion of their theory about moralistic therapeutic deism as popular religion among adolescents in the United States.

[9] Ibid., 165.

[10] Evelyn Parker, *Trouble Don't Last Always: Emancipatory Hope Among African American Adolescents* (Cleveland: Pilgrim, 2003), 35–36.

[11] José Casanova, *Public Religions in the Modern World* (Chicago: University of Chicago Press, 1994), 35.

[12] Ibid., 11–35.

[13] Mark G. Toulouse, *God in Public: Four Ways American Christianity and Public Life Relate* (Louisville: Westminster John Knox, 2006).

[14] See Smith with Denton, *Soul Searching*, 162–163.

[15] Delores Williams, *Sisters in the Wilderness: The Challenge of Womanist God Talk* (Maryknoll, NY: Orbis, 1993/2003), 6.

[16] Monica A. Coleman, *Making a Way Out of No Way: A Womanist Theology* (Minneapolis: Fortress, 2008), 86.

[17] Robert Michael Franklin, "A Great Ordeal" (sermon delivered at the Fall Convocation of Candler School of Theology, Emory University, September 2, 2003).

[18] Duncan Forrester, "The Scope of Public Theology: What is Public Theology?" in *Forrester on Christian Ethics and Practical Theology: Collected Writings on Christianity, India, and the Social Order* (Burlington, VT: Ashgate, 2010), 441.

[19] However, I must add that public theology and the public engagement of issues of faith is a modern/postmodern invention. Without the proceeding separation of our lives into public and private realms and the attempt to relegate religion (and by extension theology) to private spheres, we would not need to discuss public theology.

[20] This is an important distinction to make about public theology versus any type of religion in the public square, because we have seen examples of religious communities having to interact with governmental agencies and policy makers to protect the rights of its members to practice as they believe or to worship where and how they want to worship. However, public theology or the work of the public theologian is not primarily driven by an attempt to protect the rights, and otherwise private beliefs and practices, of religious communities.

[21] Clive Pearson, "What is Public Theology?" http://www.csu.edu.au/faculty/arts/theology/pact/documents/What_is_Public_Theology.pdf, accessed May 26, 2013.

[22] Toulouse, *God in Public*, 186–187.

[23] For a more complete discussion of the passions of youth and the ways that many youth are demanding that religious communities and traditions respond to these needs, see Kenda Creasy Dean, *Practicing Passion: Youth and the Quest for a Passionate Church* (Grand Rapids: Eerdmans, 2004).

Chapter 14: Inheriting the Earth – Ben Lowe

[1] See Genesis 1 and Genesis 2:15.

[2] Mark 12:29–31 (TNIV).

[3] Quoted in Ken Wilson, *Jesus Brand Spirituality: He Wants His Religion Back* (Nashville: Thomas Nelson, 2008), 59.

[4] Colossians 1:19–20.

[5] The Cape Town Commitment, Part 1, Section 7a. It's available at http://www.laus anne.org/en/documents/ctcommitment.html.

[6] Matthew 5:5 (TNIV).

[7] Personal communication with the author.

Chapter 15: Bringing Sexy Back: Forging a Theological Framework – Dave McNeely

[1] It is worth noting that, while writing this chapter, congressional representatives in my own state introduced two separate legislative bills that became known by the following monikers: "Don't Say Gay" and "Gateway Sexual Activity." Apparently, institutions other than religious ones are experiencing an awkward disdain regarding current realities.

[2] Christian Smith with Kari Christoffersen, Hilary Davidson, and Patricia Snell Herzog, *Lost in Transition: The Dark Side of Emerging Adulthood* (Oxford: Oxford University Press, 2011), 150. See also Mary Eberstadt's brief but insightful *Adam and Eve after the Pill: Paradoxes of the Sexual Revolution* (San Francisco: Ignatius, 2012) for a critique of the consequences of the sexual revolution from a uniquely Catholic perspective.

[3] See Adelle M. Banks, "With High Premarital Sex and Abortion Rates, Evangelicals Says It's Time to Talk About Sex," http://www.huffingtonpost.com/2012/04/23/evangelicals-sex-frank-talk n 1443062.html, accessed May 26, 2013,, which includes this shocking revelation: "Eighty percent of young evangelicals have engaged in premarital sex . . . And almost a third of evangelicals' unplanned pregnancies end in abortion."

[4] Grey Matter Research Consulting, "Most Americans don't feel the Christian faith positively impacts racism and sexuality in society; the perceived impact of the Christian faith on American society is explored," http://www.greymatterresearch. com/index_files/Impact.htm (accessed July 9, 2013), which cites the following: "The most negative perception [among respondents] is how the Christian faith impacts sexuality in society. Just 26% feel the faith has a positive impact in this area, while 37% see no real impact, and 37% believe it has a negative impact."

[5] Laurie A. Jungling, "Creation as God's Call into Erotic Embodied Relationality," in *The Embrace of Eros: Bodies, Desires, and Sexuality in Christianity*, edited by Margaret D. Kamitsuka, 217–30 (Minneapolis: Fortress, 2010), 220.

[6] Ibid., 223.

[7] Jungling writes, "I submit that such freedom without faithfulness actually threatens the possibilities for discovering the fullness of erotic life . . . Without faithfulness, a life-giving relationship can devolve into an attempt to escape space or time in a search for unencumbered eros, which constitutes, theologically speaking, a suppression of creatureliness and of the human calling as God's image. . . Faithfulness, I propose, does not have to exclude freedom; instead, it can open new doors to experiencing it." Ibid., 226.

[8] Stanley Hauerwas, "Sex in Public: How Adventurous Christians Are Doing It (1978)," in *The Hauerwas Reader* (Durham, NC: Duke University Press, 2001), 481.

[9] I have in mind here an eroticism that is not reduced solely to sexual desire. Rather, in the words of poet Audre Lorde, eros is a "creative energy" with the capacity to provide "the power which comes from sharing deeply any pursuit with another person . . . whether physical, emotional, psychic, or intellectual." Audre Lorde, "Uses of the Erotic: The Erotic and Power," in *Sister/Outsider: Essays and Speeches*, 53–59 (Freedom, CA: Crossing, 1984/2007), 55–56. For a more theological appraisal of this view of eros, see Margaret D. Kamitsuka, ed., *The Embrace of Eros*.

[10] *Catechism of the Catholic Church* (Liberia Editrice Vaticana, 1997), 1015.

[11] Jenell Williams Paris, *The End of Sexual Identity: Why Sex Is Too Important to Define Who We Are* (Downers Grove, IL: InterVarsity, 2011), 128.

[12] Stanley Hauerwas, "The Radical Hope and the Annunciation: Why Both Single and Married Christians Welcome Children (1998)," in *The Hauerwas Reader*, edited by John Berkman and Michael Cartwright, 505–518 (Chapel Hill, NC: Duke University Press, 2001), 514.

[13] Linda Woodhead, "Sex in a Wider Context," in *Sex These Days: Essays on Theology, Sexuality and Society*, edited by Jon Davies and Gerard Loughlin, 98–120 (Sheffield: Sheffield Academic Press, 1997), 106.

14 Jana Marguerite Bennett, *Water Is Thicker than Blood: An Augustinian Theology of Marriage and Singlehood* (Oxford: Oxford University Press, 2008).

15 Galatians 5:22–23: "By contrast, the fruit of the Spirit is love, joy, peace, patience, kindness, generosity, faithfulness, gentleness, and self-control" (NRSV).

16 For example, so-called "Royal Covenants," involving one or more parties who wield more power in the covenantal relationship, lend themselves easily to such abuse. Nevertheless, the selfish use of covenants can work both ways. Just think of proverbial "gold-diggers" who manipulate covenant laws to their advantages even as these covenants may preserve patriarchal privilege over females.

17 Paraphrase of 1 Corinthians 13:1–3.

18 Robert Grimm, *Love and Sexuality* (New York: Hodder & Stoughton, 1964), 33.

19 Smith et al., *Lost in Transition*.

20 Eberstadt, *Adam and Eve*. Eberstadt writes, "The sexual revolution . . . has fallen heaviest on the smallest and weakest shoulders in society – even as it has given extra strength to those already strongest and most predatory" (Introduction, Paragraph 10). (e-book).

21 There is much current debate about the nature of adolescence and emerging adulthood and this discussion undoubtedly has a profound effect on how we understand the relationship of these rituals to adolescent transitions. It is beyond the scope of this chapter to address this topic, except to note that however we view this issue, the triangulation between biology, culture, and ritual matters deeply in the lives of teenagers as well as the church as a whole.

22 Actually, this shouldn't be the "finally." One of the greatest tragedies of recent Christian teaching on sexuality has been its obsession with teens and young adults, leading many young people to the unfortunate conclusion that marriage is a magical threshold that grants freedom from sexual confusion, frustration, and immaturity. On the contrary, marriage often exacerbates such tensions and increasing life expectancy has created even more uncharted dimensions of sexuality, namely that of the senior adult. In truth, a new kind of sexuality will only be helpful to the degree that it also addresses the sexual challenges of adulthood and senior adulthood, but it is beyond the scope of this chapter to go into detail on these areas.

23 Lauren Winner, *Real Sex: The Naked Truth about Chastity* (Grand Rapids: Brazos, 2005). Other recent voices engaged in the task of reimagining Christian sexual ethics, while not appropriating the burdened language of chastity, have posed the challenge of exploring commitments and boundaries within sexual expression. Such voices include Margaret Farley, *Just Love: A Framework for Christian Sexual Ethics* (New York: Continuum, 2010) and Kathy Rudy, *Sex and the Church: Gender, Sexuality, and the Transformation of Christian Ethics* (Boston: Beacon, 1998).

[24] The literature on this is extensive, such that I hesitate to even make a recommendation. Nonetheless, a great starting point is Kenda Creasy Dean and Ron Foster, *The Godbearing Life: The Art of Soul Tending for Youth Ministry* (Nashville: Upper Room, 1993), and the work of Christian Smith and the National Study of Youth and Religion (www.youthandreligion.org) is an invaluable contribution to an understanding of this subject.

[25] For an interesting take on gender segregation practices and gender equality, see David M. Csinos, "Will Boys Be Boys and Girls Be Girls? Correcting Gender Stereotypes Through Ministry with Children," *Priscilla Papers* 24, no. 2 (2010): 23–28.

[26] Unfortunately, little beyond the cloistered walls of monasticism, and much less since the Reformation, has been written about the rich possibilities (not to mention wise counsel) of inter-gender friendships. One notable recent exception is Dan Brennan, *Sacred Unions, Sacred Passions: Engaging the Mystery of Friendship Between Men and Women* (Elgin, IL: Faith Dance, 2010). While directed more toward the nature of adult friendships, Brennan's work is undoubtedly a valuable asset as new directions are sought.

[27] Daniel Bell's valuation of such works of mercy is particularly instructive: "Works of mercy produce and provide, not for the sake of empowering the insatiable desire of autonomous individuals to pursue private goods and interests, but for the sake of expanding communion. The goal of the works of mercy is not self-sufficiency but participation in the circle of giving and receiving." Daniel Bell, *The Economy of Desire: Christianity and Capitalism in a Postmodern World* (Grand Rapids: Baker Academic, 2012), 209.

[28] It is worth noting here the connection Lauren Winner makes between the sexuality of teenage girls and their involvement in team sports. Citing research that identifies participation in team sports as the greatest predictor of girls remaining "chaste," Winner notes the logic of the correlation: "Through [team sports], those girls are learning how to inhabit their bodies in good, robust physical ways...They are learning . . . that their bodies should be celebrated, because their bodies do great things." Winner, *Real Sex*, 96.

[29] Elizabeth Stuart, "Sex in Heaven: The Queering of Theological Discourse on Sexuality," in *Sex These Days: Essays on Theology, Sexuality and Society*, edited by Jon Davies and Gerard Loughlin, 184–204 (Sheffield: Sheffield Academic Press, 1997), 204.

Chapter 17: Jesus on the Autism Spectrum – Dixon Kinser

[1] The statistics come from a 2012 study of the Centers for Disease Control and Prevention: http://www.cdc.gov/Features/CountingAutism/, accessed May 26, 2013.

[2] *Diagnostic and Statistical Manual of Mental Disorders vol. 4.* This is the definitive source of the American Psychiatric Association and remains the "industry standard" for defining mental disorders. To be diagnosed with Autistic Disorder, certain criteria that must be met are laid out in the *DSM IV.* A new version of the *DSM* (the *DSM V*) was published in 2013 and includes changes to the criteria for ASD diagnosis. More information about conversations and debates surrounding diagnosis is available at http://www.autismspeaks.org/what-autism/diagnosis.

[3] A wonderful resource from Johns Hopkins University about ASD, the mystery of its origins, and it's increasing prevalence can be found at http://www.jhsph.edu/research/centers-and-institutes/center-for-autism-and-developmental-disabilities-epidemiology/Facts/autism.html.

[4] Facts about Autism," http://www.autismspeaks.org/what-autism/facts-about-autism, accessed May 26, 2013. There is also informationabout this on the Centers for Disease Control and Prevention website, http://www.cdc.gov/Features/CountingAutism/.

[5] This will, of course, not be the case for every child with ASD. Because of differences in severity, some children do best in specialized schools or learning environments dedicated solely to ASD and more practical therapies. I only draw from my experience at playing with practices for approaching and inviting youth with ASD who want to be part of youth ministries.

[6] Matthew 12:46–50.

[7] Luke 14:25–26.

[8] John 19:26–27.

[9] Initiating a meeting like this should be handled with care. Not all parents want to admit or accept that their child in on the spectrum and some parents may be offended at such a suggestion. Likewise, a leader could be wrong in guessing a teen has ASD. To circumvent this awkwardness, I make "open calls" during my bi-annual parents meeting during which I ask parents to let me know if their teens have any special needs of which I should be aware. While this usually yields positive results, sometimes I find that I need to be the one to raise the topic. When this is the case, I approach parents only after I've collected some solid data on how their teen interacts with the community and where I see the issues. Then when I sit down with the young person's parents, I can explain what I've noticed (my data) and ask them when strategies they would recommend (or have used in the past) to make their teen's integration into the community more smooth.

Also, some parents might expect a call about their child to be a confrontation about discipline issues or something similar. I like to assuage these fears by letting the family know that I want them to teach me about their teen because their integration into our youth ministry is as much my responsibility as it is anyone else's.

Ultimately, I remind myself that my goal is not to discover a hidden diagnosis or convince parents that their teen is on the spectrum and they're in denial. My goal is to serve and disciple this particular young person. Keeping this in mind releases me from feeling like I have to play armchair psychologist and it keeps the task at hand actually at hand.

[10] I have an SF-IEP meeting at least once a year with each family with a teen on the spectrum. However, if things are not working or goals are met quickly, it can be helpful to meet throughout the year.

[11] Here is an example of a schedule:

6:30–6:40	Snacks and mingling
6:40–6:55	Welcome and names game
6:55–7:00	Announcements
7:00–7:30	Bible study
7:30–7:40	Singing
7:40–7:45	Closing prayer

Chapter 18: Let's Say Grace – Joy Carroll Wallis

[1] Available at https://archive.sojo.net/index.cfm?action=magazine.article&issue=soj98 11&article=981151.

[2] See Joy Carroll Wallis, *The Woman Behind the Collar: The Pioneering Journey of an Episcopal Priest* (New York: Crossroad, 2004) and Jim Wallis, *Faith Works: Lessons from the Life of an Activist Preacher* (New York: Random House, 2000).

[3] Jim Wallis, *On God's Side: What Religion Forgets and Politics Hasn't Learned about Serving the Common Good* (Grand Rapids: Brazos, 2013).

Chapter 19: Yours, Mine, and Ours – David M. Csinos

[1] Neil Bissoondath, *Selling Illusions: The Cult of Multiculturalism in Canada*, rev. ed. (Toronto: Penguin, 1994/2002).

[2] Lawrence Hill, *Black Berry, Sweet Juice: On Being Black and White in Canada* (Toronto: HarperCollins, 2001), 75.

[3] Bissoondath, *Selling Illusions*, 81.

[4] Himani Bannerji, "Geography Lessons: On Being an Insider/Outsider to the Canadian Nation," in *Dark Side of the Nation: Essays on Multiculturalism, Nationalism, and Gender*, 63–86 (Toronto: Canadian Scholars' Press, 2000).

5 Clifford J. Jansen, "Canadian Multiculturalism," in *Possibilities and Limitations: Multicultural Policies and Programs in Canada*, edited by Carl E. James, 21–33 (Halifax: Fernwood, 2005).

6 Bissoondath, *Selling Illusions*.

7 Ibid., 108.

8 Traci C. West, *Disruptive Christian Ethics: When Racism and Women's Lives Matter* (Louisville: Westminster John Knox, 2006), 112.

9 The Gospel and Our Culture Network (http://www.gocn.org/) is one organization dedicated to ongoing exploration about how culture shapes and reshapes Christian faith, practice, and mission, as well as biblical and theological reflection. Although it focuses on contemporary Western culture, it provides a useful model for such engagement.

10 Executive of the General Council, The United Church of Canada, *A Transformative Vision for the United Church of Canada* (Thunder Bay: The United Church of Canada, 2006), 140.

11 Roger C. Hutchinson, *Ethical Choices in a Pluralistic World* (Camrose, AB: The Chester Ronning Centre for the Study of Religion and Public Life, 2009), 11.

12 Ibid., 5. Hutchinson offers an approach for intercultural ethics and conversation that includes four levels of clarification: "rigorous attention to the validity claims about facts, attention to the persuasiveness of claims and arguments about rights, attention to claims about consequences, and attention to what an issue symbolizes." Hutchison, *Ethical Choices*, 13.

13 Danielle Shroyer, *The Boundary-Breaking God: An Unfolding Story of Hope and Promise* (San Francisco: Jossey-Bass, 2009).

14 Elizabeth F. Caldwell, *God's Big Table: Nurturing Children in a Diverse World* (Cleveland: Pilgrim, 2011), 4.

15 Although not specifically geared toward ministry with young people, *That All May Be One*, edited by Greer Anne Wenh-In Ng (Toronto: United Church Publishing House, 2004), is a tremendous resource for beginning to reflect on and address some of these issues. See also The Canadian Ecumenical Anti-Racism Network, *Cracking Open White Identity Towards Transformation: The Canadian Ecumenical Anti-Racism Network Examines White Identity, Power, and Privilege* (Toronto: Canadian Council of Churches, 2012).

16 Sandy Eisenberg Sasso, *Cain and Abel: Finding the Fruits of Peace* (Woodstock, VT: Jewish Lights, 2001).

17 Martin Luther King, Jr., *Strength to Love*, (Philadelphia: Fortress, 1963), 102.

Chapter 20: Drawing Future Maps in Pencil – Melvin Bray

[1] "If there is no struggle, there is no progress. Those who profess to favor freedom, and yet depreciate agitation, are men who want crops without plowing up the ground. They want rain without thunder and lightning. They want the ocean without the awful roar of its many waters. This struggle may be a moral one; or it may be a physical one; or it may be both moral and physical; but it must be a struggle." From a 3 August 1857 speech by Frederick Douglas in Canandaigua, New York on the 23rd anniversary of the West India Emancipation, available at http://www.black-past.org/?q=1857-frederick-douglass-if-there-no-struggle-there-no-progress.

[2] Proverbs 6:27 (NASB).

[3] Pseudonym of Christopher Lee Rios, an amazingly gifted Latino hip-hop lyricist of the late-'90s/early 21st century, who died just before he could fully experience the luxury of his newfound fame.

[4] By *myths* I mean the stories around which we organize our lives.

[5] Romans 8:31 (KJV).

[6] Joseph Campbell, *The Masks of God, vol. 4: Creative Mythology* (New York: Viking Penguin, 1968), 609, 611, 621, 623.

[7] William H. McNeill, "The Care and Repair of Public Myth," *Foreign Affairs* 61, no. 1 (1982), 1–13.

[8] In using this term, I make no assumptions that all children are pouty and petulant, whether or not they're in the sky.

[9] Russell is founding minister of House of Mercy, a church in St. Paul, Minnesota.

[10] I introduced myself to Russell out of sheer jealousy over the fact that he had written a far more interesting version of a book that had been banging around my head, about an off-beat pastor on the verge of psychotic break who told stories that baffled some and bewitched others, enraged and enlivened. Russell's character is Rev. Richard Lamblove, whose exploits can be found in his books, *Post-Rapture Radio: Lost Writing from a Failed Revolution* (San Francisco: Jossey-Bass, 2005) and *Midrash on the Juanitos: A Didactic Novella* (St. Paul: Cathedral Hill, 2010). My character is Sent St. Common, affectionately known as Revelations. His exploits can be found at http://melvinbray.com/category/village-half-wit/. Our characters subsequently became friends and Rev. Lamblove had been known to grace Revelations' pulpit on occasion.

[11] Rathbun. *Midrash on the Juanitos*, 100.

[12] For a far more comprehensive consideration of the many different aspects of a story that can be re-imagined, see Susan Burt's chapter in this book. My primary con-

cerns are the sharing of better stories with one another and how doing so better shapes us as people of the Way.

[13] To learn more about *The Stories in which We Find Ourselves* and *Stories that Compost,* visit www.findourselves.kidcultivators.org.

[14] Paraphrase of Philippians 4:8.

[15] That was a bit of a joke for contributors to this volume who, for better or worse, had to acquiesce to the use of Google Drive as the most efficient means by which they, Dave, and I could collaborate in the process of putting together this book over significant geographical distances.

Signpost 4: Mapping a Lifelong Journey

[1] Bryan Moyer Suderman, "Disciples-in-Training," from the CD *New World Coming.*

Chapter 21: So the Gift Can Be Given: The Journey of Faith Formation – John H. Westerhoff, III

[1] William Faulkner, *Requiem for a Nun* (New York: Vintage, 1950/2011), 73

[2] G. Stanley Hall, *Adolescence: Its Psychology and its Relations to Physiology, Anthropology, Sociology, Sex, Crime, Religion and Education* (New York: D. Appleton and Company, 1904).

[3] I have discussed these different conceptions of childhood in *Will Our Children Have Faith?* 3rd ed. (Harrisburg, PA: Morehouse, 2012).

[4] As mentioned, these are social constructions, so people may add, remove, and change these chronological phases as necessary.

[5] This does not mean that I am against Sunday school. I was branded the enemy of Sunday school for about 25 years. But I actually love Sunday school. I just think it should be a different kind of place than it is in most churches.

Permissions